250

The Dodgers and Me

THE INSIDE STORY

ZIFF  DAVIS
PUBLISHING COMPANY
Chicago . New York . Los Angeles

★

ZIFF-DAVIS LIMITED
London

★

ZIFF-DAVIS-PATEL LIMITED
Calcutta · Bombay

Leo Durocher, Manager of the Brooklyn Dodgers.

The DODGERS AND ME

The Inside Story

by
LEO DUROCHER

ZIFF-DAVIS PUBLISHING COMPANY
CHICAGO

PRINTED IN THE UNITED STATES OF AMERICA
AMERICAN BOOK–STRATFORD PRESS, INC., NEW YORK

TO LARAINE

THE MANAGER'S MANAGER

Acknowledgment

The author wishes to express appreciation of the help and cooperation of those people who have given unselfishly of their time, and who have made available files, records, and photographs without which this book would not have been possible. In particular, the author wishes to acknowledge the help of Harold Parrott, Lou Niss, J. W. Taylor Spink, Marty Martyn, the fans in Brooklyn who mailed him their precious pictures, and the management of the *Brooklyn Eagle* and the *Sporting News*.

Contents

The Dodgers and Me

THE INSIDE STORY

Chapter 1

EVERYTHING HAPPENS AT EBBETS FIELD

It was April. Baseball was in the air, though the season hadn't started. I sat in the boss's office, working with him on the Dodgers' roster. We were trying to make up the team that I would pilot in the 1947 National League race and, I hoped, lead to a pennant. The boss was, of course—who else? —Branch Rickey. He sat behind his big desk, a cigar in his teeth. Around him clustered Branch Junior, our three coaches, and Harold Parrott, our traveling secretary.

All that spring we had been together, in Havana, Panama, Venezuela, and Florida. We had worked hard and now were fairly confident that we were ready to play ball. At the moment we were talking about Jackie Robinson, the Negro boy. Could he do the job for us at first base? There were other problems, too. Should we trade Kirby Higbe, should we—

Suddenly the telephone rang.

Branch—other people give him the "Mr. Rickey," but to me he's always been "Branch," first impertinently, then with real admiration—turned to answer it.

We continued to talk as Branch said, "Hello . . . Oh! . . ." The cigar jerked, and then he was listening, his mouth tense, his eyes flashing. Something was in the air. That much anyone who knew Branch Rickey could tell. But hardly any one of us could have foretold what was actually being said at the other end of the line.

With a bang he let the phone down. He sat up and faced us.

"Harold," he nodded grimly to Parrott, "the Commissioner has fined you five hundred dollars for writing and talking."

Parrott stiffened. I could hear him suck in his breath.

We all began to jabber at once. In the complaint hearing

which Larry MacPhail, President of the Yankees, had demanded against us from Commissioner A. B. "Happy" Chandler, we thought we had won out. True, Parrott had made a few cracks in the *Brooklyn Eagle* that had caused MacPhail to holler "Copper!" to Chandler. But we had been so confident that we were in the clear that Parrott had wired home after the hearing, "Dodgers win another!"

With a wave of his hand Rickey silenced us. "The Commissioner has fined me too," he added, "and he has also fined the Yankees two thousand dollars."

As that sank in, we glanced at each other. Something in Branch's tone intimated that there was more to come. I felt a chill steal down my spine.

Branch took a vicious bite at his cigar, and rocked his swivel chair. He leaned over until his bushy eyebrows were nearly in my eyes.

I would have drawn back except that what he said next nearly froze me to the spot

"Leo!" he boomed. "The Commissioner has *suspended you from baseball for one year!*"

Thus was rudely ended—for a time, at least—the incredible dream that my playing and managing in Brooklyn had seemed to me.

It had been like a dream because I had discovered that Brooklyn was out of this world, at least out of the baseball world I had known when I played with the Yankees, the Reds, and the Cardinals.

Sure, I thought I knew it all. Hadn't I played with great teams like the world's champion Yankees and the world's champion Cardinals when they were at their peaks? I talked loud, and plenty. I'd been around, I had seen everything—Yeah, that's what I thought!

Then it had happened. I had dropped through a trap door, off the high-flying Redbirds and down to sixth-place Brook-

At Ebbets Field opening, April 9, 1913. Left to right, Charles H. Ebbets, Jr., Stephen W. McKeever, Charles H. Ebbets, Edward J. McKeever, Henry Medicus, and Clarence van Buskirk, architect.

Ebbets Field, home of the Brooklyn Dodgers.

Both photos, courtesy *The Sporting News*

lyn. I had learned things in Brooklyn. Better than that, I collided with things and with people—the wonderful people who make the Dodgers more of a religion than a ball team in a city that's built around a shrine called Ebbets Field.

Life in Brooklyn, I had found, might be explosive and unpredictable, but never dull. As Red Barber, the Cracker philosopher, so often advertises over the radio, "Everything happens at Ebbets Field."

Just about everything did happen to me at Ebbets Field. Most of it was good. Some of it was unbelievable. Altogether, it was priceless and accounts for the thrills of my lifetime.

Brooklyn! I'm no long-haired guy, but about that town I think even I could sit up and write a poem. It wouldn't be about the buildings, or the business, or even about the box office we draw. It would be about people, just plain American men, women, and kids who talk free and easy, and have hearts as big as any in the world.

When I walk down the streets the folks say, "Hi, Leo!" There's no "Mr. Durocher!" It's straight "Leo." Why not? They're Brooklyn, and I'm part of them. "Dem Bums" is more important than anything else that happens in Flatbush. Baseball is their meat and drink. If the guys who run politics knew their stuff half as well as Brooklyn knows ballplaying, the world wouldn't be in such a mess.

They cheer for us, weep for us, razz us—once in a while—and second-guess all the time. I'm proud that they like me. In fact, I'm crazy about them.

That calls for a word about some of the characters to whom Ebbets Field is more than a place where you watch a good ball game.

Hilda is a female colossus with a thundering voice, a sharp tongue, and an undying loyalty to the Dodgers. She carries a bell that rings like a scissors-grinder's. She doesn't need the bell. She can collect a crowd quicker than a guy scattering ten-dollar bills.

Hilda sends us on the field with a pat on the back that would floor a frail man. She welcomes us back at the dressing-room door after the game, and between times she hollers insults at the opposition. She makes a living packaging peanuts for the Stevens Brothers, concessionaires at Ebbets Field.

Struck by her devotion to the team, I once offered her a seat in my box behind the dugout.

"Sit with them plush-lined bums, Leo?" she nearly shrieked. "Never! My friends is back there." She waved toward the unreserved seats.

Before I could enter a defense of the "plush-lined bums," Hilda rasped, "Who come to see me when I was sick in the horspital, Leo? Who figures the battin' averages, an' sends Peewee Reese a present on his birthday? Not them box-seat guys, but the real fans, that's who."

I dropped the subject fast.

Hilda is tougher to debate than an umpire. She has a regular barrage of snappers which she fires at Dodger-baiters. She delivers them with a smile that always gets the crowd on her side, even when she's in hostile territory, like the Polo Grounds, or Philadelphia, or Boston, where she often follows her darlings.

"Walker, you're all washed up!" a grandstand jockey barked in Philadelphia, the first day I encountered Hilda. "Why don't you hang up your spikes?"

"Ah-h-h!" snorted Hilda, warming up for the rebuttal. "Look where *he* is, and look where you are, ya bum ya!"

Thrown for a loss, the Phillies fan, who couldn't point out as many sterling qualities in his own team, resorted to "I'd like to be at Ebbets Field next week when those Cardinals take your Dodgers apart!"

"An' if ya don't show up," snapped Hilda, "we'll still open the park, ya bum ya!"

Hilda isn't the only one who makes a rhetorical sandwich out of what she has to say. The various cab drivers, and all the authentic Brooklyn characters who help me manage the Dodgers, do that.

Jo-Jo, the cigar-smoking midget who thumps the drum in Shorty's Ebbets Field Sym-phony, said to me one day when he returned from a road trip, "Gee, Leo, it's good to be back home. In the Philadelphia ball park they push ya around, they push ya!"

Brooklyn bugs manufacture more words in a season than a roomful of Harvard professors could do in four years. They are the ones who created the word "rhubarb," meaning ruckus, trouble, or mix-up. For they talk their own idiom, and it is not that awful lingo that passes for Brooklynese in the movies or on the radio. The real stuff is much more picturesque and racy. It's American.

Here, too, Shorty's Sym-phony Band, like which there is nothing anywhere else, grew up like Topsy.

Shorty Laurice is a shipyard worker who corralled a few battered instruments and the musicians to man them, and started a unique career of bedeviling the Dodger opposition. When an opposing hitter makes an out and starts his somber dogtrot back to the dugout, Shorty and his ensemble give him that gal-ump! gal-ump! treatment, beating out each stride musically. If the victim goes to the drinking fountain to cover his confusion, the Sym-phony cuts loose with "How Dry I Am." If the victim postpones taking his seat on the bench, Shorty and his men hound him until he does. It may be one strike, or one out later, or perhaps a whole inning later, but a loud thump on the drums and a clash of the cymbals announce that the victim has seated himself.

The Sym-phony has made strong men bite their nails in the visiting dugout at Ebbets Field. The fact is, the Toscanini of Section Eight is more concerned with the psychological havoc his tunes wreak than with their rating as pure music.

A guest at Ebbets Field remarked to Shorty when the Cubs

were being harassed, "I like your musical effects."

"Yeah," said Shorty, puffing up with pardonable pride, "it sure affects them Cubs. We never would of swept this series wit'out our horns!"

Is it fun? I'll say it is. For at Ebbets Field all of Brooklyn gathers to root for "Dem Bums." We are members of one family, and, like relatives, we sometimes needle each other, but we stick together in the face of any foe, in the National League—and the American League, too, when World Series time rolls around.

After carrying on like this, you might think I broke my neck to get to the Dodgers. The reverse was true. *Broth-err!* And how!

Chapter 2

I BECOME A "BUM"

BACK IN 1937, IF ANYONE HAD TOLD ME THE TIME WOULD come when my heart would nearly break at the thought of leaving Brooklyn—for any reason—I would have given out with a horselaugh, king size.

Managing a big-league ball club was the fulfillment of all the baseball dreams I ever had since the day I first talked back to an umpire. But time was when the whole Dodger setup looked like a nightmare—in technicolor.

With the Cardinals I had been riding high for four and a half seasons. Alongside the Deans and Pepper Martin, and Frank Frisch, who managed the club and played second base beside me, every day was a picnic. Frisch had been my pal, even though, after the 1934 World Series, in which we walloped the Detroit Tigers, I kidded him a lot about needing a wheel chair. I used to call Frank's attention to every ball I fielded on his side of second base. For my part, it was just ribbing. I dished it out and I could take it.

For spring training in the fateful year 1937, Frisch and I drove to Florida together. We roomed together and played golf every day at Daytona Beach. We were pals, I thought, until—

One day, after our training chores for the day were finished, Branch Rickey called me over.

"You and Frisch had a fight?" he asked.

"No, sir!" I replied. "We hit it off great."

"Well, he wants to trade you!" snapped B. R., belching a cloud of cigar smoke that would probably have floored me, even if his statement had not. Rickey smokes cigars that smell like burning upholstery.

7

My jaw dropped. I said no more, but I felt as though I had been hit by a pitched ball.

After that Frisch and I slowly drifted apart. The break came when Frank fined me and suspended me for the rest of the season. Rickey insisted that he did not want to break up his infield. Frisch, however, stood his ground. One of us, he said, had to go. Naturally it wouldn't be him.

"All right," Rickey finally decided. "I don't want to make this trade, but if you put it on a personal basis, I'll have to do it."

Once before, at Frisch's request, Rickey had shipped a player. That had been Jimmy Wilson, a fine catcher, also a pal of Frank's and formerly his roommate.

I was stopping at the Hotel Warwick in New York in October, 1937, when I read about the deal in which I was sloughed off: *Durocher for Joe Stripp, Johnny Cooney, Roy Henshaw, and Jim Bucher!* What a collection of baseball players!—has-beens. They might as well have included Mordecai Brown and Nap Lajoie, too, I thought.

Then the rest of it hit me. "Brooklyn!" I bellowed, as if Rickey had sent me to the Black Hole of Calcutta. "I won't report!"

That minute the boss popped up. As usual, he beat me to the punch. "Didn't think you were worth so much, Leo," he said, with a twinkle in his eye. "Imagine getting four men for you—"

I started to scream, but he shut me up with, "Just go there and keep your nose clean, Leo. You have ambitions beyond being just a player, haven't you?"

Right then it didn't sink into my fat head because I was so mad. Later it developed that Rickey had ideas about my managing and really wanted to give me a break. I wasn't through; he could have made a better deal for me elsewhere. But he picked my spot.

Three years before, I had kicked up a fuss after he grabbed me from the Cincinnati Reds to play shortstop. B. R. had calmed me. That time (May, 1933) I invaded his bedroom and dirtied up his clean white bedspread as I blurted out that I didn't want to play for his "cheap" organization, meaning the Cardinals.

Rickey squinted at me and said, "I have heard, Leo, that you don't make friends easily. Now I can understand why!"

I snapped, "I had one friend, Miller Huggins, but he went and died on me." Huggins had managed the Yankees when I played with them.

"Well," returned Rickey, "I'll forget all the stories I've heard about you. All I want you to remember is 'Rickey took me because he wants to win the pennant. He's trying to make a champion out of me.'"

So B. R. hit me in a vulnerable spot. Next to living, I like winning best, no matter what game it is. He sold me the idea that I was going to play for him on a *championship* team.

Strangely enough, I had started my Cardinal career in Brooklyn. That day in June, 1933, the Cardinals were playing the Dodgers. I hustled over to Ebbets Field. The game had already started when I reported in uniform to Manager Gabby Street. The next time we took the field he sent me out to shortstop. I remember the surprised look on Frank Frisch's face as he stared over from second base and said, "Who invited you?"

A lot of things were to happen to me in Brooklyn. But for a long time, in my mind it was to be a joke town, and a joke team. Looking back, it's easy to see why.

There was the time in 1934 when Dizzy Dean beat the Dodgers 3 to 1 after hitting a home run as well as pitching a classic. Before the game he had visited the Dodgers and Casey Stengel, their humorous manager, in the clubhouse, and calmly told them every spot he was going to try to make while pitching to their line-up.

Then Paul Dean, his brother, pitched the nightcap against the Dodgers, and got himself a no-hitter!

When the last game was over, Dizzy, instead of being elated, for we were speeding on our way to a pennant, threw his glove away. "You had no right to do that without a-tellin' me, Paul," stormed The Great One. "If you'd'a told me I'd'a pitched a no-hitter too!"

I had a suspicion Dizzy might have done it, too. In my book, you see, the Dodgers were buffoons. A comedian for a manager, and a clown team. Brooklyn? A terrible place to be traded to—if you liked to win more than you liked to laugh.

Why shouldn't I have looked at the Dodgers as a daffy team in a daffy town? I'd heard about the Brooklyn cab driver who stalled his hack outside the Ebbets Field bleachers and shouted up to the fans: "Howz our Bums doin'?"

"Last of the sixth," a Brooklyn fan bellowed down, being careful not to turn his head and miss any action on the field. "Scores tied! Two out and we got three men on base."

"Which base?" cracked the hackie.

That was Brooklyn, wacky from 'way back.

Squire Charley Ebbets, the first in a long line of comedians, managed the 1897 Dodgers into tenth place *wearing a top hat*. The name of the Brooklyn team—"Superbas"—came from a vaudeville troupe famous at the time. Rumor had it that the original Superbas were jugglers. That seemed to fit Ebbets' team, too.

In an even earlier Dodger day Ebbets had sold peanuts and score cards. He had been given a little stock in the club by George Chauncey, who had backed the team. Ebbets worked hard and saved his money. He acquired more stock and finally, when he was elected president of the club, got to put on a top hat, which, at that time, all the baseball magnates wore.

Charley took the helm with great zeal, and in the same

manner the Dodgers progressed—toward tenth place. In those days the National League had twelve teams. But it was still tenth place, no matter how you looked at it.

On the way to tenth place, Ebbets fired a couple of managers—Bill Barnie and Mike Griffin. This procedure later became a popular custom with the Dodgers. In one stretch, the Brooklyn club paid *six* salaries for *four* years of management of the club. One year, 1937, Casey Stengel was paid $15,000 for *not* managing the team, twice as much as Burleigh Grimes received for managing it!

I always got a kick out of the picture of Ebbets managing in a top hat. He was not a funny man as comedians go—unlike "Uncle Robbie" Wilbert Robinson and Casey Stengel (who once tipped his toppiece to let a live bird escape and embarrass an umpire), but he must have looked funny. At any rate, a lot of us have blown our toppers managing the Brooklyn club, and Ebbets blew his, too, after going to the bench at the end of 1897. After that he hired many good men, including Ned Hanlon, Patsy Donovan, and Harry Lumley, and later, of course, Robinson himself; but Ebbets never returned as manager.

When he was only a little guy in the picture, Charley had seen the team moved from old Washington Park to East New York, so when he got control, one of the first things he did was to move it back to South Brooklyn, to new Washington Park. That was in 1898.

In those days he had many a bitter pill to swallow because the Giants, a swashbuckling, insulting crew under the iron hand of John McGraw, regularly beat Brooklyn's ears off and landed at, or around, the top of the league. Ebbets had a lot of ballplayers like "Whitey" Alperman, a clown outfielder who could hit, but who gave even the simplest fly ball a thrilling waltz before he captured it.

When Alperman made a simple catch, the fans needled him by cheering wildly. The poor fellow would tip his cap gratefully, while the knowing Dodger fans yowled: "Put your cap on, Alperman, you bum, who do you think you are, anyway?" (Doesn't that immortal line have a familiar ring?)

Ebbets did not have too much luck. In 1907 the Dodgers had the pick of the Augusta club in the South Atlantic League and chose Nap Rucker, a pretty good pitcher. But they could have taken another ballplayer from the Augusta roster: a certain Ty Cobb.

However, the fans liked the zany Dodgers, and Ebbets, warming up, became convinced that Washington Park was too small. Scouting around, he chose a garbage dump in a part of Brooklyn they called Pigtown, bordered by Bedford Avenue, Sullivan Place, and Montgomery Street. He quietly began to buy up parcels of land in that neck of the woods. Then word of his plans leaked out, and poor Charley had to pay double.

He had started to buy land for the new park in 1908. By 1911 he was out of money. That brought in the McKeever Brothers, Steve and Ed. Having made a fortune in contracting, the McKeevers ventured into baseball because they had a hunch the new ball park would be successful and so would the Dodgers. They were willing to back their hunch with $100,000, enough cash to get Ebbets out of the clutches of his creditors. For their share the McKeevers received 50 per cent of the club's stock. Dearie McKeever Mulvey, Steve McKeever's daughter, and Jim Mulvey, her husband, still own 25 per cent.

As could be expected, there was a zany touch to the new ball park. Ebbets showed the plans to the "Four Kings," the four most influential baseball writers in the Brooklyn picture. These men, Abe Yager of the *Brooklyn Eagle*, Len Wooster of the *Times*, Bill Granger of the *Citizen*, and Bill Rafter of the *Standard Union*, had often rapped Charley for his deals and for his handling of the club. But they were his friends, nonetheless.

These gimlet-eyed guys inspected the blueprints, checked the details, and enthusiastically okayed everything.

When the structure was nearly completed, someone discovered that everybody, including the trained observers from the press, had forgotten to include a press box!

Ebbets Field opened in 1913. In 1914, Uncle Robbie came in the back door. This set the tempo for Ebbets Field for years. It certainly helped put the cap and bells on the Brooklyns for fair.

Oddly enough—the Dodgers were always doing odd things —Robbie sort of sneaked up on the manager's portfolio. Ebbets and the McKeevers had hired him to be coach, planning to make Hughey Jennings manager after Bill Dahlen resigned.

But they failed to land Jennings, and so they promoted Robbie from coach to manager, although he hadn't yet started to coach! In New York Robbie had been McGraw's pal and coach for years. Earlier he had refused to come to Brooklyn from Baltimore, where he was catcher while McGraw played short. Now he waddled over in a hurry because he and McGraw had fought all through 1913, and were washed up as friends.

I knew Robbie, of course. But I knew him by "ear" even better than I knew him by sight. For years I had been hearing how he ran the club backwards.

He couldn't remember his players' names, much less spell them. One day a new outfielder named Oscar Roettger reported. Robbie always played his new men immediately, on the theory, I suppose, that nothing could be as bad as what he already had.

In this case he also had a right fielder named Dick Cox. When Roettger reported and Robbie said he could play right away, the sports writers wanted to know how to spell Oscar's handle. Robbie made several stabs at it, and became flustered. In disgust he said, "Hell, let Cox stay in right field!"

Brooklyn became a baseball synonym for confusion. The club had a scout named Larry Sutton who had sent up good ballplayers like Zack Wheat (1908), Casey Stengel (1912), and Ed Pfeffer and Sherry Smith (1914). But when they got to Flatbush they all seemed to be bitten by the daffy bug.

Robbie had a rockheaded shortstop named Ivy Olson who not only drove the fans crazy, but even argued with Robbie in the clubhouse afterwards. One day, in a jam, Olson failed to lay down a bunt. Robbie was boiling. He said he'd show him how to bunt. The next afternoon, at practice, Robbie grabbed a bat, told Duster Mails, one of his own pitchers, to fire the ball, and himself laid down a perfect bunt, although Mails tried to prevent it. Robbie puffed out his chest as he walked away from the plate. He'd shown these bushers!

"If he can bunt, so can I," announced Sherry Smith, the Dodgers' classy left-hander who was to pitch that afternoon. Smith grabbed a bat. Mails pitched one high and inside—and hit Sherry right between the eyes. They carried Sherry off. They almost had to carry Robbie off, too!

Robbie had a huge pitcher named Pea Ridge Day who became more famed as a hog-caller than as an artisan on the mound. This was understandable because the first hog-call that Day emitted in Ebbets Field occurred in an exhibition game in July of 1931 against the Yankees, and was greeted by a home-run drive that Babe Ruth walloped far and away over the right-center-field wall.

Hog-caller Day was a strong hayshaker, and he had a trick of expanding his chest to break any of the players' belts that they would agree to fasten around him. It was Pea Ridge's turn to pitch the next day when Del Bissonette challenged him with a particularly strong leather belt. Day strapped it around his huge chest, and he huffed and he puffed. There came an ominous sound of something giving 'way, but it wasn't the belt. Pea Ridge had cracked three ribs, and he couldn't let out a good hog-call, much less pitch a ball game, for a month!

Robbie liked big pitchers who could fire that ball, and he liked long hitters. But his teams were short on brains. They got into unbelievable mix-ups on the bases. Twice in one season his players hit home runs with the fabulous Babe Herman on base, and twice Herman came home alone. The home-run hitter had been called out for passing the star-gazing Babe loafing on the base lines en route!

I had seen great plays made by the champion Yankees, and I had watched the best in the National League. But all the great plays weren't talked about half as much as a certain Brooklyn play. To me it came to be the most famous play in baseball history, and it remains in my mind as being typical of the Brooklyn of that day.

It was on a Sunday afternoon in 1926. Boston was the visiting team. With the bases filled and one man out, Babe Herman belted the ball against the Ebbets Field right-field wall. The runner on third scored. But Dazzy Vance, who had been on second, passed third, started home, got confused, and scurried back toward third. Chick Fewster, the runner behind Vance, saw Dazzy hesitate, and stopped between first and second.

Herman, happy with his base hit, sailed merrily past first, past Fewster, rounded second in high, and slid into third just as Vance returned there. So the double off the wall became a double play!

Vance was a strike-out pitcher whom the Dodgers came up with unexpectedly when they sent Larry Sutton to look at a minor-league catcher. He, too, became part of the daffy legend that was Robbie and the Dodgers in those days.

Dazzy was a hulk of a man with undeniably great natural ability. He was twenty-eight before he made good. He pitched 187 victories for the Dodgers and was paid just

$187,000 in salaries. But he refused to pitch in Baker Bowl. The telephone-booth dimensions of this Philadelphia ball park were responsible for many pop-fly home runs. Daz said the place would hurt his record.

One day Daz was pitching against these same Phillies in Ebbets Field. Burt Shotton, later to run the Dodgers in my place in 1947, was managing the Phillies. Shotton had a great hitting club with players like Hurst, Klein, Whitney, and Schulmerich, but Brooklyn was leading by two runs. Phillies were on second and third. Two men were out and Klein was at bat. Robbie pointed at first base, which was open, and gestured for Vance to put Klein on.

Daz shook his head. He wanted to pitch to Klein rather than to Pinky Whitney, the next hitter.

Robbie insisted. Still Daz demurred. Robbie popped out of the dugout, gesturing violently: he was the manager. Vance shook his head, refusing to obey, like a stubborn schoolboy.

Finally Robbie had his way. He sent a messenger out and insisted that Daz walk Klein.

Now the bases were full of Phils, and Daz was pouting. Shotton relates that the first pitch to Whitney came in as big as a balloon.

Whitney hit it into the upper deck in left-field center.

On the mound, Vance turned his hands upward in a "Well-I-told-you-so!" gesture. He was happy; he had won *that* argument!

The Dodgers made so many blunders that Robbie, in a moment of inspiration, founded a "Bonehead Club." Each mental fumble committed by the boys was to bring a contribution to the treasury of the "Bonehead Club." At the end of the year the funds were to be used for a farewell party.

Enthusiastically, Robbie told the writers all about his new idea. It would eliminate boners and encourage clear thinking. Then, at game time, he wrote out the line-up and had Coach

Otto Miller fetch it up to the umpire. On the card, Robbie wrote "Lombardi, c." But for some reason he sent Al Lopez out to start the game. That boner resulted in an automatic out!

So Robbie, quite flustered, became the first contributor to his new "Bonehead Club." The first and the last. For that evening, after the game, he dissolved the club. "That stuff is all right for college kids," he huffed. "But we're grown men. That's out!" By then he probably had forgotten that he had started the club himself!

Robbie wasn't the only Dodger who thought up bright ideas which backfired.

Charley Ebbets installed the first public address system ever tried in a ball park. It was the sensation of Ebbets Field for years, although not in the way that Ebbets had hoped. Ebbets' scheme was to have the umpire equipped with a lapel microphone which would be hooked up when he stepped on a metal strip behind home plate. The umpire could make all the announcements of player substitutions in that way instead of by using a megaphone.

The big experiment got off to a miserable start. The only sounds to come out of the loud-speakers were crackling noises described by Tom Meany, the Number One wit of the Dodger press box, as something like "a thousand eggs, frying simultaneously." So they turned off the static and the gadget was temporarily forgotten. But in the fifth inning, when a player was cussing the plate umpire, and vice versa, over a called third strike, the device suddenly began to work *loud and clear!* What came out of the speakers made frail women blush and strong men grip their seats.

The next day Ebbets scrapped it all and Ebbets Field did not have a public address system again until 1936.

Robbie and the Dodgers I knew and heard about were

famous for their mistakes. The old gent had quarreled with
Joe Vila, powerful Sports Editor of the *New York Sun,* and
Vila had assigned baseball writer Eddie Murphy to follow the
Dodgers and criticize Robbie. I said "follow" because Murphy did not move with the team like other baseball writers.
He tailed the team like a gumshoe sleuth, and made his own
railroad and hotel arrangements. Every day, without men-
tioning Robbie's name, he referred to the "Falstaffian leader
of the Dodgers" sarcastically, and detailed each of the blunders the manager had committed during the day.

It impressed me that Murphy was able to fill an entire column each day and hardly ever repeat himself. Truly, Wilbert
Robinson must have been the blundering-est of all baseball
men!

Things became no saner in Brooklyn when, after a short
interlude under Max Carey, Casey Stengel was handed the
managerial reins.

Stengel, it seemed to me, was expected to run the club like
an Olsen and Johnson routine. He obliged. One of his first
"finds" was "Frenchy" Bordagaray, who had qualified to be
a Dodger by racing a horse around the bases in a Coast League
ball park.

Frenchy reported to the Dodgers wearing a Vandyke
goatee and carrying a violin under his arm. He could run fast,
too, an ability which was to be invaluable to him when he
became involved with indignant managers. There were plenty
of the latter, for Frenchy blew through baseball like a gust
of wind, testing, and I do mean testing, the White Sox, Reds,
Cardinals, Yankees, and Dodgers, as well as assorted minor-
league clubs. Frenchy was tossed out of baseball in 1947—I
got tossed that year, too, but for different reasons. An umpire
in the Sally League said Frenchy spit at him. Mrs. Bordagaray
explained later on that Frenchy's mouth always waters when
he thinks of lemons, or gets mad.

One fine day with the Stengel Dodgers, Frenchy was picked off second base while *standing on the bag!* He was tapping his foot on the bag and the opposition's second baseman, strolling over, ostensibly for a chat, applied the ball to him like a poultice. The umpire cried "Yer out!"

In the dugout Stengel nearly collapsed.

"What happened?" he asked Frenchy.

"Dunno, Casey," said the Frenchman, who had been in jams like this before, "I guess he musta got me between taps!"

In an interview after that, Stengel was asked who was the fastest player on his team.

He gave this some thought. "Bordagaray is the fastest man I've got," Casey replied. "Running to the wrong base!"

These were the Dodgers. They did everything backwards. Running to the wrong base was their trademark. They had always been buffoons.

And now, I thought bitterly, I was to become one of them. What a comedown!

Chapter 3

OVER THE TOP—IN SEVENTH PLACE

How I hated Frank Frisch—and Branch Rickey, too—for selling me down the river to Brooklyn, this baseball bughouse! I delayed reporting as long as I could.

I was still holding out when the Brooklyn club was playing its 1938 spring exhibition games in Clearwater, Florida. But there wasn't anything I could do about it. I had to be a Dodger whether I wanted to or not.

If only I had known then into what a bed of clover I was being pushed!

To be sure, Brooklyn was no soft spot. The has-been and never-was ballplayers in Dodger suits had dropped sixteen out of their last seventeen games in the 1937 season; they were to blow their last seven decisions in the soft 1938 citrus circuit. They looked pretty bad to me when I was still loafing on the sidelines. I was holding out for a $12,500 contract and a chance to make an additional bonus of $2,500, as I had done in St. Louis. But they must also have looked pretty bad to Larry MacPhail, the Rickey protégé who had built up the Reds and now was reviving Brooklyn. For he finally gave in, and, in his Packard car outside the Clearwater ball park, signed me up. I remember he tossed in a set of Bobby Jones golf clubs, too.

Maybe I was supposed to be the Napoleon who was to lead the boys out of seventh place. But I knew I was no ball of fire. My legs had begun to bother me. I had trouble with my throwing elbow: bone chips. Then I split my hand, and was out for a few weeks. Since, with me on the sidelines, the boys kept on kicking games away in Florida, the illusion grew in the mind of Burleigh Grimes, our manager, that I would be a wonder-worker or something, and that the team would start climbing upward as soon as I was in the line-up regularly

One fervent Dodger fan, who had brought his family to Clearwater with him, stopped me in the lobby of the Harrison Hotel and said, "You're our man, Leo. We've been waiting twenty years for you!"

I thought he was nuts.

"We haven't had a shortstop for twenty years," he sighed. "Every time we thought we had one, something happened. First it was Joe Tinker. Ebbets thought we had the deal made, but Garry Herrmann of the Reds had to back down and couldn't deliver Tinker, whom he'd actually sold to Brooklyn for $20,000.

"Then Larry Sutton found Ollie O'Meara, and he looked great. But Ollie broke a leg and that was the end of him.

"We got Davey Bancroft," he went on sadly. "Too late. Davey was through. So was Rabbit Maranville all washed up when we got him."

It was a grim recital. Who was next, I wondered?

"We gave up a hatful of cash and six players to get Johnny Butler," my informant continued. "But Butler couldn't do it. He collapsed. Ulcers. Nearly bled to death."

Next?

"We gave Jess Petty to get Glenn Wright," the fellow moaned. "What a hitter that Wright was, and what a guy! But my six-year-old daughter could throw harder than he could. You could run a load of hay under every one of his pegs from short. He couldn't throw out a guy who ran to first backwards."

"So," he summed up, "at last we got you, Leo. You're our guy."

With a jinx like that following the Dodger shortstops, I felt ready to collapse right then. I didn't feel any better the next day when a pudgy catcher named Paul Cervinko outran me in a training-camp race.

But with me on the sidelines the boys continued to lose, and in reverse, you might say, it built me up to be quite a hero. For some reason, everybody was convinced that when I played short this would turn into a dandy team.

After watching awhile I had a few ideas of what was wrong with this sick ball club. But when I got in the game I really found out. The first day I played, I fielded a double-play ball and shot it to Tony Lazzeri, who was covering second. The ball whizzed by Tony's ear, into right field. I was sure he never saw it.

Lazzeri raised his glove to his face. "Take it easy, Leo!" he said out of the side of his mouth. "I'm not as fast on those things as I used to be. You'll have to throw the ball slower."

So I began to lob the ball to Lazzeri, and we missed the man at first by a full stride or two.

I thought I had played with a weak ball club at Cincinnati, but nothing like this one. I could see it was going to be a tough year all around.

It opened tough for Grimes. I was for him, because I knew he had been for me when MacPhail said he had a chance to get me from the Cardinals. "Old Wirewhiskers" they called him when he was pitching, because he never shaved the day he was due to pitch, choosing to look rough and tough out there on the mound. Many a time when I was with the Cards I had ridden Burleigh, only to have him bark at me, right from the mound: "Be ready, Busher, because I'm going to knock you on the seat of your pants when you get up there to hit." He almost always did knock me down, too.

But Burleigh must have liked me, too, for he made me field captain. We saw that we faced a tough year. And right at the start Grimes got in bad with MacPhail, which was not hard to do.

It was Larry's first year in full charge. He was throwing off sparks as he ripped Ebbets Field apart, tore out the moldy corridors and the Ebbets-McKeever heirlooms, and put in the press bar, which later was to become known as "Larry's Saloon and Gymnasium." It was on that very bar, incidentally, that MacPhail once wrote me an order, so hard and with such anger that reporters could read the indented words in the mahogany weeks later.

One of Grimes's faults was his frankness. When the writers asked him how his awful team was going to do in the National League race, he told them. He said he didn't think this club, as it stood, could beat the Bloomer Girls. Where was the pitching? he demanded, obliging with the questions himself. He couldn't expect to win many games with old men like Heinie Manush and Kiki Cuyler in the outfield alongside of Buddy Hassett who hadn't played out there before. Long Tom Winsett? What "Old Wirewhiskers" said about that guy was unprintable.

Where would the team finish? the writers asked.

"A snappy eighth," "Boily" Grimes retorted. "Maybe seventh, by a miracle," he hazarded.

MacPhail read that interview and bounced out of Brooklyn as though he was riding a rocket. The 1937 team had finished sixth; if, after all the MacPhailian magic, it was going to drop to seventh, what did that make Larry look like? He commanded the unlucky Grimes to leave the team in charge of coaches Andy High and Jess Haines, and to meet him in Greensboro, North Carolina, where no writers would hear him roar. MacPhail announced in Brooklyn that if his team was seventh on May 15, there'd be changes made. Grimes knew what "changes" meant.

The unhappy Grimes told MacPhail that he had been misquoted. But when he got to Richmond a reporter on a local paper quoted him as saying the New York writers who traveled with the Dodgers were "a lot of heels." Twice as miserable now, Grimes denied that, too. But the rumors had started. The team hadn't yet opened the season and the boys were already predicting that soon I would be the manager, or

that Babe Ruth would. The *Brooklyn Eagle* ran a picture of
MacPhail with his arm around Grimes, and captioned it,
"Will you love me in September as you did in Florida?"

Every time we lost, which was almost daily, MacPhail got
on the phone and burned up the wires. One day the Boston
Braves belted us 15 to 1. That night Grimes and Secretary
John McDonald blew town. They had been ordered to try
to sign a few of the ballplayers whom Commissioner Landis
had made free agents in "purging" the Cardinal farm system.
But those ballplayers were not ready. They were years away.

Grimes was doing his best. He had been a great competitor
and he could not understand why other ballplayers did not
have that same driving power.

Burleigh was Branch Rickey's type of pitcher—a "captain."
Rickey had told me that a baseball team was not unlike an
army. "You've got to have a leader, and it must be the
pitcher. He must want to take charge out there on the
mound. If he doesn't, he will always be a private. This Fiddler
Bill McGee we have will always be a private. Maybe he
might become a corporal. But he could never be a captain,
like Grimes or Dean!"

Yet here was Burleigh, a captain in the Mahatma's book,
with hardly any army to boss. Burleigh's athletes were all
soldiering, all right—and most of them were 4 F or overage!

We lost five of our first seven games and Van Lingle
Mungo, who had been one of Grimes's big hopes, wound up
in the repair shop, as he had been doing off and on since he
first began to have trouble with his arm. This time an osteo-
path in Philadelphia tinkered with the Mungo arm. But Van
could not throw the overhand thunder he had once con-
trolled. Now he threw sidearm.

Max Butcher got drunk and was fined $500. The next time
he pitched, Max shut out the foe—and hit a game-winning
homer with a man on. It was that kind of a club. But it did

not draw customers, and a clicking turnstile is about the only thing known to science which can lull MacPhail into silence.

Our biggest crowd in Florida was 2,000. On our first Western trip, 6,800, in Pittsburgh on a Sunday, was tops. Strangely enough, we seemed to win on the road, where we played better than .500; we won sixteen and lost fourteen. At Ebbets Field, we won only five out of our first twenty. The joint was all painted up, but nothing happened.

MacPhail had decorated the park in loud colors and when we first saw it, Babe Phelps, our catcher, blinked and pointed to the paint job with a shrug.

"Turquoise," said a reporter. "Ain't that something?"

"Don't try to kid me," said Phelps menacingly. "Turquoise ain't a color, it's a animal."

The team got no better. Our infield was not bad, with Camilli on first, Coscarart on second, myself or Johnny Hudson at short, and Harry Lavagetto on third. But the outfield came down to Cuyler, Koy, and Hassett, and I do mean came down. Koy could not hit at Ebbets Field, although he did all right on the road.

Phelps was slugging, but there was always something wrong with him. He caught only sixty games. And he was our only .300 hitter.

The pitching was horrible. Fitzsimmons worked occasionally, and Luke Hamlin was throwing home-run balls. They won about ten games apiece. Waite Hoyt drifted off to join the Bushwicks after getting his ears pinned back. Pressnell, Mungo, Butcher—they were all alike.

Grimes, although I was strong for the guy, was not exactly a streamlined manager, either. He always kept a red handkerchief in his hip pocket, and gave his signals with it.

"Boily" also had a habit of conducting the longest clubhouse meetings I have ever attended. Every day, before he sent his aged team creaking out on the field, he kept them for perhaps half an hour, reciting what they had done wrong the day before, and how they must win today. They were old hands, these fellows, and they had been through this for years. So, first they fidgeted, and then they talked back.

One day after a rather stormy clubhouse meeting in which Waite Hoyt and some of the older hands had talked back sarcastically, Burleigh called me into the trainers' room. As the two of us stood there, tears of frustration came to his eyes. He said, "I don't know what to do with them, Leo, I don't know how to make them win!"

I wanted to help him. I distinctly remember saying, "Don't let those clunks talk back to you like that, Burleigh, or the team will get out of control. You are the boss, and if they don't show you respect and follow orders, take their money, and they'll show more respect."

Chapter 4

MEET THE MANAGER OF THE DODGERS

NOBODY BUT GRIMES AND MACPHAIL WAS EXCITED ABOUT this 1938 collection of Dodger misfits. Certainly the Brooklyn fan wasn't interested. The attendance made MacPhail no happier than the final scores.

But not for nothing were they to sing about MacPhail later at the Baseball Writers' Dinner as the man with the "Pocketful of Schemes." One verse went:

> When mortgage-holders squall
>   I introduce a yellow ball—
> Oh, I've got a pocketful of schemes!
>   When there's no one in your park
> I can fill it after dark
>   Oh, I've got a pocketful of schemes!

Now, when he needed revenue and something to pep up the customers, MacPhail pulled the same electric-lighted rabbit out of his hat that he had produced in Cincinnati.

In Red territory, he had needed all his oratory and the backing of youthful, progressive National League president Ford Frick to get the other magnates to let him play seven games after dark. Here in Brooklyn the job was not so difficult. But MacPhail's plans leaked out. Les Scott wrote the facts about the ordering of the steel towers for the lighting system—even that they would cost $110,000—weeks before MacPhail gave out the news. However, Scott worked for a seed catalogue known as the *Brooklyn Citizen*, and although the *Citizen* printed the story, hardly anyone saw it.

Before the opener with the Reds, MacPhail staged a pre-

view of his lighting plant, and the Cincinnati writers pro-
nounced it better than their own.

Larry wanted the opener to be a memorable night. He got
Jesse Owens to run an exhibition race and Bill McKechnie
of the Reds promised to put in Johnny Vander Meer, who,
on his last time out, had pitched a no-hitter against Boston.

MacPhail, as I said, wanted it to be a memorable night: He
got his wish, in spades!

All Vander Meer did was pitch *another no-hitter*, with side
thrills thrown in. He had the parkful of Dodger bugs on the
verge of nervous breakdowns.

In the ninth, with everybody rooting for him, Vandy, who
thereafter became known as "the Dutch Master," got Hassett
out. He walked the next three men. This brought up Ernie
Koy. The usual Indian war cries in the stands to encourage
Ernie were fewer this time. Everybody knew he was poison
for Vander Meer. A few weeks earlier Johnny had beaten us
with four hits, and Koy had belted three of the hits, one a
home run. Now, here he was again. But this time everybody
wished he were back in Texas. The Brooklyn fans, always
fair-minded, wanted Vandy to get his second no-hitter.

Koy, however, rolled out meekly enough. And who do you
suppose came up as the potential twenty-seventh out? Nobody but yours truly, old Leo!

I never tried harder. Vandy was wild, and with three on, I
had him in a hole. Then I got the ball I wanted to hit—but I
belted a long foul into the left-field stands. Finally, I did hit
the ball hard. It was a drive which hung just long enough for
Harry Craft to get under it in center field. I am not so sure
many other center fielders could have caught it.

It certainly was a big event. Big, because we jammed the
park, as we were to jam it with an average of 27,151 fans a
night for seven night games. Big, too, because it signalized the
real birth of the new MacPhailian era.

Present to note the passing of the old regime was Mrs.

Minnie Ebbets, then eighty, first wife of old Charley. How her thoughts must have sped back to Washington Park and East New York and Ned Hanlon and Uncle Robbie that night! It was the last game she was to see. She had come into Ebbets Field quietly and unannounced, and she left with hardly anyone noticing that she had been there.

When the novocain which Vander Meer had administered had worn off, the pain returned and, in the cold gray dawn we realized that we had lost another. As a matter of fact, the Dodgers were to lose the first six night games they played in Cincinnati and Brooklyn.

We were also losing the day games too regularly. Mac-Phail wouldn't hold still, and I watched for the storm signals to go up. Larry grew more impatient with Grimes and with the team, and with the small daytime crowds. By mid-June I knew he had something up his sleeve.

One day in June, 1938, after we blew another, Larry waited for me at the bottom of the steps leading from the dugout. As we trudged back to our clubhouse, he popped the question:

"How do you think Babe Ruth would go on this club?"

I couldn't have been more surprised if he had asked me about exhuming Abner Doubleday. Everybody knew Ruth was through.

Larry saw the question in my eyes, because he quickly countered, "I mean as a coach—and just to hit a few out of the park in batting practice. Don't you think he would get the fans in here?"

I admitted that Ruth would draw the people if he was carried in by rickshaw. I added, "What does Burleigh think about this? Have you told him?"

MacPhail hadn't, but he said we'd have a big meeting in his apartment.

I passed the word to Grimes, and he was against hiring

Ruth. However, we were having a bad year and he was willing to do anything to help the gate and MacPhail. I said that if Burleigh didn't want the Babe, now was the time to talk up. But he said no, he guessed he'd just go along.

The meeting that evening at MacPhail's apartment on Columbia Heights, overlooking New York Harbor, was a corker. Ruth was willing to join the club for $25,000. MacPhail said no: most of the season was over, and Babe would have to take $15,000. They argued back and forth, and finally Christy Walsh, Babe's man, signed for $15,000.

That first night it became apparent that the Babe had managerial aspirations. He drew me aside in another room, and said, "I'll be the boss around here before too long."

This made me see red for two reasons. First, Grimes was my man, he had been nice to me, and I was doing everything I could to help him. He confided in me, had made me captain, and I felt responsible, and pretty bad that we weren't doing better.

Second, by now I had a few ideas myself, and while I never wanted to cut in front of Burleigh, I quickly let the Babe know that the line for aspiring Dodger managers formed over on the right, and that he would have to get behind me.

We had not exactly been pals when we were on the Yankee team together. Now Ruth told me that he did not like me. I thought we were going to have a scrap right then and there, but it blew over.

About a month later, Clay Bryant of the Cubs was shutting us out with one or two hits. He had two men out in the ninth, a 2-0 lead, runners on second and third, and Harry Lavagetto at bat. Ruth was coaching at first as usual, and I was waiting to come up after Lavagetto.

First base was open. Gabby Hartnett, the Cub catcher, turned to look scornfully at me, as much as to say, "Put Lavagetto on, and we will pitch to the All-American out." But there is a cardinal rule in baseball that you must not put the

winning run on base. The Cubs were soon sorry they had followed that rule.

Lavagetto hit a one-hop line drive off Billy Jurges' leg at
short, raising a lump the size of another kneecap. As the ball
rolled into short left field, both runners scored, and the ball
game was tied up.

Lavagetto and I had a private hit-and-run sign. As he led
off first base I flashed it to him. Suspecting something was up,
Bryant pitched out to me. As Lavagetto broke, I threw my
bat at the ball.

The Durocher luck held up. I hit what ballplayers call a
"squibbler," just inside the line down behind first base. Lavagetto scored, and the game was over.

After the game the writers came in and asked for the details
of the victory. One question was, "Did the Babe flash the hit-
and-run sign?"

I said no, Ruth hadn't. No more than that.

The writer, however, went back to his office and did a big
piece about Ruth being as useful as a wooden Indian coaching
down there at first base. Why, he pointed out, Babe hadn't
even given the sign for the play that won the game—or so
Durocher had said.

The next day we played at the Polo Grounds. As Grimes
began his clubhouse meeting, Ruth got up and said he wanted
to talk.

Burleigh declared that he was running the team, and that he
would run his meeting. If Ruth wanted to say anything, he
could have the floor later.

I just sat there. I wasn't wise to what was going on; I hadn't
seen the piece in the evening paper. Ruth had seen it, though,
and he was hotter than a firecracker.

When Grimes finished, Ruth stood up. "Durocher," he
began, "I've wanted to slap you down for a long time—"

I looked up. "What's eating you?" I asked.

He referred to the story in the paper, and added that I had belittled him by saying that he hadn't given the sign.

"Well, did you?" I barked.

The Babe repeated that he had been wanting to slap me down for a long time, and it might as well be right now.

I leaped up off my seat; we tangled.

It was all over in a moment, as those things usually are, but the scuffle left a mark under Ruth's eye. As the team went out on the field, Grimes called me back for a minute.

The story leaked out to the writers, who were in the dugout. There was Ruth—marked up. There were rumors of a fist fight in the clubhouse, and I was the only player who hadn't appeared on the field.

When I finally showed up they bombarded me with questions. "We gotta have the story," they insisted. "Did you belt Ruth?"

"Are you guys crazy?" I hollered with a straight face. "Look at the size of him, and look at me. What would I be doing fighting a heavyweight?" I shrank down as I said it, to make it more plausible. The whole thing was soon forgotten.

The Babe and I forgot it, too. We are friends and I have met him many times since. There is no doubt that this great-hearted fellow is the biggest idol our game has ever known.

As I said before, Brooklyn was a sick team, and it just about died on poor Burleigh a month before the season ended. With about three weeks to go, MacPhail gave him the bad news. The afternoon Grimes told me he was out he turned to his locker and began to throw his stuff into a suitcase. He was going home right then.

"Burleigh, don't do it!" I pleaded. "Never quit under fire. There will be other years and other baseball jobs—"

At last he saw it my way, and decided to stay. That night as we talked, he suddenly said, "Leo, you're the man for this job. With that tongue of yours you could jab some of these prima-donna ballplayers awake. Why don't you go up and ask MacPhail?"

I thought about it. I said I would never cut in front of him. "But if you'll go visit MacPhail with me, we'll see what happens."

Grimes was as good as his word. In fact, he threw the idea at MacPhail like a bombshell. "Here's your man, Larry," he urged. He put his arm around me and went into a long recital of what I could do. According to him, I was just what the doctor had ordered.

MacPhail brushed off the idea as only he could. He rattled off five reasons why I could never manage this club. I am sure he was making up reason Number 2 while he was still reciting reason Number 1. I lacked experience . . . I wouldn't be able to keep order or discipline . . . and so on.

The World Series was in Chicago that year. Of course, we attended. Our rooms were at the Congress Hotel.

One evening Larry called me to his suite. I entered. He was lying on the bed with a highball in his hand. "What now?" I wondered.

He called to his brother Frank, a fine fellow, now dead.

"Come in here, Frank," he said, with a sly grin on his reddened pan, "and meet the 1939 manager of the Dodgers."

That was the way Larry MacPhail loved to do things. When he had made up his mind I couldn't tell. But I was in.

Chapter 5

IN AGAIN—OUT AGAIN—FINNEGAN

THE WINTER OF 1938–39 BROUGHT THE DODGERS RED BARBER, Whitlow Wyatt, and Durocher, manager. I soon had the distinction of being the first one to be fired, as well as the one most frequently to be given the gate. The first time, at Hot Springs, Arkansas, where I took the pitchers for early conditioning, we hardly had time to get a cup of coffee before MacPhail bounced me. That was a story.

Larry had brought Barber on from Cincinnati, where he had made a hit broadcasting baseball. The Ol' Redhead was a quick click in Brooklyn, too.

Incidentally, Barber's is a real Horatio Alger story. He once told me that he was practically broke when he landed in Cincinnati for an audition broadcasting the Reds' games. He had come up from Tallahassee, where he had been fooling with a microphone at a college radio station. Because he wanted to make a good appearance at the audition Red splurged on a hotel room and had his suit pressed. But after those luxuries he had only about two bucks left. However, he got the job, and it became his springboard to Brooklyn and success. Barber is now probably a $100,000-a-year man!

Wyatt had been a so-so pitcher in the American League. He had been short on control and had had arm trouble. Now he was about thirty, but they said he had finally learned to pitch. The year before at Milwaukee he had won twenty-three and lost only seven.

The first day at Hot Springs we galloped over the mountains and took the baths. As a result we were pretty tired that night. Still, the place was like a morgue, so I went over to a joint called the "Belvedere Club" to play bingo, of all things.

34

International News Photo

Vilbert ("Uncle Robbie") Robson, former Dodgers president.

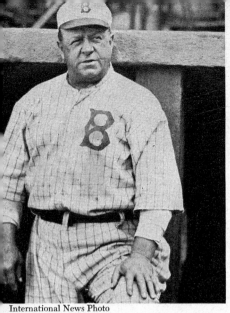

Shot of Babe Herman loaned by Dodgers fan J. L. Hoffman.

Leo Durocher when he played shortstop with the Cardinals.

International News Photo

Burleigh Grimes pauses to chat with Babe Ruth at Ebbets Field.

Press Association Photo

Famous fan Hilda Chester gets bracelet from Dodgers. Surrounding her are Mickey Owen, Chuck Dressen, John Griffen, and Max Macon.

The Dodgers' Sym-phony Band, the unique "musical" organization which claims a large share in Dodgers success.

Dodgers rooters are loyal and uninhibited.

To be first in line for bleacher seats at a World Series game Dodgers fans will camp out for as much as thirty-six hours with blankets and sandwiches.

Brooklyn pastor B. F. Benson prays publicly for a Dodgers victory.

Ladies' Day at Ebbets Field brings out loyal feminine fans.

The Belvedere was filled with folks balancing cards on their knees and filling in the numbers as they were called. About a dozen of my players were there, too, each nursing a card which cost two bucks.

I wanted to be sociable, so I bought five cards for ten dollars. Everybody gave me free advice. They said that on five cards I wouldn't be able to follow all the numbers.

I was busier than the famous one-armed paper hanger all right, but I won the second game—twenty dollars. Then came the big, final game for the sweepstakes. I captured that and the $664 prize.

Naturally it got into the papers. The next morning MacPhail was on the phone. "Night clubber!" he barked. "You're not a manager, you're a gambler! You're fired!"

I didn't know what to do. But I had a general idea of how MacPhail operated, so I went right on managing. Nothing ever happened; the incident was never referred to again.

One of our bright hopes was Red (Russell) Evans. He had pitched for New Orleans the year before, and had been named the Southern Association's most valuable player. The moment I saw Evans tossing the ball on the lawn of the Eastman Hotel where we lived, I liked him. I liked the way he carried himself. I told the writers we would take a closer look at him in the early training games.

Evans had several peculiarities. He never wanted to go to bed. He worked harder than anybody else during the day, dashing over the hills and down the valleys, and chasing fungoes until everyone else had been run into the ground. But at night he liked to go out and drink beer; not a couple of bottles, but maybe fifteen or twenty. And we just couldn't get him to bed. Funny thing, unlike most night-owl players he never lied. If you asked him where he was, and what time he came in, he told you straight. That made me like him even more.

I began to notice that when we took our jogs through the hills, Evans would be so far out in front after the first mile, that he would be out of sight. Running beside Evans every day was Whitlow Wyatt, whom I judged to be a farmer, or a trapper, from the Georgia hills. Anyway, Whitlow was an outdoor guy and knew how to navigate those crags and trails, while the rest of us stubbed our toes and puffed like vintage 1900 locomotives.

Invariably, when we straggled back to the hotel well beaten-up, Evans and Wyatt were waiting for us, looking cool and refreshed. I hated to be outdone at anything, so I was convinced that no one could gallop those twelve miles that fast. I felt that Evans and Wyatt had found a short cut and were cheating on the rest of us.

That first year I was manager I did my own detective work. This assignment nearly killed me. The next day I clung to that pair until my face was as red as a stop light and my lungs were ready to explode. All I discovered was that they really did do the distance—in a breeze. I was so mad I couldn't have talked even if I had had any breath left.

Evans was the first of the daffy bunch of ballplayers I was to collect in the next two seasons. He weighed only 160 pounds, but he could drink enough beer to float a cabin cruiser. The pay-off came one night when he borrowed fifty bucks from me and stayed out overtime.

I have always told my players that if they have good reason for staying out late, they will not be turned down—if they ask permission. This night I was hoping that Red would ask permission. As I peeled off the five tens I waited for him to ask, but he never did. So I sat up in the lobby and waited for him. Just in case I should miss him and he came in by a back door, I had the house "dick" put a plug in the door of his room, which was so crowded with empty beer bottles that you had to step gingerly to locate the floor. The detective put the plug in the lock, which meant that the key would just not fit in.

I waited in the lobby with Charley Dressen, one of my

coaches, and John McDonald, our road secretary. The midnight curfew hour passed. Outside it was raining cats and dogs. Presently Dressen chuckled, "He's out on the porch now." Charley had spotted Red in the shadows. It was about 2:00 A.M.

I went out after him, but Evans was too slick for me. He went in by another door just as I stepped out. Charley saw him streak up the stairs to his room.

I sauntered up. The hall outside Red's room was dark. No sign of him. "Better come out, Red," I said casually. "I know you're here."

Evans descended from the next stair landing. "Skipper," he said sheepishly, "my key won't seem to go into my lock."

"That's the beer!" I retorted. "You've just had so much beer you can't find the keyhole." And with that I took the detective's gadget, quickly removed the plug, and opened the door. "Good night, Red," I said. "You and I will have a conference tomorrow."

So I got ready to hand out my first fine. Just thinking about it that night I bet I didn't get as much sleep as Evans did.

When we reached the clubhouse the next day and dressed, the players, including Evans, lounged around on the equipment trunks. However, I put a single chair over on the other side of the room. "Over there by yourself, Mr. Evans," I murmured, smooth as silk. "For the present, you are not one of the players on this team. But I am going to ask the players to decide what should be done with you."

Red blinked and looked surprised. I started to outline the case against Russell Evans like a district attorney.

At one point Dressen piped up, "Evans drinks eight or nine bottles of beer a night. No player can—"

Charley got no further, for the culprit was on his feet, roaring like a bull. "You can't belittle my beer-drinking like that!" bellowed Red. "Eight or nine bottles! I had twenty-six bottles last night—"

The players conferred in a little knot. Soon Freddy Fitzsimmons, who was spokesman, announced, "We think he ought to be fined $100."

The next day Red came to me with a grin from ear to ear. "You'll never catch me again, Skip," he vowed.

I asked how he figured that.

"I just can't afford them hundred-dollar drinks of beer," he grinned.

Red was a hard-luck guy. He pitched our opening game of the season that year against the Giants, and Zeke Bonura beat him with a homer with a couple of men on.

One day soon after that he was pitching a whale of a game against the Cardinals, and the score was 0-0 in the ninth, with Pepper Martin on third.

Red took a lot of time with his delivery, and Pepper made a trial run toward the plate, skipping back to third at the last second.

"Time!" I hollered. "Evans, Martin will steal home on you if you don't watch him."

Red shook his head, sagely.

But, just as I had warned, Martin stole home on the next pitch, and we lost, 1-0!

Red lost another game in which he led the Phils, 1-0, in the ninth. He balked the tying run over.

He had enough stuff to win, but we could never get him to go to bed, and finally we had to send him to the Southern League. About a month later I got a letter from him saying that things were tough. He was broke—and could he please have back that C-note I had fined him?

I sent Evans the money.

I liked him because he always told the truth, instead of making up fables. That was one difference between him and Boots Poffenberger and Mungo, and some of the other characters I was soon to acquire for my traveling Dodger asylum.

Chapter 6

THE FABULOUS MacPHAIL

I WAS SOON TO RUN INTO TROUBLE FROM ANOTHER QUARTER: MacPhail.

This 1939 team had nothing much of anything, except the power to give me headaches. After all, Tuck Stainback, Ernie Koy, and Gene Moore were our best outfielders.

But we had a youngster named Pete Reiser. We had picked him up for a hundred dollars on a tip when the famous Commissioner Landis edict cut loose a bunch of ballplayers from the Cardinal chain. That spring, when we got to Clearwater, I took a quick look at Reiser. All the kid collected was seven straight hits, while he got on base eleven times in a row. Naturally, I wanted to see more of him. But he appeared to have a scatter arm, and I did not think he was the infielder he should have been.

Next thing you know, when we went North I had put him in center field in place of Dixie Walker. We arrived at Camp Wheeler, Georgia, on a Saturday morning. There waiting for me was a wire from MacPhail. It was an order to bench Reiser.

I was still pretty fresh, I guess. I had been talking so much about Reiser to the writers that I could not very well bench him for anything less than a broken leg. Anyway, I felt that I might as well find out whether MacPhail or Durocher was managing the team. So I shrugged off the telegram and played Reiser in the Saturday game.

Sunday morning MacPhail flew into Camp Wheeler with a full head of steam. I missed him on the first bounce, for I went to eleven o'clock Mass that morning. Not until I was pulling on my uniform for the game that afternoon did I suspect I was in the doghouse. John McDonald came to my room and said the storm warnings were up; the boss wanted to see me right away.

As soon as I stepped inside MacPhail's door he roared in one full breath: "You're through, fired, suspended without pay, out of my organization!"

Then he turned to McDonald, and ordered him to write out an announcement for the papers telling of my dismissal.

That scene I will never forget. McDonald was sitting on one twin bed, with his portable typewriter on the other. He was purposely fumbling with the keys, making mistakes and taking a long time to hammer out what MacPhail was dictating, for he was hoping that Larry would cool off.

As MacPhail noticed that McDonald was not keeping up with the tirade he had launched, he boomed: "You're incompetent, too, McDonald. I ought to get rid of you, as well!"

I sat there feeling pretty glum, when MacPhail came to the most violent portion of his announcement. I hardly heard it because I was so low.

"Larry, you can't put a thing like that in the papers!" quavered McDonald.

"Oh, I can't?" bellowed MacPhail. "Well, for talking back you're through, too, McDonald, as soon as you finish your typing."

As MacPhail went on heaping sulphur and venom into his press announcement, I came out of my trance. When he reached a particularly nasty part I bounced to my feet. I figured I was through anyway, so why should I let this guy say those things about me?

I grabbed him by both lapels; the bed was behind him, and the window behind that. I gave him a shove, and he went down in a heap, between the bed and the window. That was that! I felt better.

As I prepared to stalk out of the room, I flung at him, "Mac-Phail, you don't want a manager, you want a rubber stamp!

You had a lot of nerve, thinking you were going to write out my line-ups for me. I'm glad I played Reiser yesterday and found you out in time!"

"I only wanted to keep Reiser from getting major-league ideas too soon, Leo," returned MacPhail, pulling himself together. "He needs another year in the minors. We'll never get him to go down if he stays in our line-up."

That soothed me a bit. "Well," I growled, "if you had put your reason in the telegram, it would have been different."

The following day we were in Atlanta. I was in my room dressing when the phone rang. It was MacPhail.

"Where are you, Larry?" I asked, thinking it was long-distance.

"In the lobby," came the reply. "May I see you?" He had followed us there by plane.

When he entered the room, he had a big smile on his face. "Leo," he said—and big tears were actually streaming down his face!—"you and I understand each other better now!" Everything was hunky-dory again.

It soon became apparent to everyone that we had a wobbly club. The infield, with Lavagetto, Coscarart, Camilli, and myself, was pretty good, but the outfield was bad, and the pitching was worse.

The one bright ray of sunshine was Wyatt, who later was to get tangled in a play with Lonny Frey of the Reds, and jam up a knee that took two years to heal. The Reds, incidentally, were the sleepers of the National League. They had finished last in five of the previous eight seasons and now manager McKechnie had them on their way to a pennant.

Wyatt was great, but even that was to get us into a rhubarb. When we got Wyatt, MacPhail had sent a bundle of cash and promises to Henry Bendinger, the Milwaukee owner. But Mac-Phail neglected to send the players he had promised, and the

Milwaukee man told Sam Levy, a baseball writer out there, that he was going to appeal to Landis to have the deal declared null and void.

Harold Parrott, who was then writing a column for the *Brooklyn Eagle*, heard about the situation. . . . The sports extra of the *Eagle* containing Parrott's story arrived at Ebbets Field one afternoon just as Wyatt was putting the finishing touches to a nifty shutout.

MacPhail, standing up near the hot-dog stands at the top of the lower tier behind home plate, heard the newsboys hawking the *Eagle*, which had a big headline: LANDIS MAY VOID WYATT DEAL

Wyatt was just about the whole Dodger team, and Larry knew it. He was exploding in three different directions, when Parrott happened to come out of the press box.

Larry addressed Parrott as fourteen different kinds of a liar, and barred him from the press box, from the ball park, and, some witnesses say, even from Brooklyn.

Harold was not as accustomed to this sort of abuse as McDonald and I were. He called Ford Frick, the National League president, to make sure he would be able to get inside the park the next day.

Pretty soon a good feud was running. That annoyed the Brooklyn Trust Company which just about owned both the *Eagle*, which had been through bankruptcy, and the ball club, which was heavily in debt. George Barnewall, a big man at the bank, called a peace luncheon to get the bank's two stepchildren to bury the hatchet.

MacPhail was present, as were assorted *Eagle* editors, and Parrott. The idea was to have Larry declare that he regretted he had insulted the writer in front of so many people, and to have Parrott put out his hand and shake on it.

MacPhail bubbled over. After one cocktail he was telling how he was going to add new light towers . . . a better lighting system . . . more seats . . . better ball park. Another cocktail

and two courses later Barnewall finally managed to edge into
the torrent of the MacPhailian conversation.

"Larry, we called this lunch," began George, "because without thinking, you called Harold Parrott a —— ——— ——— in
front of a few thousand people the other day."

"Oh, that!" beamed Larry, with a generous wave of his
hand. "Why, I'm willing to forget the whole thing. Now, as
I was saying—"

It was the last that was ever heard of that incident!

Our pitching became worse and worse, and we began grasp-
ing at straws. One straw was Baron "Boots" Poffenberger. Del
Baker, who had had him at Detroit the year before, warned
me about him, but MacPhail had painted glowing pictures
about how the fellow could pitch, and in a weak moment I
agreed to take him.

The Baron was a short-armed, little guy, and I liked his
stuff. He knew how to pitch, and, at first, seemed to talk on
the level, so I signed him. He had been getting $4,000 in the
minors. MacPhail told me to get him for as little as possible,
and not to go over $8,000. I wanted to get the guy on my
side, so I gave him a speech about having heard a lot of Poffenberger stories, but that I was going to start with him fresh.
I would give him $8,000! The guy was so grateful I think he
would have shined my shoes.

Our next series was in Philadelphia. We were living in the
aristocratic old Bellevue-Stratford Hotel. Over the clerk's desk
was a huge clock, and, grouped around it, were clocks that
gave the time in cities like Tokyo, London, and Buenos Aires.

The first night in Philly, MacPhail and I were sitting just
off the lobby. He was having a drink, and talking a mile a
minute. We had won that day, so everything was okay.

It was about 12:30 A.M., and who do I see sauntering in but
Poffenberger! MacPhail did not spot him. Even if he had, he
would not have recognized him. Larry could not identify the

players even when they were in uniform, and was constantly asking who this was, and who that was.

The next day I had a little talk with the Baron. I asked what time he had come in the night before.

"Just about eleven," he said brazenly, looking me right in the eye.

"I was right there," I growled. "And the clock in the lobby said twelve-thirty."

"Maybe," he shrugged. "Maybe the clock you looked at said that. But one of them little clocks said eleven, and that was the one I went by."

I forgot the incident—until the next night. MacPhail and I were sitting in the same place, talking over another victory, and who should walk by but Poffenberger again. This time it was near 1:00 A.M. When I spoke to him the next day, Poffenberger gave me that ancient gag about an old aunt out in the suburbs, and how he had left her house at eleven, but it took longer than he figured to get back to the hotel.

When I was a busher I had used that one myself. So I told him, after this, to leave his aunt early enough to reach the hotel by midnight. Still, I was a little peeved because I had signed the guy and he had promised to behave. I added, "This is the end. From now on, if you break the rules, it costs you $200 the first time, $400 the second time, and so on."

The third night, MacPhail and I were sitting in the same place and Larry was having a few drinks on another win we had scored that day. There was no sign of Poffenberger, and at 2:00 A.M. we decided to go up to bed. Who should get on the elevator with us but the Baron! He did not bat an eyelash. But as he got off on a lower floor and MacPhail and I rode on, Larry said to me: "Wasn't that a ballplayer?"

I said, "Sure, Poffenberger."

MacPhail dragged me into his suite, and treated me to a big blast. The ballplayers, he said, were walking all over me. I was too lenient, I was an easy mark.

The funny part of it was he hadn't even seen Poffenberger wander in late the first two nights. I told Larry I'd fine him $200; but it didn't halt MacPhail's lecture.

It didn't stop Poffenberger, either.

Our next trip was to Boston. Although the night sleeper did not pull out until 2:50 A.M., the players were to be in their berths by midnight.

At 1:00 A.M. I asked "Senator" John Griffin, who checks in all the athletes, if everybody was aboard. The Senator said they were.

Just the same, I was curious about Poffenberger. I gumshoed to the Baron's berth, and found it buttoned up tighter than the Bank of England. I opened it cautiously. After my eyes got used to the gloom, I made out a shape lying under the covers.

However, I had a hunch it wasn't my man. When I felt Poffenberger's "body" it turned out to be a suitcase under the bedclothes. The Baron was wandering again!

Nobody could understand it. "I saw him in his pajamas, Skipper!" vowed Griffin.

Poffenberger had actually donned his pajamas to fool everybody and then had slipped his clothes on over them, and sneaked off. I set a sentry to await his return and report to me.

The next day I learned that the Baron had boarded the train just as it left the station. I confronted him.

He looked me right in the eye and told me he had been in his berth at 11:00 P.M.

"That was the first time," I retorted. "When did you come in the second time?"

"One o'clock."

"One hundred bucks fine!" I announced. "Now please start over."

"I got in at one-thirty!" he said.

"Two hundred dollars!"

"I got in at two o'clock!" he blurted out.

"Three hundred!" I said.

"Time out, Skipper," he pleaded. "I've had enough of this game. It's too expensive. I got on board just as the train was leaving at almost three o'clock—"

"Fine," I said. "In fact, three hundred bucks fine. Too bad you didn't tell me the truth the first time. You would have saved yourself two C-notes."

The first Western trip Poffenberger made with us was highlighted by a stunt he pulled in Cincinnati.

It was a blazing hot day. We were getting ready to charge out on the field against the Reds, who were leading the league; you know how you like to knock off the leaders. It was one-fifteen, when everybody should be in uniform in the clubhouse, but Poffenberger had not put in an appearance.

"You can tell him that'll cost him a hundred dollars," I said to the players. "And that's only the beginning!"

Suddenly, Dolf Camilli spoke up. "I saw Poffenberger in the hotel lobby as I came out here. He asked me to bring you a message."

"Go ahead, Dolf. What's the message?"

The muscular Camilli held back. "It sounds silly," he grinned.

Finally he told me. The Baron had decided it was too hot to play ball that afternoon, so he was not coming to the park. "Tell Durocher," he had said to Camilli, "that I am tired of the way he is keeping me, like a bird in a cage."

That time I suspended Poffenberger, fined him, and sent him home.

After a month he wrote asking for another chance.

I had had enough, but MacPhail talked me into forgiving him. MacPhail was like that: he would swear that some villain would never throw a ball again on his club, and the next week he would invite him back.

So I relented, and MacPhail sent Poffenberger $150 for a train ticket to rejoin us.

The Baron never came back. Neither did the $150.

We came into the final day of the 1939 season with a chance to clinch third place—if we beat the Phillies at Ebbets Field. It was a big day, for MacPhail was giving away an automobile to the fans via a raffle. However, the rain came down hot and heavy and there was some question whether we should play. We might gain third place by not throwing a ball.

We took a vote in the clubhouse and the decision was: "Let's not back into third money. Let's go out there and beat 'em!"

Soon we were in a jam. With Phils on first and second and one out and the score tied, I had to call in a new pitcher. I had Luke Hamlin and Carl Doyle all heated up in the bull pen. But when I sent word that it was to be Doyle, you should have heard the noises from MacPhail's private box under the upper tier behind home plate.

The park was crowded, and I suspect all eyes turned to Larry. He was blowing a fuse and hollering: "No, no, you nitwit; Hamlin will stop them, get Luke in there!" Larry always liked Hamlin, who was never a pinch pitcher; we were to have several fallings-out over Luke.

Now I was at shortstop, and as Doyle warmed up in the box and MacPhail still carried on, I felt that he was showing me up before the fans. So I thumbed my nose at him. If they could not see him, everybody could see me doing that. The crowd buzzed at this little sideshow. I even had the last laugh, for Doyle got us out of the jam with a double play, and we won the game as second-baseman Letchas fumbled an easy chance.

When MacPhail had signed me to manage that first year, he had raised me to $17,500 and told me I must keep on playing. He told the writers that although he was gaining a manager he was worried about losing a shortstop. I answered him by playing 116 games. He grumbled that I should have played 150!

Now, from Louisville, we bought "Peewee" Reese, a shortstop who looked like a high-school boy. The Red Sox, who had the pick of Louisville, had passed him up. But our chief scout, Ted McGrew, raved about the kid day and night. "Reese will shove Durocher onto the bench next year," he predicted.

I was happy to hear it.

Fanning with a few newspapermen one evening during the winter, I said I hoped Reese would play a lot of shortstop for our club the next season.

"What will MacPhail say to that?" asked Garry Schumacher.

"Nothing," I grinned. "Nothing. Because he'll be so mad he won't be able to talk!"

Chapter 7

BEANBALL, INCORPORATED

THE 1940 SEASON WAS NO NEARER TO SANITY THAN 1939 had been.

We had an outfielder who wore a pink corset because he had a bad back, and a relief pitcher who whizzed through our training base at Clearwater on a motorbike, giving vent to wild cowboy yells. The club developed a holdout war between first-baseman Dolf Camilli and MacPhail, which took, first a daffy, and then a violent turn. We paid $10,000 for a pitcher who stayed out late and then was on the verge of breaking me in half, and $25,000 for an outfielder who ate salads only and was so weak he couldn't wave his bat.

Our cast changed as frequently as the bill in small-time vaudeville. Players came and went as though we were working behind swinging doors.

Despite all this, we opened the season with nine straight victories. Number 9 was a nifty no-hitter by Tex Carleton, a pitcher we had picked up from Milwaukee for peanuts. It promised to be a real upside-down year.

But it was a patch-quilt team: Joe Vosmik, who had been a great hitter in the American League, couldn't always stoop far enough to greet a ground ball because of his corset. Still when Joe couldn't play, there was always a chance that Roy Cullenbine might be strong enough to sub for him.

Cullenbine, a switch hitter, and Steve Rachunok, a huge bear who pitched, were two athletes we had picked up when Judge Landis cut them loose from Detroit in another of his purges. Both men, it was soon evident, were born Dodgers.

Cullenbine confided that he had had a poor season in 1939 because he was twenty pounds underweight, and weak.

"Why were you weak?" I asked.

"My wife was having a baby," he explained.

Still I didn't understand.

"You know how they eat at a time like that," he went on. "Salads, salads, salads. That's all we had at home. Leo, funny thing I noticed about salads. You eat one, and you're still hungry. I was hungry all year."

Rachunok, a huge youngster, stood about six foot three, and weighed well over 200 pounds. It seemed as though that big body should be able to propel a baseball with dazzling speed. But Rachunok did not pitch with his body; only with his arms, as though he was directing traffic.

Rachunok and Chris Hartje, a catcher, began to stay out late. There were only two bars in Clearwater you could visit after midnight, so it was easy to find them.

The first time, I lectured the pair of them. But the very next night they stayed out again. I caught them red-handed, and fined them a hundred dollars each.

MacPhail heard about it. To my amazement, he made a crack about my clamping down too hard. "Maybe we can smooth it over," he said.

We had a rule on the club that no whisky was allowed at any time—and no beer until spring training was over. So when I caught the same pair out the third time, I was hopping mad. I didn't show it though, as I edged into their booth.

As I sat down, there was a stony silence. "Well," I began, "aren't you guys going to buy a pal a bottle of beer?"

Pretty soon I announced that it was going to cost them five hundred dollars each. With that I sent them back to the hotel.

Rachunok hustled right up to his room, but Hartje stayed out another hour.

The next day I told MacPhail what I had done. "Leo, perhaps you're too strict," said Larry. "Why not give them another chance?"

This, from the man who had almost fired me for giving Poffenberger too much rope, amazed me. I told him flatly that Rachunok and Hartje would be disciplined my way—or I was through.

Later it came out that MacPhail himself had scouted Hartje, who was thus Larry's first personal "prospect" for the Brooklyn club. Larry had bought many other players, but Hartje bore his own stamp. Naturally, he wanted Chris to make good.

But that didn't stop me. The next day, in the clubhouse, I told Hartje and Rachunok to take off their uniforms. I fined Hartje five hundred dollars, and sent him back to the hotel. He never returned to our club. Incidentally, he was killed in the summer of 1947 in a Seattle bus tragedy.

Then I turned to Rachunok. "I am socking you five hundred dollars, too, you dumb—" I began, and immediately knew I had made a mistake.

The big pitcher drew himself slowly to his full height and glared at me.

"Don't stand up there staring down at me!" I snapped, trying to sound unconcerned. Inwardly, I was wondering if the big kid was going to take me apart a limb at a time. I talked fast, but it was one of the trying moments of my early managerial career. I breathed easier when Rachunok subsided and left the clubhouse.

The next day the big Russian was back in uniform, working harder than ever. He never sulked. I liked his spirit, and a few days later I told him so. I also gave him back his $500.

The Russian Bear grinned happily. He was on my side now—and was I glad!

I didn't have much else on my side. As we got ready for 1940 we looked terrible, especially without Dolf Camilli.

The big Italian first baseman had flown into our Clearwater camp from the Coast. But before he would sign a contract, he wanted traveling expenses for his family, as well as a raise to $15,000.

MacPhail roared that he wasn't running a kindergarten, and did not intend to pay the expenses of Camilli's "eight kids."

Of course, that was a typical MacPhailian exaggeration. Camilli had only four youngsters. It made Dolf twice as mad.

Finally, MacPhail invited Camilli into an office on the lobby floor of the hotel. Elderly folks who had been dozing over their morning papers suddenly jumped up, startled. The noises that came from that "conference" must have sounded like the lion cage at feeding time. At one point there was a gurgling sound; Camilli had picked MacPhail right off the floor by his jowls. I didn't know what to do: Dolf was as strong as Strangler Lewis. I thought Larry was a goner.

Needless to say, they reached no agreement. Camilli did not like to have his family talked about, and I had all I could do to keep him from flying back to his California ranch.

This dragged on for weeks. MacPhail roared and was stubborn and Camilli threatened to go home. Meantime, we were kidding ourselves by playing Bert Haas at first. Result: I was without the first baseman I had hoped would make us a pennant threat.

Finally MacPhail growled at me: "Tell Camilli he is going to get that extra thousand bucks he is crying about, but don't let him know it is coming from me. This is one argument I want to win!"

Even at that I had a hard time with Dolf. He would have preferred to make Larry count the cash out to him in one-dollar bills.

"I'm guaranteeing you the money," I pleaded. "Don't you believe in me? I'll see that you get it. It may not be today, or next week, but you'll get it. I guarantee that."

We had a junky pitching staff. The year before, two of our pitchers had won twelve: Freddy Fitzsimmons, whose aging arm was twisting up like a corkscrew now, so that he couldn't work often; and Vito Tamulis, the Lithuanian relief pitcher who was the life of the outfit and rode his motorbike through Clearwater like a put-putting Paul Revere.

After our first fourteen victories, I couldn't have named our ace. Casey, Carleton, Hamlin, Fitz, Wyatt, and Kimball had each won two, and Macon and Tamulis had taken one apiece.

We whizzed through that first Western trip like a club on its way to a pennant, and MacPhail decided to bring the team home de luxe! Flatbush was buzzing. He chartered two airliners to transport us.

At this point we had our first trouble with our big catcher, Phelps. Wild horses could not drag him near an airplane. It was the first time I had ever heard of a blimp refusing to go up in the air. A couple of us tried to persuade him to fly. I said, "Babe, what difference does it make? If your number comes up, you're going to go, whether you're in a train, walking on the sidewalk, or in a plane!"

He looked at me suspiciously. "Yeah?" he mumbled. "Suppose you're up in a plane, and the pilot's number comes up. Where does that leave you?"

Anyway, we flew home in style—minus Phelps—and thirty thousand people milled around waiting for us at Floyd Bennett Field, down at the foot of Flatbush Avenue. I don't think there were a dozen among them who weren't sure we were going to win the pennant!

However, we soon had outfield troubles. Some of our fly-chasers could not establish contact with ordinary fly balls. Others, like Melo Almada, the Mexican, could go and get the ball, but could not hit good enough to drive it through a paper bag. Soon Almada, whom we had bought for $25,000 the year before, when MacPhail was claiming everything that came down the drainpipe, was shipped to Sacramento.

We had to give up on Cullenbine, who seemed too weak to swing a bat. His lethargy had brought him twenty-three walks in eighteen games, but he was supposed to be a cleanup hitter;

when we traded him to the Browns for Joe Gallagher, he was batting .180. Gallagher, unlike Cullenbine, swung at every- thing. He also ate everything that Cullenbine had missed, and was so big he took up more room on the bench than three men.

That year a lot of rhubarb grew in what Red Barber called, "the Flatbush pea patch." Our hard luck seemed to start when Jake Mooty beaned Peewee Reese early in June. The young- ster was in the hospital a week and out of the line-up more than three weeks.

MacPhail was shopping for a slugging outfielder. He adver- tised in all the newspapers; that is, he told the sports writers that he was willing to spend heavy sugar.

Branch Rickey answered the ads. We should have suspected something wrong right then. Branch has not let many good players get away from him, no matter what the price.

Anyway, Rickey could afford to part with Joe Medwick, who was supposed to be the best slugger in the league, because Joe had had trouble with Ray Blades, who had started the year as Cardinal manager, and the St. Louis fans were booing the Hammering Hungarian who had once been their hero.

The price was $132,500 cash and four players. Rickey threw in Curt Davis, the gaunt sidearm pitcher who had won twenty-two for the Cards the year before, but had got off to a bad start this season. The four players we gave Rickey did not amount to very much: Ernie Koy, Carl Doyle, Sam Nahem, and Bert Haas, who had been Camilli's first-base un- derstudy during the big Italian's spring war with MacPhail.

Whether Medwick had actually slipped badly before we got him, or whether what happened to him as soon as he climbed into a Dodger suit gave him his big shove downhill, I don't know.

Medwick and I had been long-time pals. I felt sure that I could straighten him out, and get him hitting again. After all, before I came to Brooklyn, he had hit .380 in Ebbets Field for the Cardinals. Since I had joined the Dodgers, he had fallen off a bit. Still people flattered me by saying I had tipped our pitchers on how to throw to him. They forget that when he was going good Ebbets Field was made to order for him. With the tremendous power he had he could paste that outside pitch up against the wall and scoreboard in right field. And he could park the inside pitch in the left-field stands.

So he moved into a suite at the Hotel New Yorker, where I lived. Joe had had a little trouble with some of the Cards, who thought he hadn't helped the club much the year before, when it had had a chance to overtake the Reds. They said he was a solo player, strictly for himself.

This came to the surface the second day of the first series we played against the Cardinals at Ebbets Field. It happened that we rode down in the hotel elevator that morning with Bob Bowman, who was to pitch against us that afternoon. I made some crack to Bowman and he replied, "I'll not have any trouble getting you out, anyway."

Medwick, who felt pretty sure of himself because he was the toast of the town, cracked, "I doubt if you will ever get to pitch to Leo. We'll belt you out of there before you get down the line-up that far."

Bowman bridled, and said something that several people in the elevator were to remember later that day: "I'll take care of both you guys. Wait and see!"

We had not been doing very well. The Reds had been in town before the Cardinals and they had cleaned us up. But now we took out after Bowman as if we owned him. The first three men lined out base hits. Two were still on, when here came Medwick.

Bowman whistled the first pitch high and inside. I can still see Medwick going down as the ball struck him in the temple. He was unconscious before he hit the ground. His back hit before his legs, which shot out in a sickening manner. He lay there, his arms outstretched.

Ebbets Field was like a madhouse. I tore out after Bowman, and there was fighting on the field. MacPhail, his face as red as a beet, came up through our dugout and went over to the Cardinal bench. He called them everything in the book, and a few new names besides. Pepper Martin and Johnny Mize tried to quiet him, but he wouldn't hold still. Trouble was brewing in the stands, too, and the police emergency squads were called. I guess MacPhail feared the indignant fans would go down and settle with Bowman and the Cards themselves.

Billy Southworth, who had succeeded Blades at the Cardinal helm, wisely took Bowman out and had him escorted back to the New Yorker by two detectives.

Now MacPhail called up Ford Frick and demanded that Bowman be barred for life for this "deliberate" act. He issued a long statement to the press outlining the "threat" that Bowman had made in the elevator. The MacPhail bulletin began, "Bob Bowman is a coward—"

All Brooklyn was up in arms. The next day the *Eagle* carried a headline on the front page fairly screaming, DISTRICT ATTORNEY WILLIAM O'DWYER TO INVESTIGATE MEDWICK BEANING. It was a good story because the reporter figured that O'Dwyer could make out a case of premeditated assault on account of Bowman's remark in the elevator. The episode snowballed into quite an atrocity yarn, because Peewee Reese was still out of action after the beaning he had received. The demand was made that the fighting O'Dwyer (quite a fan himself, by the way) investigate "Beanball, Incorporated" just as he had run "Murder, Incorporated" to earth. "Beanball, Incorporated" was represented as a league-wide move to thwart the Dodgers in their pennant bid by trying to bean key men like Medwick and Reese.

O'Dwyer, now Mayor of New York City, appointed Assistant District Attorney Burton Turkus to take charge of the investigation, and all parties were summoned for questioning. Thirty-two pages of testimony were taken, but nothing ever came of it. At that hearing, Billy Southworth made a great speech about clean baseball. I had not forgotten that speech the next day when Mickey Owen came into second base in a manner designed to cut Pete Coscarart in half as he covered second on the play. I wasted no time in calling the attention of Southworth, who was coaching at third, to this maneuver. Before I knew it, Owen, jogging past on his way to the bench, popped a punch at me. We both took a few swings, but nobody was seriously hurt.

The next man to be injured was Luke Hamlin. However, only his feelings were touched.

Luke was one of our pitching mainstays. He had a lot of stuff, but no savvy. He had the home-run habit, but bad. He did not hit homers himself. He let the other guys hit them by giving up soft pitches. He had allowed twenty-seven homers, frequently with men on. In fact, Luke was the main offender when the enemy belted us for fifty-six homers to bring in eighty-one runs, in fifty-two games.

Now Hamlin blew 4–0 and 5–0 leads in the last game against the Cardinals, and MacPhail charged into our clubhouse to call him a coward, too. Hamlin disappeared. In the writers' stories, he became "Lonesome Luke." No one could find him. Someone suggested dragging the river, but MacPhail, still fuming, said, "Hamlin's control is so bad that if he jumped into the river he wouldn't hit the water!"

With Medwick, Owen, myself, and now Hamlin, there was plenty of rhubarb in that one Cardinal series. One writer said, "Most of the trouble centered around Medwick's bean and Hamlin's lack of it."

Reese came back strong. He got a clean base hit the first time he re-entered the game. Medwick, however, returned shaky and gun-shy. Many think that the beaning ruined one of the greatest free-swingers the game has ever known, and that Medwick was never the same after it.

We realized that something was wrong shortly after he came

back, when Joe was up in the last of the ninth, against the
Pirates, the score tied, the bases loaded, three on, one out. The
game was crying to be won, but Joe pulled away from the
pitch and dribbled into a weak double play. We lost that game
in the thirteenth inning, when the Pirates got five runs.

"When we blow," wrote one of the Dodger scribes, "it's no
peanut whistle." As Joe failed, so did the whole club. Once I
had Joe batting as low as sixth in the line-up. He finished at
.301, but he did not belt the ball when it counted, or for distance. We finished twelve lengths behind the Reds, who had
had a taste of World Series money, and never wavered in their
pursuit of more of the same after they moved into first place
in July.

It had been a breathless, daffy year, but it could not end, it
seemed, without one more goofy chapter.

In late September, Umpire George Magerkurth had a bad
afternoon at Ebbets Field. As the game ended—we had lost—
and he was walking off the field, a short, stocky fan dashed out
of the stands, a strange light in his eyes. Perhaps Magerkurth
thought the fellow was about to start a friendly conversation.
At any rate, he was off his guard and before anyone could
shout a warning, big Mage, all 230 pounds of him, was down
in the dirt and on his back and this Lilliputian man was doing
a war dance on his chest.

Since the Dodgers had lost, the new excitement was sweet
balm to Flatbush hearts. To the overenthusiastic fan, Frank
Germano, who had forgotten not only his manners but his
parole—it seems he was out on some rap at the time—it brought
only trouble.

In no time Germano was in the brig again. However, the rest
of the fans, suddenly detecting in him the spirit of a champion,
did not let him down. The next day they took up a collection
in the stands, and hired a lawyer to defend him. Appropriately
perhaps, the lawyer's name was Wacke.

I still think we would have won the pennant that year except for the mishaps we suffered. Reese had been beaned, so had Medwick, and then Wyatt had still been bothered by his bad knee. Just as we pulled ourselves together for one final lunge at the pennant, Lavagetto went out with appendicitis, and we had to play Reiser at third. Then Reese went out again with two broken bones in his ankle, and old man Durocher had to go in to play short.

Meanwhile, the Reds moved calmly, behind fine pitching by Walters and Derringer, to their second straight pennant.

Around our club, there was not much calm, or peace, or quiet. In fact, you never could tell when a storm was going to blow up. It could start quite innocently. . . . We were all sitting around one night in New Orleans, during the winter baseball meetings. MacPhail was in an expansive mood. He was talking about the team he was building and about the farm system Branch Rickey, Jr., was cooking up for him.

Someone made a crack about the Cardinal players turned loose by Landis in 1938. Brooklyn had had very few good ballplayers that spring, and MacPhail had sent out every available bloodhound to track down and sign those emancipated players.

"That was the year McGrew had an extra beer!" somebody chuckled. "He missed the train out of Clearwater, and so he didn't get to Meridian, Mississippi, in time to sign Skeeter Webb—"

We all chuckled as Ted McGrew sucked his beer. Sure, that was one on old Ted. He had missed a train—and missed a ballplayer. But so what? That was two years ago, and Skeeter Webb hadn't turned out to be a whiz-bang anyway.

"That's how much you guys know!" retorted McGrew, wiping off a mustache of foam. "I'll tell you something about that story you never heard. The boss here was awful high on that Webb, and I couldn't steer him off the kid. I'd seen Webb, and I didn't like him. I was sure it would be tossing $20,000 down the drain to go that high to sign him. Well, there was only one thing to do. So I missed that train *on purpose*, and let someone else get to Webb first and have him!"

McGrew laughed.

But he laughed alone. A pall fell over the jolly group, for MacPhail was bristling like a cornered porcupine.

"Who's running this club?" he shouted, getting up from the table. "Am I running it, or is some half-blind, broken-down, washed-up umpire who thinks he can tell one ballplayer from another, running it? McGrew, you're through! Understand? I'm firing you!"

That was the longest bounce McGrew ever got from Mac-Phail—being fired *for something he hadn't done two years before*. But, fortunately, it didn't stick. The boss cooled off and Ted stayed with us.

Chapter 8

MUNGO VERSUS DUROCHER

ALL IN ALL, 1940 WAS NOT A LOST YEAR, ALTHOUGH IT CER-
tainly was a daffy one. We had been in seventh place when I
played under Grimes, third in my first year as manager, and
now we were second. So the fans looked ahead, and chanted,
as they had for the past twenty years, "Wait'll next year!"

One reason the Brooklyn fans were always looking ahead
hopefully was Van Lingle Mungo, a mumbling, muscular
young man from South Carolina. Big things were expected of
Mungo. He never lived up to them.

Quite another case was "Dixie" Walker.

Brooklyn fans could look back with satisfaction on the 1941
season largely because of Walker. When we picked him up
out of the waiver ash can in 1939, nothing was expected of
him. But he delivered brilliantly for more than eight years, and
became a better and smarter ballplayer each year.

First of all, Dixie had charm, he could kiss babies, sign autographs, and talk at smokers and at meetings of the ladies' aid
societies. He developed a tremendous personal following. Mac-
Phail and I soon discovered that to leave Walker out of the
line-up was to play with fire. The fans were wild about him.

Every spring we tentatively handed Walker's job away to
Pete Reiser, to Paul Waner, or to some rookie. Ordinarily this
could be called good figuring, because Dixie was thirty-ish
when we inherited him from the American League, and after
thirty, ballplayers usually move downhill, especially when they
have been busted up and sewed up as often as Dixie Walker.
But he fooled us all. He moved uphill instead of downhill. At
almost thirty-seven, just before we traded him to Pittsburgh
in 1947, Dixie had played in 148 games and had hit .306.

So, every year when Walker came back from the "grave" to snatch his job away from the youngsters, what a bird Mac-Phail and I got.

Once, when we benched Dixie in the South, MacPhail got a telegram with 5,000 names of indignant fans signed to it! That sort of popularity never hurt anybody.

It was amazing that the same run-of-the-mine ballplayer who had reported to Dressen and me in mid-season of 1939 and had made so little impression on us, could work himself up to become such an important figure in the Brooklyn picture. The Dixie Walker we had greeted was pitiful in our way of thinking. He could not start, he could not stop, and he could hardly move in the field. He had had an operation for a trick knee, and his throwing-arm had been stitched where they had tied it together after he had had a collarbone crack-up. Dressen took one look and said to me: "Where's the wheel chair that came in the deal with this guy?"

But we had little outfield strength, and so we kept Dixie longer than we otherwise might have. Before long he had worked out his troubles, and by 1940 was a serviceable ballplayer again. He batted .308, leading the club in hitting, and maneuvered better than before in the outfield. Later, of course, he was to become a real surprise package. He led the league in hitting and in runs batted in, and played our carom-shot right-field wall the way Eddie Duchin plays that piano.

To get back to Mungo—he was the opposite of Walker in every way. Mungo wound unpredictably like some bright string accidentally woven through the Dodger crazy quilt. He had appeared in the Thirties and was still there when the club zoomed to success.

In the Thirties, to mix up a few metaphors, the string that was Mungo was any minute expected to fatten into a rope up which the Dodgers could shinny to a pennant. But he didn't develop, and the Dodgers didn't climb.

I suspect that he was "carried" on the roster from force of

habit. The baseball writers, always quick to see behind the curtain, had a character named "Larry MacPhail" sing in their annual show:

> "I pay fifteen grand to Mungo
> Just to hit an occasional fungo—"

Mungo was the last of the Uncle Robbie "finds." Manager Wilbert Robinson appraised his pitchers by size or volume. He ignored all "shrimps" because he assumed they couldn't throw the ball through a brick wall. Many a time I thought Mungo would ram his head through a brick wall—and wished he would.

When Mungo first joined the Dodgers, some of the dozen-odd—and I do mean odd—writers had grave doubts that this huge specimen, who talked like a man at the bottom of a well, could either read or write. The questionnaire which the *Sporting News* sent to all rookies remained untouched in his mailbox at the Brunswick Hotel in Boston, where the Dodgers were playing. Some of the more playful writers called his attention to it but he ignored the hint. Finally, Mungo got a bright idea. He told the writers they could fill it in if they wanted to; he would tell them the answers.

The boys gave him the works. They invented all manner of embarrassing questions that Publisher Taylor Spink would never have thought of putting in his questionnaire. Pretending to read from the sheet, Eddie Murphy of the *Sun* asked, with a stern look and the voice of a district attorney, "Were you ever in jail?"

Mungo looked as though he were being tortured on the rack. "No!" he fumbled. "Well, once."

Promptly, Murphy demanded all the details.

So it came out that Mungo had been watching a high-school football game in his native Pageland, South Carolina, and had run out on the field and belted the referee.

"Why did you do that?" pursued Murphy.

"Because," mumbled Mungo, "he was a cheater!"

Obviously, Mungo would never develop into the kind of pitcher who finesses the hitter by using his noodle. He was strictly a thrower.

Late in the 1940 season, Mungo, who had been carried most of that year with a sore arm, got in trouble on a Pittsburgh–St. Louis train trip. I had gone on ahead of the team. Several of the boys were playing poker in a drawing room. Mungo, who had had a few drinks of hair tonic, insisted, like a playful mastiff, on coming in and mussing up the cards. The boys nudged him out of the room and locked the door.

Enraged by the snub, Mungo swung his mallet-like fist through the frosted-glass window of the drawing room. He broke up the game, the glass, and his pitching paw.

When I saw Mungo the next day, I asked for an explanation. He had a dandy, one he never could have dreamed up if he had remained in Pageland and not trained with the Daffy Dodgers of those days.

"The porter, Leo," he said, shaking his head, "that darn porter said something nasty about—who do you think? Yeah, about you, Leo. I swung at him, and he ducked, and my fist went through that glass—"

I told him we would start all over again. If he repeated the same fairy tale, it would cost him a hundred dollars. Quick as a flash I got the truth.

But I laid down the law. It had been laid down to this big guy before, but now the law had adhesive on it. I assured him the fine would stick, and I would be tough after that.

He got it! He went on the wagon for the rest of that season. I was told that he did not take a drink through most of the dull winter months in Pageland, either.

Now to pick up the Mungo story in the spring of 1941 at Havana. Mungo was still on the wagon and looking great. He showed me that his arm had come back. Optimist that I was, I dreamed that he would be my Number One pitcher.

What a nightmare that dream turned out to be!

The Cleveland Indians were coming over to play a week-end series with us in Havana. We had assurance that Bobby Feller, the modern wonder boy, would pitch Sunday's game. So, a week in advance I told my own wonder boy to get himself ready. Mungo flexed his muscles, and assured me that he'd "show 'em."

He showed 'em, all right. But not what we expected. In many respects that was the weirdest week end I ever spent with the club.

Mungo asked me for late leave Wednesday and Thursday. I granted it without the slightest suspicion.

When he asked me if he could stay out late Friday night again, I became a little curious, and did some gumshoe work. I finally spotted him sitting at a table on which there was a foaming beaker of beer. He was locked in earnest conversation with a female named Lady Vine. Upon what intellectual level that scion of society met the farm boy from Pageland, I never did find out. But little Leo was not born yesterday; I concentrated on the glass of beer rather than on the lady. Sure enough, as I circled in the shadows, I discovered a hooker of whisky hidden behind the beer. Mungo was drinking boilermakers! To me that meant what storm warnings run up all along the coast would mean to a transatlantic skipper.

I cautioned Mungo the next morning, but I felt that my words were not sinking in. That evening, which was Saturday, MacPhail and I went to the Casino. As we watched the roulette wheels spin, Larry had an urge to spin them himself and make it a gay evening.

I pretended a headache, and begged off. I had grave fears for the pitcher I was going to use on the morrow, and hustled back to the hotel.

By midnight there was no Mungo on the horizon. When the rest of the athletes headed for the hay, I got word that my hero was looking *for me!*

At 12:15 A.M. he appeared. He bounced off the walls twice, and wavered before me. "Shkipper!" he mumbled. "Woosh you gimme p'misshun—"

"Time!" I barked at him. "Mungo, I've given you all the permission you're going to get. Now if you're not in your room in five minutes it'll cost you two hundred bucks!"

As luck would have it, Mungo's room was at the top of a long flight of stairs from the lobby. Traveling Secretary John McDonald had put Mungo, the night owl, in the same room with Curt Davis, who was perhaps the quietest man ever to come to the big leagues. "Ol' Coonskin" was probably reading in bed, and worrying about his missing roommate.

Now I pointed majestically to the stairs. "Five minutes!" I repeated, and folded my arms like Napoleon. "Git!"

Five minutes wasn't too much time. Like the fellow who wondered if having to go to the poorhouse wasn't tough enough without having to climb the hill on which it sat, Mungo started. He negotiated those stairs as if they wound up Mount Everest.

He made it, and I turned away. Still I had a hunch, and turned detective again. My room overlooked the driveway. I went up and just sat at the window. Something told me that, even at this hour, Mungo's flair for trouble would lead him out of his room, and out of the hotel.

I did not have to wait long. Suddenly, I saw Mungo appear in front of the hotel—with a companion. They hailed a taxi and went off. I took four quick turns around my room, I was that mad. Right then I made up my mind I was through with the big guy. If anything was needed to bolster me in that decision, I got it the next day.

When our bus left the hotel at 11:00 A.M. for the ball park, Mungo was not with us.

I was on Doc Wilson's rubbing table in our clubhouse getting loosened up, when in Mungo walked.

Tense moment in a Card-Dodgers game. Padgett has returned safely to second base and Reese is making the catch.

Courtesy *The Sporting News*

Reiser slides safely into home while Reese stands by. This photo was made by Dodgers fan Albert L. Esposito.

Durocher arguing with Umpire Goetz.

Upper photo by N. Y. *Daily Mirror;* lower, International News Photo

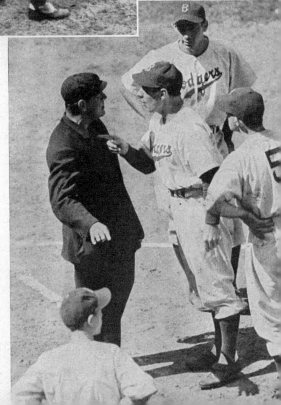

Leo emphasizes a point to Umpire Sears.

"Missed the bus, huh?" I growled. "That'll be two hundred bucks—"

"Bus went off and left me," he grumbled.

That really set me off. "The bus is all right for forty other players," I shouted. "What do you want, a limousine for yourself?"

It was then that I first noticed it: Have you ever seen a man come in from the intense cold, and try to unbutton his coat? Mungo seemed to have no feeling in his fingers. He fumbled with the buttons on his shirt as though he were asleep.

The temperature in Havana was 90 degrees. Mungo was not cold. He was numb, full of firewater. So I told him not to bother about getting into his uniform. I ordered him to go back to the hotel and to bed, before he got into more trouble.

"That's two hundred dollars for missing the bus," I bellowed, "and another two hundred for breaking training rules. And if you don't keep out of trouble, that four hundred I'm socking you will grow!"

It grew quicker than either of us figured.

For now Mungo wanted to fight. Doc Wilson, our trainer, thought the big guy, with the strength of a grizzly bear, was going to annihilate us. Doc grabbed an ice pick.

I told Wilson to put down the ice pick, get out of the room, and close the door. In a loud voice I announced that Mungo and I would fight it out alone. I wasn't being brave at all. Mungo could hardly stand up. I don't believe he could even see me; maybe to him I looked like a dozen Durochers. He certainly, in his condition, couldn't lay a hand on me.

Then Mungo quieted down and purred like a tabby. "Aw, gee, Skipper," he blubbered, "you and me been pals—"

I shooed him out of the dressing room. I went down to the field, where the rest of the team was at batting practice. I was pretty mad, not because Mungo was drunk, but because I had lost the guy I had figured for my Number One pitcher.

I had hardly reached home plate when a big shout arose in left field, where the dressing room was located. I wondered who could be making the commotion. I had just come from there.

Who could it be but MacPhail, running down the third-base line toward us, with his coattails flying. The clubhouse was six hundred feet out along the third-base line, but he was yelling so loud his voice carried to me.

It was a great show for the 20,000 Cubans already seated in the stands. But I was mad and I did not like it.

"Durocher!" MacPhail yowled. "I just saw Mungo. He's drunk! He's up there on the hill picking a fight with a taxi driver. He's drunk, I tell you—"

I told him I knew all about it, that I had just sent Mungo back to the hotel and fined him four hundred dollars.

"It's not enough!" screamed MacPhail. "I'm making it one thousand bucks. And I'm sending him to Macon tonight." That was banishment. The Montreal club was training at Macon, Georgia.

We hit line drives to all corners of the park off Feller, and won the game, but I was far from happy.

I thought I was through with Mungo, but he missed the boat to Miami that evening. At 12:30 A.M. I met him in front of the hotel. He was still having a hard time walking a straight line.

Van was fined and suspended now, and he was sure nothing else could happen to him. So he walked up bravely—I'll never forget what he said.

"You again, Skipper?" He rubbed his eyes to dispel the haze. "Don't you never get no sleep?"

Again I thought that that was the last I'd see of Van Lingle Mungo; again I was wrong. At seven the next morning a frantic hotel manager awoke me. He said a guy with a knife was outside Mungo's door threatening, in Spanish, to kill him.

I threw on my dressing gown and dashed to Mungo's room.

There was the male member of the dance team which had been appearing in the hotel floor show. He cried, "Mungo!" and waved the big frog-sticker, with which he obviously wanted to let some daylight into my erstwhile twirler.

It was time for fast action. I called my trusty agent, Babe Hamberger. Babe smuggled Mungo out of the room via a window, and hid him in the cellar among some potato sacks. Pretty soon the place was alive with police, each carrying a bayonet. They all chanted one name: "Mungo!"

That afternoon Hamberger sneaked Mungo down to the dock where the flying boats left for Miami. He hid the big guy behind a door until the plane was ready to take off. Then they made a run for it. Mungo scrambled aboard in safety and the Cuban cops never did get their man.

Nor was that our last brush with the authorities on the island. When we finally packed up to leave, our plane was late. Some of the boys started a poker game at the airport. One of the Cubanolas drifted over, pulled out his wallet, and said a few words in Spanish.

Thinking the guy was showing off his cabbage and making a bid to get into the game, Hugh Casey gave him the quick brush. "Scram!" is practically the same in any language I guess, because the fellow got the idea and did not like it. When the boys looked up, he was waving a big cannon under their noses and shouting his head off. I had to get some influential friends down to the airport to square that one, because the policeman, instead of wanting to get into the game, had been showing his badge in the wallet and had been trying to tell the boys that no gambling was allowed. I wondered whether they would ever let us out of Cuba that day; they could be very stubborn about such things. Fortunately, everyone calmed down, and we, too, left.

Mungo wasn't the only night owl we had. MacPhail had hired a flatfoot to shadow our boys as they searched out the hot spots at night. This dick had a unique way of identifying his quarry. He numbered each man according to the numbers they wore on their field uniforms.

His reports the next day were likely to read: "Number 10 and Number 18 went together to 14 Obispo. They met two more parties and came away with a package." The dick handed these tail reports to John McDonald, who was supposed to give them to me.

When we landed at Miami, McDonald had a pocketful of these cryptic reports. The customs men, searching him, came upon the notes and promptly turned them over to the F.B.I. After all, it was wartime. John had some job explaining these documents. For a little while he seemed to be heading for the clink.

At times it must have seemed as though we were all bound for a padded cell. What a psychopathic season 1941 was to be!

Chapter 9

SO YOU WANT TO MANAGE THE DODGERS?

MAYBE YOU THINK YOU COULD HAVE HANDLED MUNGO BETTER than I did!

A manager is supposed to be a buffer between the players and the front office. He is supposed to be boss and still to hold the team together. He is supposed to crack the whip and also to be a diplomat. Some job? I'm not complaining.

This 1941 Dodger team was stuck together with glue. It was a collection of so many peculiar characters that I doubt if the Voice of Experience, with assists by Dorothy Dix, Angelo Patri, and Mr. Anthony, could have solved its problems. I couldn't. I couldn't even solve MacPhail

The Mungo episode in Havana was only the beginning. MacPhail had sent him away for good. However, in a few weeks, Larry was asking me to take him back. To the newspapermen he said, "Only if Durocher gives his okay will Mungo get another chance."

That was enough. I said, "No, never again, thank you."

The next day Mungo joined us anyway.

I was fit to be tied. "If Mungo ever takes another drink," I snapped to the newspapermen, "either he is through, or I am!"

It didn't take long. Pretty soon Mungo was on his way to Montreal again.

That was only one shuffle. I doubt if ever in the history of baseball had a team been so often juggled, torn apart, rebuilt, and finally sent spinning on its way to a pennant.

These daffy goings-on had begun during the winter when MacPhail made a secret deal with Gerry Nugent, owner of the Phillies. Larry agreed to give Nugent a bag with $100,000 for Kirby Higbe, a rubber-armed, right-handed pitcher, if

71

Nugent would agree to keep it quiet. That was in November, 1940

MacPhail wanted to keep the deal from the ears of only one man: Branch Rickey. He needed secrecy because Rickey's Cardinals were figuring to win in 1941 if the Dodgers did not get too strong. At the same time, MacPhail was making passes at Arnold "Mickey" Owen, a catcher on Rickey's pay roll.

MacPhail reckoned that Rickey would think it safe to sell Owen to the Dodgers for $80,000 if we got no other help. Rickey knew that Brooklyn needed at least another front-line pitcher to win in 1941. If he found out that MacPhail had also landed the extra pitcher in the person of Higbe, he would not sell us Owen!

To keep Rickey in the dark, MacPhail had to enlist the help of half-a-dozen other men, including Baseball Commissioner Kenesaw M. Landis. Normally, all deals are noted in the regular bulletins from league headquarters. MacPhail wanted this one hushed up another month, until he landed Owen.

We finally nailed Owen. That was in no small part due to Nugent, who hush-hushed the Higbe deal so well that the Giants still thought they had a fine chance to buy Owen after he had already become our property! As a matter of fact, in Toots Shor's Restaurant on the eve of Armistice Day, Horace Stoneham was telling his cronies that he would surely nab Higbe.

An opportunity like this, MacPhail lapped up. As soon as he had Owen, Larry called a press conference. He began his announcement to the writers with these dramatic words: "The New York Giants, despite what they say, have no chance to land pitcher Kirby Higbe from Philadelphia. Higbe is owned by Brooklyn!"

Larry should have been an actor.

Now we had Higbe and we had Owen. But we lost Phelps. The year before, the "Blimp" had been in hot water because he had refused to go up in the air. Now he was sulking in his home at Odenton, Maryland. I guess he did not like the idea of us getting Owen.

Phelps had told me that he would not fly to training in Havana. I told him to come to Miami, and take the boat across.

Later, I found out that the big guy got as far as Miami. But he must have taken one look at the dock and the water, and decided that he was no more of a sailor than he was a flyer. For he promptly turned around and went right back to Maryland. He said he was suffering from a cold, and that it had got worse when he hit Miami.

It puzzled us how Phelps expected to cure his "cold" in the frozen North instead of in sunny Cuba, but maybe a psychiatrist could not have figured it out either. Once I thought I should have roomed one of those filberts with the "Blimp"; I bet the psychiatrist would have come out screaming.

MacPhail blew his top every time he thought of Phelps. Larry ordered a specialist from Johns Hopkins Hospital in Baltimore to Odenton to examine his prize specimen. The medico found the 240-pound catcher in great shape. There was only one shape like it in baseball, and I sure would have enjoyed having him with us in Havana. After all, Phelps's hitting was his strong point. Most of the experts figured that Owen could never have held the catching job permanently because of the power of Phelps's big bat.

Incidentally, the moment we announced we had both Higbe and Owen, a lot of these same experts began to pick us to win the 1941 pennant. Frank Frisch was one of the first to tab us as his pick to beat out the Cardinals.

At the Baseball Writers' Show in February one of the hit songs, "That's Why Dodgers Are Born," kidded us for failing to win in 1940. But it contained a prophetic line. The verse went like this:

Someone had to finish second,
Even though a pennant beckoned;
—But in '41 our winning will be done . . .
That's why Dodgers are born!

Later in the season Phelps, as temperamental as a prima donna, was to miss an important Western trip. Third Baseman Lew Riggs, who lived with the big guy, said Phelps actually had his bag down in a cab in front of the hotel, but, at the last minute, changed his mind and went back to his room.

When Phelps did not show up at the train, MacPhail slapped a $1,000 fine on him, and suspended him. Eventually the case wound up in Judge Landis' office, and we had a hearing when we reached Chicago. The team was already at Wrigley Field, dressing for the afternoon's game when we went before the Judge: John McDonald, Phelps, and myself.

The discussion revolved around whether Phelps was actually sick that day he failed to make the train. Phelps, who had always worried about heart trouble, insisted that when he lay in bed in the still of the night, he could hear his heart skip a beat. He was worried that it might skip three or four, and he would cash in his chips.

If he had told the Judge that he was sick and worried, I know Landis would have been easy on him. Instead, Phelps denied the story Riggs had told us. He swore he was sick in bed, that he had never gone down to the street, put his bag in cab, and then changed his mind.

The Judge eyed him shrewdly and croaked to his secretary, "Get player Riggs on the telephone at Wrigley Field."

Apparently Riggs repeated, in a straightforward manner, everything that he had witnessed of Phelps's actions. Phelps, although he could not hear what was being said at the other end of the wire, began to perspire like a man digging a ditch.

The Judge said nothing when he hung up the phone—nothing, that is, except "Harrrrumph!" He gazed at Phelps as though he were a freak from another planet.

I suspect that Phelps puzzled Landis as much as he puzzled the rest of us. Eventually, the Judge put him on our ineligible list in September—after the Babe had changed his mind several times about rejoining the club, and had passed up his $10,000 job playing baseball, with an additional crack at a $7,000 World Series check. He retired to smash baggage in Odenton at fifty bucks a week.

MacPhail had been sore at Phelps. Now he got into a big huff at Mickey Owen, and both staged a long holdout battle. Larry offered $9,000 and Mickey, who had a broad streak of zany in him and used to ride around the minor leagues in a flaming red roadster with his name blazoned on it in big gold letters, asked $13,000.

It was great for MacPhail to rant and rave. In the meantime, I had no catcher. We tried Herman Franks, and imported Angelo Giuliani from the minors.

At last Owen came to terms. We held a press conference. I was as nice as pie to my brand-new catcher, and Mickey seemed happy enough puffing on a big cigar. But I never knew what he would say next. Leave it to Mickey to say something!

One of the writers, looking for a story, wondered aloud how I thought Mickey would do at the plate. Before replying, I asked Owen how he had hit in the 1940 season.

Mickey's eyes twinkled as he applied the forced draft to his big cigar. "It ain't how much I hit," he chuckled. "It's WHO I hit!" He was referring, of course, to our 1940 bout, which had taken place at Ebbets Field. A nice crack.

Owen got into shape, and Franks promised to become a good Number Two man, so we had to get Angelo Giuliani back to the minors. The latter and MacPhail had had a big rhubarb, so it was my job to talk him into going to Montreal.

I thought I had all the answers. Angelo, however, soon stumped me.

"I won't report to Montreal if you send me there," he began.

I was sure I had the answer to that. I told him about the money he would get.

"It's not the money," he said. "Don't you know there's a war on?"

I couldn't figure what that had to do with his case.

"I'm an Eyetalian!" he blurted out. "And Canada is at war with Italy. If I went to Montreal those Frenchmen would come right down out of the stands and kill me on home plate!"

Do you still want to manage the Dodgers? There are times when the job even has international complications.

That spring, catchers weren't our only problem. We were weak at second base. Alex Kampouris and Pete Coscarart debated rather feebly who should hold down the sack. At short, Peewee Reese hadn't yet got his feet on the ground; and Old Man Durocher was having more aches and pains than Sloane's Liniment is supposed to cure.

Our outfield made us moan plenty, too. Walker was our center fielder. Yet, somehow he had never mastered the handling of that job, although he was a dandy in right field. In center, he could not catch a ball below his belt. Aware of that, he would start in for almost everything, and the line drives sailed over his head.

Paul Waner, who had the lead on Pete Reiser in right field, didn't bother much with training rules. Medwick, who seemed to be slashing the ball as he had before Bowman beaned him, was surly. He was mad at everybody, even his teammates.

We leaned heavily on Wyatt, who was thirty-two, and on Hamlin who was thirty-five. No one in our club thought Luke could pitch under pressure. If a ball was batted through the box, Luke would worry about being decapitated. He would lose his head figuratively, if not literally, and I would have to yank him out in a hurry—even if we were ahead, 10–0.

Wyatt was troubled with stiffness in his arm, his bad knee bothered him, and he was temperamental. Here we were trying to beat out the Reds, who had won the pennant two years consecutively, and Wyatt, our Number One pitcher, had lost to them five times straight the year before. I tried to build Wyatt up. He moaned, "It's no use, Skipper, they've got a jinx on me. Why, I pitched a two-hitter against them last year and that dratted Lonny Frey hit a phony homer that beat me, remember?" He was a psychological problem.

I remembered, all right. Wyatt had no love for Frey. Two years before he had tangled with Lonny and had come out of the fracas with the bad knee which nearly ended his career. And it had to be Frey who beat him in the toughest game we lost in 1940. The homer Wyatt referred to was a high fly to right which went into our screen in right field, hit the concrete at the base of the wall, and bounced up and down tantalizingly, as if it were on a rubber band. Finally it came to rest *on top of the wall*, like a coin standing on end. I had never seen anything like it. Our outfielders stood by helplessly, like a bunch of mourners. The ball did not come down. For a time I thought Wyatt would collapse; eventually we got him calmed down.

We had no such troubles with Higbe, our new man. When he reported, he notified me that he could pitch one day and relieve the next. "I'm as strong as an ox, Leo," he said. "And twice as smart!" Hig always pitched his heart out for me. If he had ever learned control, he would have been one of the all-time greats.

Meanwhile, MacPhail was up to things. He tried to force the visiting clubs to stay in Brooklyn hotels, rather than in Manhattan, where they had always put up. That irked the Cincinnati Reds. They sent him a hot wire charging that there were "too many bars" in Brooklyn hotels.

"Where do you keep your players in Manhattan," Larry snapped back over the wires, "in church?"

Another of his campaigns which did not win him friends was his drive to keep our opponents from "beanballing the Dodgers out of the league." He bought us all plastic helmets, "guaranteed to withstand baseballs propelled at a hundred miles an hour." "Now let them throw at my boys," he challenged the world. "They can't hurt us!"

We opened the 1941 season against the Giants. A ball sailed over Walker's head and we lost one game. We lost the next two, also, largely because Peewee Reese kicked a few at short. Harold Parrott wrote in the *Brooklyn Eagle*, "A week ago any Brooklynite would have licked Peewee's boots. Today, the team's a civic calamity!"

After we blew those three to the hated Giants, whom Mac-Phail had taunted publicly for failing to get Higbe, life was not so beautiful to Larry. He squawked his head off because I was not playing short, instead of Reese. He told the writers I was a "prima donna." He roared, "There's going to be some changes made around here!"

I knew what "changes" meant, just as Burleigh Grimes had known. Now I knew how it felt to have the edge of the guillotine on my neck.

How about it? Do you still think you'd like a job like that—running the 1941 Dodgers?

Chapter 10

"THERE'LL BE SOME CHANGES MADE"

"Changes," did MacPhail say? "Earthquake" would have been a better word!

By May, Paul Waner and Alex Kampouris, who had started the season as regulars, had been fired. Tex Carleton, our no-hit hero of the year before, was in Montreal.

Back came Vito Tamulis, the little Lithuanian pitcher whom we had traded to the Phillies. We added Mace Brown and Newt Kimball, a handsome blond giant. These three did not add up to one really good pitcher, but they were the best MacPhail could find.

When, after our horrible start against the Giants, we straightened out and won fifteen out of seventeen, Larry returned to something like normalcy. However, he began to erupt again when we lost six in a row.

He screamed at me. I screamed back. I said whatever happened to float to the top of my mind. Since I was worried about second base, I hollered for Billy Herman, then with the Cubs. That was like asking for the moon. "Get me Billy Herman," I wailed, "and we'll win the pennant!"

A couple of days later, my phone rang. It was 5:00 A.M., but what could that mean to the Big Man? It was MacPhail, all right. I was just about to tell him off, when he cooed: "Say hello to your new second baseman!" I almost fell out of bed as Billy Herman got on the phone and told me he was reporting that very afternoon.

This surely was one of the most amazing deals ever made. All night in the Hotel Commodore MacPhail had bellowed and pretended to drink until he got the details set. Finally, the late Jim Wilson, then managing the Cubs, and Jim Gallagher, general manager, thought they had their man ready for the kill. They had come to trap MacPhail. But he had poured his drinks down the sink all night (no mean sacrifice in itself for a man like MacPhail) and now, at 4:30 A.M. he was still fresh—and wily. So instead of being taken, MacPhail slyly clipped his foes. He palmed off Charley Gilbert, a young outfielder, and also Johnny Hudson, a stand-in for Reese and me at short. Hudson had hit a thumping .217 in 1940. For these two prizes he got the best second baseman in the league.

Suddenly a terrifying thought hit MacPhail. Suppose the two Cub officials awoke at noon and could not remember the swap?

He made them scratch out the details on an envelope and had them sign it!

Herman hopped us up. For the Cubs he had been hitting .194. In his first twenty games for us he belted .386. I moved him up to hit second, put Reiser (now in right field) third, and Camilli fourth. Dixie Walker dropped to sixth in this batting order.

We won nine games straight. But the Cardinals were streaking, too. They won eleven in a row. However, when they reached Brooklyn, we walloped them three out of four.

Suddenly, we fell into a losing streak, and MacPhail hit the ceiling. Our pitching began to fall apart. Every day for a week Higbe was in the bull pen because when I started him he couldn't get out of the first inning.

I told the baseball writers traveling with us that I liked a kid who had tried out with us one day in Chicago. The youngster had given ten other clubs a look, and the bids were up to thirty grand. "I would match it," I said.

Back in Brooklyn, MacPhail roared and reached for the telephone. "What are you trying to do, Durocher?" he screamed. "Spend my money for me?" By the way, the kid was Dick Wakefield.

Wyatt was knocked out twelve straight times. We staggered through twelve games in a row without finding a pitcher who could go nine innings.

Each time we blew one, MacPhail got hotter and hotter. "There'll be some changes made!" he roared. There were.

In a waiver deal with the Browns we got Johnny Allen, who had been a great pitcher for the Yankees. Johnny was thirty-six, but he knew all about pitching. He would step on your face if he had to do it to win. We also picked up Tom Tatum, a young right-handed-hitting outfielder, and Tom Drake, a night-owl pitcher from the Nashville club.

Tatum was supposed to be the medicine for the left-handed pitching we had to face day after day; for Reiser, Walker, and Camilli were being rendered null and void by one southpaw after another.

His first time up, Tatum doubled. In the late editions that evening he was hailed as a new sensation. Yet, by August, he was to be back in the minors.

Down the waiver chute came Augie Galan, who had played in less than twenty games with the Cubs all season. He was practically on one leg; he had a bad knee and wore a brace. What a pickup "Goo-Goo," as we called him, turned out to be!

The Cubs also cut Larry French loose. We took him on the theory that anybody might help.

It was August, and we were seesawing up and down for the lead with the Cardinals who, fortunately, were also having their troubles. At one time Slaughter, Moore, and Hopp, the best outfield in baseball, were completely on the shelf with injuries. The Redbirds had infield troubles, too, and Slats Marion at short showed signs of cracking under the strain of the tight pennant race.

MacPhail continued to emote—and to promote. He rounded up a bunch of scantily dressed models and introduced a new type of curve on the pitching mound at Ebbets Field. They say old Abner Doubleday did a complete spin in his grave that afternoon.

Wyatt, pitching a whale of a game against Cincinnati, thought the trainer was handing him a drink of water, and swallowed a glassful of mouthwash. He became deathly sick. Casey had to relieve, and although we won the game in sixteen innings, MacPhail wanted to fire the trainer. I can't even guess what he would have done had we lost the game.

At Ebbets Field, I never knew what I might find. One day a fan brought a flock of pigeons for me to release from home plate—for good luck. I wouldn't refuse for fear of stirring up a jinx.

One day, I thought Peewee Reese would commit suicide. We had beaten the Cards three straight at Ebbets Field, and in the fourth game of the series, Freddy Fitzsimmons produced a real classic. Just when we were about to nail the coffin lid on those St. Louis pests for good, Peewee kicked one, and it cost the game.

Two hours later, Reese was still sitting with his head in his locker, crying his heart out. Everybody had left the clubhouse after saying a kind word to get him to snap out of it. Even Fitzsimmons, who would have cut off his right arm at the elbow to win that game, begged Peewee not to take it so hard. "You'll make a great play next time and win for me," he said.

Still Reese sat there. I didn't know what to do.

Finally, I decided that since kind words didn't help, I'd bark at the kid. "Come on, Reese!" I snapped. "Do you think that's the last error you're ever going to make for the Dodgers?"

The youngster shook himself. He glared at me. But as it sank in he got dressed, and seemed to feel somewhat better.

He was having a tough year, making the mistakes that all youngsters make. The only difference was that they attracted special notice because every play meant so much in a pennant race.

Everything happened to us. I thought I had seen it all, till one day big Ernie Lombardi, who was about as quick as a turtle, stole second base on Kirby Higbe, when the pitcher forgot himself and wound up. Big Lom hadn't stolen a base in four years!

Brooklyn was red hot. Every place you went, the Dodger bugs talked pennant. In the first game of a double-header with the Giants at Ebbets Field, we were trailing by a run. Ducky Medwick slashed a terrific blast to left. It would have sailed into the seats for a home run, but a woman leaned out over the rail. The ball struck her, and was deflected back onto the field. Nobody bothered to notice whether the woman was injured or not, but we certainly were hurt when Camilli, Lavagetto, and Walker failed to bring Medwick in from second base. That was where he had been forced to stop when his drive was cut down from a homer. So we lost that game by one run. The fans were so frustrated they didn't know what to do.

Between games an usher came down to me in the clubhouse. He was out of breath from running, but he had a plan. "You can't hit a woman, Leo," he opened up with sincere regret in his voice, "but don't you think they should of trun out the guy what brung her?"

Our pitching was as thin as the margin that separated us from the Cardinals. First, French seemed to have nothing left in his arm. Second, we couldn't get Drake to go to bed. Third, Fitzsimmons' arm crooked up like a coat hanger after he pitched, and he couldn't work for the week following. Fourth, Wyatt and Higbe both showed signs of overwork, although each had won twenty games.

On August 30, the Giants beat us twice, while, for the Cardinals, Lon Warneke pitched a no-hitter against the Reds. That left us half a game out in front. MacPhail blew all his fuses every day.

We ran so short of pitching that on September 3 we had to start a kid from Durham in the Piedmont League. His name was Eddie Albosta. I remember him, not by his curve or his fast ball, but by his Adam's apple which jumped up and down as he pitched, like a yo-yo on a string.

I could feel it: MacPhail was about ready to explode. He did, mostly in the direction of Branch Rickey. Blond Ernie White, a kid left-hander who had won eight straight, and had beaten us four times, had been Rickey's best pitcher all year. Now Rickey dug, as only he could, into that farm system of his and came up with another left-hander, a classy-looking kid named Howard Pollet. Branch brought Pollet up from Houston. When he, too, clicked, MacPhail nearly disintegrated.

Larry held a press conference "for the good of baseball." "Rickey is ruining the minor leagues," he told the writers, "by raping a good farm club like Houston. His taking Pollet off a team that has a fine chance to win in the Texas League is bad for baseball."

The reporters, of course, confronted Rickey with this unusual statement. I got a kick out of his reply.

Rickey leaned back in his big chair behind the desk across which I had so often faced him in St. Louis, puffed on the ever-present cigar and said, with mock sympathy, "Boys, I'm genuinely sorry if Pollet is hurting MacPhail. Mac is a bright boy, and I do not like to see him suffer. I put him in baseball, you know. He still does not know much about the game, but he is learning fast. It's funny to hear him complain about my taking Pollet from a team which is twenty-four games in the lead in the Texas League. If I see him, I'll remind him of how, just a year ago, he lifted Pete Reiser and Ed Head off an Elmira club that was in a hot pennant fight. The Elmira owner telephoned me and begged for a player or two to repair Mac-Phail's raids!"

Rickey puffed, and laughed some more. Then he added: "On second thought, boys, I probably will never bring the matter up with MacPhail. I hate noise!"

That was the first real breach between master and pupil. It was patched up. But how it was to widen later—into the rift that made the big baseball news of 1947!

The only thing that kept the Dodgers up near the top in those tough days was spirit. We had that "Let's-go-out-and-knock-'em-down" drive. As a consequence, we had few pals around the league. We brushed good hitters back from the plate, but most of the time we also picked baseballs out of our own teeth.

One day, Richard Merriwell Erickson, a pitcher for the Braves, worked against us. He hit Medwick on the arm. He hit Reiser on the shoulder. Then he bounced a curve ball off Camilli's plastic helmet.

I thought the incident was over. But when the inning ended, Camilli charged at Long George Kelly, the Braves' coach. When I got there, Camilli was snarling, "Don't you ever laugh at me when I get hit on the head!" Kelly turned white—and promised not to laugh again!

That was one fight I was sorry did not take place. It would have been something to see the muscular Camilli double "Highpockets" up like a folding ruler.

Every time we lost a game, MacPhail blamed me. The reasons were monotonously the same: I yanked a pitcher too late. I yanked a pitcher too soon. Or I was on the bench when I should have been playing short instead of Reese. He told so many people he had paid me $25,000 for managing the club and an additional $5,000 for staying in shape to play short, that I decided to get in there and take some of the pressure off Peewee.

We had a big week-end series with the Giants. Then we were to begin our last Western invasion of the year, the most important Western trip the Brooklyn club had ever taken.

In the first game against the Giants, I took the field. I planned to work myself into shape to play the important series against the Cards in St. Louis, the second stop on our trip. I had one big reason for wanting to be in that crucial series against the Cards, myself. I had rested Freddy Fitzsimmons so that he would have eleven days' vacation before he warmed up for the opener. Reese had kicked away the last two great games that Freddy had pitched. I figured Peewee might still be brooding about that; one more boot behind Freddy might send the kid into a tailspin from which he would never recover.

So, I played that Saturday game against the Giants. It was a neat win for Curt Davis. Vander Meer licked the Cards that day, so our lead grew to two games. Then on a big Sunday afternoon, as the Cardinals split, we beat the Giants twice. We therefore had a three-game lead as we turned westward.

But as we sped toward Chicago, I suffered a painful Charley horse. I worried. Would I be able to play the Thursday opener in St. Louis, behind Fitzsimmons?

If I had known what was going to happen on that trip, I would probably have stayed home. It was to be a haywire, hysterical road trip.

Chapter 11

RHUBARB IN THE WEST

THE FIRST DAY IN CHICAGO IT RAINED. THAT MEANT A DOUBLE-header on the schedule. But it should have kept on raining. It didn't. Still, our three-game lead shrank as if it had been left out in the downpour. That Black Wednesday the Cubs beat us twice. When the Cardinals took two from the Phils, our margin shriveled to one game.

I really blew one of those games myself, for I yanked Higbe too soon in the opener. I was anxious to get Whitlow Wyatt in to save the game, but when I finally did, Whit flopped on me. I played that game over and over again that night in retrospect, especially after Erickson beat us in the nightcap.

Back home, the *World-Telegram* ran an article about "bounce." We had bounced back from the slough of despondency before, the writer said, and we must do it now, for the fair name of Brooklyn was at stake. MacPhail bought forty *World-Telegrams*, drove them to LaGuardia Field himself, and put them on the plane, so that every man on our team would have one in St. Louis the next morning.

In the opener against the Cards we had to face Ernie White, who had licked us four straight. However, Fitzsimmons was ready. He came through with a corking game, huffing and puffing on every pitch.

Yet, for a while it did not seem as though even Fitz's great pitching could save us. For the umpiring was weird. We were to have some terrific battles with the umpires in Cincinnati.

Reese was at bat facing White; the count was three and

one. The next pitch was so low, there was no doubt about it; but Umpire Al Barlick called it strike two. Instead of getting his walk, Reese flied out. What we hollered at Barlick from the dugout made him red and white by turns.

When Reiser, the next hitter, tripled, we renewed our attack on Barlick, because now we felt that, with his screwy decision, we had lost a run that was rightfully ours, in this still-scoreless, bitter game.

By this time, Barlick was probably upset by our remarks. However, White, the pitcher, wasn't exactly calm about Reiser, who was on third. He knew our man could run like a scared rabbit. As White got ready to deliver the ball, Reiser made a trial run toward the plate. In a moment of uncertainty, White hesitated in his pitching motion. Then, as Reiser scuttled back toward third, he continued and delivered the ball. It was an obvious balk. But Barlick did not call it. In anger we rushed him.

His explanation was a classic. "You're not going to win a big game like this on a technicality," he sputtered.

For many years since that episode Al Barlick has been one of the best umpires. Perhaps he was a good umpire then, too, but just temporarily off his trolley. When he heard Al make that crack about a "technicality," I thought Old Freddy Fitz, pitching his heart out through that crooked old arm of his, would go off his trolley, too. Every inning Freddy's arm seemed to tighten up more and more, and get shorter in his sleeve. He just grunted and nodded when I asked him: "Can you go one more?"

Freddy got into his big trouble late in the game. Two were out, three were on, and Johnny Mize was up. The score was tied: the game hung in the balance. Freddy's arm was in bad shape, but he did not want to leave, not in that jam, although I had Hugh Casey all heated up and ready. Mize, according to Freddy, was his boy, and he wanted to "take care" of him, as only he could do. One of the most spectacular pieces of pitching I have ever seen followed.

I don't know quite why, but Freddy never liked Big Johnny Mize. He always called Big John "Tomato Face," and he uttered it with a sneer. Now, as he prepared to pitch, Freddy walked in toward the plate to get the ball from Mickey Owen. Coming up, he warned the big slugger.

"Be ready, Tomato Face!" he snapped. "I'm going to take your cap off!"

The first pitch sailed right at Mize, and John really hit the dirt with his shoulders. His bat flew one way, his cap another. He shook himself like a big Airedale that has rolled in the dust. I could see that he was not happy.

The next pitch was a knuckle ball, right through for strike one.

Now Freddy walked up again. As he took the ball from Owen, he snarled, "Down you go again, Tomato Face."

I did not really think Freddy planned to low-bridge the big guy again; I thought he was bluffing.

Again, Mize got out of the way just in time. Before the big fellow could get off the floor again, I was out at the mound, pleading with Freddy. "You might hit him," I argued. "And remember, the bases are full. If you do hit him, or if the pitch gets away from Owen, the winning run will come across. It's great to brush the guy back with the first pitch, but don't take chances."

Fitz nodded. He was like a man in a dream, and I knew he wasn't listening by the way he looked. He was always mad at everybody when he pitched. He was mad at the umpires, mad at the other players, even at his own teammates. Now he was good and mad at Mize—and mad at me, too, for interfering.

The next pitch was right through and again Mize took it. The count was two and two.

Once more Freddy came in close to take the ball from

Owen. Once more he snarled insults at Mize. "Right at that thick skull of yours," I heard him say.

The funny thing is that Mize, big and strong as he was, would never talk back to Fitzsimmons. He would not say a word. He just puffed his cheeks and blew, like a traffic cop on a cold day.

None of us had the slightest idea that Fitz would knock his victim down again. But the pitcher carried out his threat, and Mize went sprawling. The count was now three and two, with the bases full. I felt like taking Fitzsimmons out. But I knew if I did, I would have to bring a strait jacket to the mound to make him obey and get out.

Again Freddy, huffing and puffing more than ever, walked in toward the plate. I wondered what he was going to say this time. "It'll be right through there," I heard him sneer out of the corner of his mouth. "And you'll probably never get the bat off your shoulder!"

Mize just blew out more wind and waited, bat ready. Freddy fussed around on the mound like a hen on her nest.

Now when Fitzsimmons threw his fast ball, he always grunted, like a man digging a ditch. This time he spun toward second base as he always did, flapped his short arms, and let loose a grunt that must have been heard in the upper deck. But instead of the fast ball that Mize had been looking for, up came a curve—a slow, s-l-o-w curve! Johnny started to unload, held back, changed his mind again—and then it was too late. The curve ball cut the plate.

As the "St-rrr-ike three!" call came, Freddy folded his glove, stuffed it into his back pocket, and waddled in. He spit in front of home plate without even looking at Mize, and went on into the dugout.

That was the game's big crisis. Fitzsimmons continued on to win, though he got into trouble in the last of the eleventh, after we got him the run he needed. Then Casey came in and saved the day. Our lead was up to two games again.

The next day, gambling for a sweep of the series, I made a last-minute switch from Wyatt to Curt Davis and they beat us with Pollet.

So the third and final game of the series was to be the big one, and who would I rather have had in there than Whitlow Wyatt? That contest stands out in my long memory as one of the real pitching classics of baseball history, produced under pressure. We went into the game with only a one-game lead at the head of the league.

Reese got Wyatt into a jam early, and we had Cardinals on second and third, and no one out. But our pitcher really had the stuff, and the heart of a lion. He turned on that something extra, which every truly great athlete has, and fanned Mancuso and Mort Cooper, who was pitching a top game himself. Then he nabbed Jimmy Brown on an easy infield chance.

After that, the Cardinals worked another man into scoring position and sent Enos Slaughter, who had been out with a broken shoulder, up to bat. Ordinarily we pitched Enos high. I ran out to the mound to remind Whit to keep the ball up. On a high fast one, Slaughter might have even more trouble than usual getting around.

"It won't matter where the pitch is, Skip," Wyatt reassured me. "This guy ain't going to see it!"

With that he delivered three fast balls that were the swiftest I believe I have ever seen a pitcher deliver. Feller and Grove included. Slaughter, a fine hitter even then, struck out. In fact, he never even got to foul one!

It is box-score history, of course, how Billy Herman and Dixie Walker put together two doubles for the run that won that game for us, 1-0. Herman's double was a fly ball which fell just short of the fence. I am convinced that Terry Moore would have caught it had he been in the game. Walker's rap, on the other hand, was belted high against the screen, and nobody could have got it.

We were still in danger. While we won one game in Cincinnati the next day, the Cards won two. Our lead was down to a mere game and a half.

It was truly a nerve-racking road trip. Every stop we made brought more incredible developments. But one game that will always remain in my mind is the second we played at Cincinnati— As we began, our margin over the Cards was a game and a half. Since the Redbirds were idle that day, we would come out either two games ahead—if we won—or only one—if we lost.

The game started on a stormy note. One strike was called on Walker before he led off for us, in fact, even before he went to bat. Dixie was arguing about something with Umpire Larry Goetz. Larry got hardheaded and commanded Paul Derringer to pitch the first ball of the game before Dixie stepped into the batter's box!

Johnny Allen, who had pitched strongly for us since we picked him out of the Browns' ash can, started this game. He gave an indication of what kind of a battle it would be by announcing that the first pitch would be high inside. Sure enough, he knocked Billy Werber down. It was open war from then on.

Allen pitched like a champion. He gave one hit in the first nine innings. After the seventh, he tired faster and faster. At the end of each inning, as he came in, I said, to give him a lift, "Hold 'em right there, Johnny. We'll get you a run now!"

The eighth, ninth, tenth, eleventh, twelfth, and thirteenth innings went by, and still no run. After pitching the fourteenth, Allen came in, soaking wet. I gave him that same line about our getting a run for him. This time Johnny turned to the other players and with a wry grin moaned, "I'm beginning to think the Skipper's kidding me!"

Paul Derringer had been pitching Reiser "on the fist," as we say, which means close, and belt-high. I knew that Paul always took his eyes off the hitter as he wound up. He seemed to stare at a spot about ten feet in front of the mound. In the last of the fifteenth Reiser was first up, so I said to Pete, "After this guy starts to wind up, jump back a foot or two. If he pitches you in the same spot as before you'll have room to get around on the ball."

On the second pitch Reiser tried it—and hit a four-hundred-foot home run *for the first score of the game!* The Reds immediately went into a stall. Dusk was coming and they hoped there would not be light enough to complete the bottom of the inning. In that case the score would revert to what it had been at the end of the fourteenth inning—o-o.

Werber circled under a pop fly which a little girl could have caught, and let it fall for a hit. The Reds wouldn't tag us out. We were anxious to get the inning over, but they let us make four more runs, still hoping to have the game called.

Allen was about dead. Finally, in the last of the fifteenth, I put Hugh Casey in. Hughie tried to pitch too fast, and walked three men to fill the bases.

I ran out to the mound, waving my arms.

"Take it easy, Leo," said Umpire Goetz. "We're going to finish this game if we have to put miners' lights on all their caps." Goetz was no dummy. He saw what the Reds were trying to do, and he had the courage to let them know that we were going to finish the game, no matter what.

When Reese finally dashed to his right to come up with a ground ball, it was too dark even for me to see. Still he threw out the Red runner for the final put-out of the game. By that time you couldn't even make out the outline of the scoreboard in left field. But we had won the game.

The next day we did not play, but the Cardinals did. They won again, and our lead was once more down to a game and a half. They won two the next day. We finally won ours in Pittsburgh, but it was another breath-taker. This was the battle about which Tommy Holmes wrote in the *Eagle:* "Personally, I couldn't look, but they told me later that Hamlin had fanned Fletcher."

Everything broke loose in that next game in Pittsburgh. After we had scored five in the top of the inning for a 5-4 lead, Hamlin was in Dutch again in the last of the inning. He threw two buckshot fast balls past Vince DiMaggio. Then he lobbed one in as big as a balloon, and when DiMaggio smacked it for a base hit, I felt like smacking Luke. However, all I did was yank him, and in came Casey.

With DiMaggio on third and Al Lopez up, Casey started to deliver his first pitch. Lopez, a smart hombre, moved out of the batter's box. Casey hesitated, and Lopez hopped back in again. Instead of calling "Time!" when Lopez stepped out, Umpire Magerkurth called it a balk, and *waved the tying run in from third!*

I ran out. I screamed, "Lopez pulled a job on us and only a chowderhead umpire like you would let him get away with it!"

Umpires are less rough on you when they know they have kicked a decision. That was probably the only reason that big Mage did not tie the can to me right then. Bill Klem, the "Old Arbitrator" and umpire-in-chief of the National League, was watching from the press box. Mage knew it, and all the rest of us knew it. What we did not know was that MacPhail and Ford Frick were listening to the game on the radio together, back in New York. As events unfolded, I would have liked a transcript of what went on there.

Later, someone said to MacPhail: "You were lucky you didn't make that Western trip, Larry, and watch those nerveracking games. You'd have been a wreck!"

"Lucky!" snorted MacPhail. "Lucky, did you say? Did you ever kick a three hundred dollar radio apart?"

When Magerkurth called that balk on us and the Pirates tied the score, I was blind with rage. Only a few minutes before I had been told that Manuel Salvo, a second-rater, was pitching for the Braves against Mort Cooper in St. Louis. I felt sure that the Cardinals would win their game while we were blowing ours. The last of our lead would go out the window.

What I wasn't wise to was that the usually calm Casey was mad as a hornet himself. Hughie's next two pitches were over the batter's head. The catcher couldn't even get near them, but the umpire almost did. Mage walked out after Casey, said something about being a target, and added, "One more like that and you are out of the game!"

I realized I'd have to do something drastic to take the heat off Casey. I ran out to scream at Magerkurth that I was running this club—and that I, and not any blind, fumbling umpire, would make the pitching changes.

Have you ever been so mad that the words wouldn't come? I mean the right words. Somewhere along the line, though, I called him "Meathead!" Magerkurth never could stand that word. So he put me out of the game.

I remember stumbling along the tunnel to our dressing room. I broke every electric light bulb on the way, and heaved a chair that went through the transom of the umpire's dressing room. I got to our clubhouse. It seemed only a few seconds when I heard the clatter of spiked shoes, and they told me we had lost. Anderson had tripled for the winning run.

Anderson! That was the last straw! This Anderson hit off his front foot, swinging his bat as though he was waving a wand. I knew that sometimes I used to look bad at the plate. But the first day I began to play, I never looked as bad as Anderson did in the big leagues. He didn't have enough power to drive the ball through a tissue-paper infield.

"Anderson!" I screamed over and over. "Anderson! What did he do to get a triple, hit the ball into a hole?"

Still, we were the ones who were in the hole. We all knew

it. We felt pretty low, thinking the Cards had surely finally wiped out our lead.

Then someone came in and said that Salvo had beaten Mort Cooper, 4-1. At first we thought some wag was playing a cruel joke, and wouldn't believe it. But it was true, and we still had that precious one-game lead. It was a thin-enough margin, like walking a tightrope over a canyon. But it was something.

So was that next series in Philadelphia. *Broth-err!*

Chapter 12

A PENNANT—AFTER 21 YEARS

I MUST HAVE LOOKED LIKE A BOWERY BUM WHEN WE ARRIVED in Philadelphia. I had worn the same pair of slacks, and the same sport coat and tie for almost three weeks. I hadn't shaved for that long, either. As long as we held the lead I wasn't taking any chances on changing our luck

We had hardly checked in at the Warwick Hotel in Philadelphia when I had a fist fight with Ted Meier, a newspaperman from the Associated Press. He was pestering me for a story. I guess I was on edge, and it was my fault. But from the publicity given our short bout in an alley alongside the hotel, you would have thought I had won a decision over Joe Louis.

The way things were going, I'd have popped a few punches at MacPhail, too, if he had shown up and second-guessed me. Larry was too smart for that, however. He stayed away from us until Saturday night—after we had won a double-header that day from the Phillies, with Wyatt and Higbe.

Not long ago I saw an old clipping with an account of that part of the pennant race. In it, I was quoted as saying, "I announced that I was going to pitch Allen and Davis Sunday, for I had about made up my mind that I was through with Hamlin. However, in the second game that day, something made me start Luke."

"Something," is right. That was the whole story, which the clipping did not tell, and which probably has never been told before.

Saturday night I dragged myself to a buffet supper for club officials and newspapermen. I was wearing the same old outfit. I needed a shave, and my eyes were deep in their sockets, because I never can sleep when we are playing those tight ball games. But we had won two that day while the Cardinals split, and we were two games out in front.

All the visitors were happy. Jim Mulvey, one of the owners, was there with his family. So was Joe Gilleaudeau, another director of the club. So was Ted McGrew, our chief scout, who had been fired by MacPhail almost as often as I had. And, of course, MacPhail, the great man himself.

Larry lost no time. He asked me to outline my pitching plans for the morrow, and the day after.

It was true that I had decided to shelve Hamlin, particularly as I had all my money pitchers ready to work: Higbe and Wyatt the first day, Allen and Davis Sunday, with Fitzsimmons left for the single game Monday. When I laid it out, MacPhail grunted, but offered no objection.

Sunday our followers, including Shorty and the band, descended on Philadelphia in force. Usually, the Phillies attracted just about enough people to start a game of bridge. This day the park was crowded—there were more fans from Brooklyn there than from the City of Brotherly Love.

The Brooklyn bunch loved us. Down on the field it was like a church social. Players were chatting with fans who ordinarily got no closer than Section 8 at Ebbets Field. The fans got their autographs, and had pictures taken of their children with the players, and so on. But the Philadelphia police could not clear the field, and we were not getting our hitting practice.

I mentioned this to Shorty. He lost no time going into action. Grabbing the announcer's microphone, he bawled: "Everybody offen the field. We want our Bums to get some practice!"

As if by magic, the Brooklyn cohorts dissolved into the stands.

Johnny Allen pitched the first game, and won it as easy as shooting fish in a barrel. The Cards won theirs, so we were

Dodgers victory parade of 1941. Mac-
Phail and Leo are in the lead car.

During contract signing, Durocher
lends an ear to Larry MacPhail.

The 1941 pennant-winning Dodgers.

still two games out in front. Between games we all felt pretty good. Curt Davis was on the trainer's table, getting the kinks rolled out of his arm before he went out to warm up for the second game, when who should pop his head into the clubhouse but McGrew. "I got a message for you," he said. "Let's go into the other room where we can talk."

I didn't know what to expect. When McGrew said, "MacPhail wants you to pitch Hamlin in this second game," I really exploded.

"I did pretty good up to now, and kept us in first place," I roared. "So now he's going to step in and take charge, and claim credit for winning the pennant, is he?"

McGrew shrugged. He said that all he was doing was to carry the message from headquarters: "Pitch Hamlin!"

"The hell I will!" I snapped. "Davis is the pitcher!"

But after McGrew left, I began to think about it. After all, MacPhail was the boss. If Davis got beaten, and we should blow the pennant, I knew MacPhail would second-guess me to the newspapermen, the directors, and to everybody else, for the rest of my life!

So I walked over to where Davis was getting ready to go out to warm up, and said, "Curt, that rub didn't take anything out of your arm, did it? I mean, if you didn't work today, you could warm up and pitch tomorrow without any bad effects, couldn't you?"

You know the Davis type: always helpful, cooperative, and understanding. Curt said yes, he would pitch Monday, if I preferred it that way. Still I knew that, good competitor that he was, he was dying to pitch this one.

I shouted to Freddy Fitzsimmons, who carried my instructions to the pitchers, to go out to the bench and tell Hamlin he was going to work, and to hurry and get heated up.

The ball club was a little upset when they saw Hamlin going to work. Billy Herman and Camilli spoke to me. They had no faith in the guy, and you could not blame them. I did not tell them the reason I had made the switch. I just said I was playing a hunch, and that Davis would pitch the next day.

While Luke was warming up something happened. If I had known about it, I probably would have switched right back to Davis. Freddy was watching Luke warm up. It was getting close to game time, and still Hamlin had put nothing on the ball. "Bear down!" Freddy said fiercely. "Put something on the ball. It's almost time to start!"

Hamlin mumbled something about not wanting to pitch, anyway. On this club they never told you when to be ready. . . . He didn't care much what happened. With that, he gave a temperamental shrug, and lobbed another ball to the warm-up catcher.

Fitzsimmons told me later that he was on the verge of popping lackadaisical Luke on the chin. What a sensation that would have caused! Anyway, Hamlin saw the look in the old war horse's eye, because he started to warm up in earnest.

"Old Strongheart," as we derisively called him, got into a quick mess of trouble in the first inning. In a flash there were three Phillies on bases and long-ball-hitter Danny Litwhiler came up. Luke wasn't going to walk this guy, too. So he lobbed up his specialty—the home-run ball. Danny promptly belted it into the seats for four runs.

We all went numb. It was a terrific shock. We had been beating the ears off these Phillies all year, by lopsided scores.

We got Hamlin out of there in a hurry, and put on a few flurries of our own that made it close, but we didn't take this one. Also, the Cardinals won, and that slashed our lead back to one full game.

After that game I walked down between the silent lines of sweating players to Hamlin's locker. I told Luke what I thought of his heart, of his head, and of his pitching. I had one spiked shoe off, and was unlacing the other, when who should appear in our clubhouse doorway, but Ted McGrew!

Ted is a great fellow. Of course, he felt as bad as anybody

about what had happened. But he was not as smart as Mac-
Phail, who had hustled back to New York on the first train.
Larry knew enough to get out of range before I told him what
I thought about his masterminding of my pitching staff. Any-
way, I was blazing, and here came McGrew to remind me of
the whole episode.

"You!" I roared, "you stool pigeon! You got the crust to
come in here? Where's MacPhail, that lamebrain boss of
yours?"

With that, I let fly with what I had in my hand—the spiked
shoe. Ted ducked, which was fortunate. The shoe took the
hat right off his bald head, and carried it through the open
door. Ted hustled out as fast as he could.

Tony Martin, the singer, was following us around. That
night he took me to Philadelphia's finest restaurant to buy me
a steak and try to make me forget. Inwardly, I was boiling so
hard at both Hamlin and MacPhail that I could have chewed
nails. So I must have made a charming dinner companion.
Tony got us a nice table in the corner of Bookbinder's
Restaurant, the walls of which were hung with historical
documents and mementos of earlier American days. I was half
through giving my order and the waiter was beaming, when
I gave out with a yell like a Comanche on the warpath. I
jumped to my feet, pulled off the tablecloth and spilled the
silverware on the floor. Everybody in the place looked up.
The waiter, I'm sure, thought I was nuts. Perhaps he wasn't
far wrong, at that.

What had touched the nerve was that I had glimpsed a
framed election placard over where we sat. In large letters, it
shouted LINCOLN AND HAMLIN. Hamlin, as I didn't
know then, had run for Vice-President on the ticket with
Lincoln. I screamed how they had shot the wrong man, and
that I would not eat where I had to face the name of Hamlin.
So the proprietor calmly led us to another table. Finally, I
cooled off enough to take some nourishment.

It was weeks before I could look at Hamlin and stay rational.

Monday, the Cards were idle, but we won our game in Philadelphia with ease. Davis pitched a dandy. That only made me twice as peeved about having made the switch to Hamlin on Sunday. Anyway, we now had a game and a half lead, with less than a week to go.

Monday night, I met Joe McCarthy of the Yankees on a radio broadcast. It did my heart good to have him whisper, "You're in now, Leo. Congratulations, and we'll be meeting you in the Stadium!"

I told Joe I didn't think we were sure of the pennant at all. With only a slim lead like that and the Cardinals right behind us, anything could happen.

"If you were going to blow it, you'd have blown in that Philadelphia series," Joe said wisely. "Now you're straightened out!"

We got to Boston, and I still had not visited a barber. I remembered what Casey Stengel was supposed to have told a Brooklyn barber as he stepped into the chair one evening after the Dodgers had dropped a double-header: "Once over lightly, please, and never mind cutting my throat. I will attend to that myself, later in the evening."

Reese kicked one early in the first game in Boston and the Braves went ahead. But Dixie Walker won it with a three-run triple in the eighth.

The papers were full of "if" stories, and how we would be *in* "if" we won the next day and "if" the Cardinals lost. I tossed and turned all night, wondering "if" I ought to yank Reese out of there the next afternoon.

I must have looked pretty drawn and tight the next day because Wyatt, walking over to warm up, patted me on the back, and said, "Get me one run today, Leo, and it will be enough!"

He was right, too. We got a quick run as Walker singled,

took third on two infield outs, and came home when Medwick beat out a tapped ball to third. Next time, Walker came
up, Owen was on second. Dixie hit a short single, too short for
Mickey to come in on. But Walker got himself in a run-up
between first and second, and before they caught him, Owen
had sneaked home. The Braves were tight. Because they hated
us, they tried so hard to pin our ears back that they played
bad ball. In the third inning, Carvel Rowell, playing second
base, made three straight errors, and we got another run.

We didn't need it. In the first seven innings, Wyatt gave
only three hits, and not a man reached third. Eddie Murphy,
of the *Sun*, kept signaling me during the game, wigwagging
that the Cardinals were losing. Rowell got the only other hit
in the eighth, but Herman retired the Braves with a great play
on a drive by Demaree.

Now Murphy signaled that the Cardinals had lost. The
boys were whooping and hollering in our dugout, but I told
them to take it easy, we hadn't nailed it down yet. With a
5-0 lead and Wyatt pitching like a world-beater, I still didn't
feel sure. That's how jittery I was.

Then Wyatt breezed through the ninth, and we carried
him into the clubhouse on our shoulders.

It is strange to see strong, swearing ballplayers cry, but we
all did. The nervous strain of the terrific race and the rhubarbs we'd been through together had worn us to the ragged
edge. Now at last it was over, and the reaction had set in.

We had to hurry to catch the special train which John
McDonald had ordered. He had loaded it with thick steaks,
beer, whisky, and even champagne.

Lavagetto started through the train like a little boy who
had just been let out of school. With his knife he cut everybody's necktie off at the knot.

At New Haven, I shut off the liquor supply, and chased the
boys into the diner to eat. I wanted them to look like heroes
to the Brooklyn fans, who were gathered, the conductor told

us, at Grand Central Station. There were supposed to be more than 30,000 of them. We heard later that they were getting bulletins on our progress. Every time it was announced that we had passed New London, or Bridgeport, or New Haven, a mighty cheer went up. For an hour before we arrived and a half hour after, not a train could leave Grand Central, so terrific was the jam.

Meanwhile, Peewee Reese, in the diner, received a chocolate ice-cream shampoo.

Tony Martin, who stood up to make a speech congratulating us, got a steak, mushrooms and all, full in the face.

"Sit down!" commanded Lavagetto. "This is our day, not yours!"

Tony sat down.

After that he was as quiet as Luke Hamlin, who ate his meal without even cracking a smile, completely ignored, and apparently oblivious to all that was going on around him.

One of the newspapermen wanted to get off at the 125th Street Station. I heard some of the players buzzing among themselves that that would be a good way to avoid the crowds. They could sneak off at 125th Street, and take the subway.

So immediately I told the conductor to eliminate the stop at 125th Street and let the train highball right through to the Grand Central Station. I felt that the Brooklyn fans who had waited twenty-one years for a pennant, and who had followed us so faithfully all year, and now thought enough of us to pack a railroad terminal at midnight, were entitled at least to see their conquering heroes.

How was I to know that MacPhail, with Branch Rickey and Sam Breadon, the defeated Cardinal chieftains, had taken a taxi to the 125th Street Station to board the train there and congratulate us? How was I to guess that they were on the platform as our train swirled through, leaving them in a cloud of dust?

I thought it funny that MacPhail, who always loved a picture, missed all the crowd shots, and all the congratulations in the Grand Central. I did not think it was funny later, when I ran into him in the New Yorker Hotel.

He wore a scowl that made his face look like a July thunderstorm. We posed for the newsreel cameras. I thought it was odd that he hadn't even congratulated me on winning the pennant. But, I said to myself, that's Larry, unpredictable as ever.

Quietly we went upstairs to his suite. Still not a word on our victory. He and John McDonald and I talked over the last two weeks of the pennant race as calmly as though we had not gone through a trying season.

"It was just as well I had you pitch Hamlin in Philadelphia," Larry had the nerve to say. "If you had worked your pitchers in any other order, we might not have won!"

I held my temper.

Then he beckoned me into the next room. I advanced confidently, expecting a big pat on the back, or maybe a bonus.

But when we were alone, he staggered me with: "Who gave the order to have that train run through the 125th Street Station without stopping?"

I blinked. "I did, Larry."

"Didn't you get my wire that I was going to get aboard there?"

"No," I replied. "I didn't." I was tired and pretty well fed up because he hadn't congratulated me. So I added, "I'm running a ball team and not a train, anyway."

"Oho!" he roared. "You're not even running the team now, Durocher. You're fired!"

Fired? Now of all times! I had all I could do to keep from hitting him. But I got out of there without starting a rhubarb, and went to my room. I was bluer than blue. I was sure nothing like it had ever happened before. A manager getting fired on the eve of the World Series. But nothing like MacPhail had ever happened before either, I consoled myself. So, on a night when everything should have been peaches and cream, I really hit bottom.

In a little while, McDonald knocked on the door. "The newsreel guys want you and MacPhail for some more pictures," he called. "Come on down!"

I said, "Go away!" How could I pose for pictures when I wasn't even the manager?

At eight o'clock that morning, my phone rang. Sleepily I answered. It was MacPhail. He sounded mild, even sweet. On my way to the ball park the next morning would I stop by his office at Boro Hall?

"Yeah!" I snapped. "What do you want to do—give me my severance pay?" And I hung up.

I found him behind his desk. He wore a new blue suit. He looked as though he'd had a full ten hours of sleep. He even had a carnation in his lapel.

"Well, Leo," he grinned, "guess I got a little out of line last night, uh?"

I grunted something.

"Well," he went, as nice as pie, "pull up a chair here, and we'll figure out how to beat those Yankees."

That's the way the man was, so emotional that he could drive you to distraction and twist his own destiny into hairpin turns. And when you rode with him, your life went dizzy, too!

I had been crushed, but my old bounce came back quickly. That afternoon the newspapermen cornered me and asked if the late afternoon shadow in the Yankee Stadium would bother my players.

"The shadow?" I sneered. "Who's afraid of the shadow? Don't tell me they got Superman on their side, too!"

I wouldn't have been half so cocky if I had an inkling who WAS lining up on their side for that big series. No one else but Lady Luck!

Chapter 13

THE 1941 WORLD SERIES

THE 1941 WORLD SERIES REMINDED ME OF TWO GUYS WALK-ing down the street. One had worked hard all day to earn a five-dollar bill. The other said, "Why bother?" and reached down into the gutter and picked up a double sawbuck. For the Yankees, this World Series was like picking up money in the street.

We had things all figured out. Curt Davis instead of Whit-low Wyatt would start the first game. That would leave us in great shape to take the series if the boys did a little hitting behind Curt. Then we would surprise them with Fitzsimmons instead of Higbe in the third game. And so on. But, as they always ask, "How did you come out?" The answer was: *Second!*

Remember the guy who said he would rather be lucky than be President? It's no disgrace to be lucky, not in my book. I have been lucky in baseball all my life. But in this World Series the Yankees were the lucky ones, lucky to catch us in a slump.

We could not get the runs. Not that the Yankees pitched correctly to us; they didn't. They threw fast balls to Med-wick right up at his face, where ordinarily he would have murdered them. They fast-balled Camilli right where he usually hit home runs. They struck Reiser out, and Walker did not get a hit until the seventh inning of the third game.

Still, these were the guys who had belted the ball out of shape all year. Reiser had hit .343 to become the youngest man—he was twenty-two—ever to lead the National League in batting. And Walker had hit an important .311, placing his hits in the spots where they counted.

To help us with our bad luck, Hugh Casey was not himself. He pitched as if he was still peeved about the Magerkurth incident in Pittsburgh. And luck again, the whole series revolved around Hughie. That's the long way around to figure anything, I know.

In the first game, we simply did not hit for Davis, who pitched well enough, but he was up against Ruffing, McCarthy's best. Joe Gordon drove in two of the runs, one a homer that beat us, 3-2. It was Gordon who murdered us with his bat during that series.

We got back on our feet when Wyatt beat Chandler in the second game, 3-2.

Then our bad luck started to catch up with us. Maybe it wasn't that; maybe, perhaps, we just weren't wide awake. I insist that, as I said earlier, the Yanks picked up the money in the street. But maybe if we had been more alert, we would have seen it there first.

It was tough luck for Russo to hit a line drive off Fitzsimmons' kneecap in the Saturday game, the third one of the series. That was a real human interest story. The next day the *Eagle* ran a front-page picture of pretty Mrs. Fitzsimmons crying her heart out as they led forty-year-old Freddy, the oldest man ever to start a series game, to the repair shop. He was limping, cursing, and groaning.

Owen's muff was a tough break, too. Still, it was not tough luck that let the Yanks knock Casey's brains out in the eighth inning of the third game. That was Hughie's carelessness. First, he did not cover first base on Henrich's drive. Camilli went for it, but Coscarart got it. Then Hughie got bullheaded and wouldn't step off the mound to throw to Coscarart. He could have picked Rolfe off clean, but he didn't throw.

Later I asked Hugh in the clubhouse about that play.

"I don't know why I didn't throw, Skipper," said the big Georgian. "I wanted to, but I just froze!"

Casey slumped badly, but all the boys played as if they were in a coma. Probably they were tight and strained from the grueling pennant race we had gone through.

Ted McGrew was an old hand. He had been through baseball as a player, manager, scout, and big-league umpire. However, hardened as he was, Ted could not stand and watch us—and his particular baby, Reese—in the World Series. He just disappeared.

During the first series game, MacPhail suddenly set up a holler for McGrew. Messengers were dispatched all over the Stadium, and down to the clubhouse, but Ted couldn't be found.

That night, Larry spied Ted talking into a tall beer in the World Series headquarters.

"Where were you this afternoon?" barked MacPhail.

"Oh, I was around," McGrew returned evasively.

"Around where?" snapped MacPhail. "You weren't at the ball park!"

"No," returned Ted, casting discretion to the winds. "I couldn't stand it. I had to get away. I went to the race track. Out there I got the score by innings."

MacPhail blew up. "McGrew, you're fired!" he screamed, "and you're never coming back. Here we're fighting for a world's championship—the biggest moment in the club's history—and you are out there betting your money on a horse race! You're through! I never want to see you around here again."

It wasn't leaving MacPhail that hurt Ted so much. It was the thought of leaving Reese, whom he had plugged for stardom, and encouraged and advised even when things looked blackest. The next morning he said good-bys all around, had his bags packed, and was ready to go when the telephone rang.

MacPhail talking: "McGrew, I want to see you right away."

Ted faltered. "But you fired me."

"Oh, forget about that," said Larry, a master at brushing off things that crush other people. He paused. Then he added, "Say, you got anything good at the track today? Bring your racing form with you, will you?"

The ax fell in the fourth game. Larry Goetz had actually called strike three on Tommy Henrich. That was the third Yankee out in the top of the ninth. So we had won the game, 4-3, and tied up the series, I thought, at two games all. Then that low inside curve ball got away from Catcher Owen, and rolled over toward our dugout.

There has been a lot of discussion about that pitch, but I know definitely it was not a spitter. It was a curve ball with a little something extra. When Owen did not shift his feet, but gave it a casual reach with his glove—the roof fell in on our heads.

The fact that Henrich was on first with two out and no-body on was not too important. The fact that Casey did not wait to get his feet back on the ground, but pitched quickly to DiMaggio, and that DiMaggio singled to left, was not fatal either. The big thing was that Casey, pitching, was numb with anger, and I did not realize it. The same thing occurred now as had happened in Pittsburgh when, without any out-ward indication of his feelings, Hughie had begun to blow up.

Now he got two strikes on Charley Keller. I thought, "Shall I go out there and talk to Hugh?" I voted against it. I didn't want to get everybody on the ball club unnerved. So instead, I just whistled to Casey, as I had done a thousand times before, and motioned across my chest. I wanted Hugh to loosen Keller up, once or even twice, with a high inside pitch. Then, I figured, Charley would be looking for that fast one, and we would give him the big curve.

Everyone knows what happened. At two strikes and no balls, Casey, the control artist, the heady pitcher, did what he almost never did. He gave Keller a fat one through the middle, and Charley belted it against the wall for the two runs that won the game for the Yankees. The base hits that followed weren't important. When, finally, we came in, we sat on the bench and stared straight ahead of us without seeing anything.

It's strange, whatever it is that happens to pitchers in such spots. Maybe psychologists ought to go to work on the problem. One day in 1947, when Burt Shotton was managing the Dodgers, I saw Casey, who was his best pitcher and his only control man all year, walk three men in a row in a night game in St. Louis. The Dodgers blew their 10-0 lead, but, happily, they won the game, 11-10.

After that fourth World Series game something happened to MacPhail. He charged into our clubhouse, among the saddest bunch of guys I ever saw, and he waved his arms and shouted they would still win the series—not to get down or discouraged.

Then the newspapermen trouped in, and Larry cracked: "Don't read the papers tomorrow, boys. When things look black, never read Dan Parker, Stanley Woodward, or Red Patterson. They make things look worse!" Patterson was standing there when MacPhail said it, and began to splutter. This is the same Arthur Patterson whom MacPhail later fought with in the Press Club—and still later made Road Secretary of the Yankees, when he moved to the Stadium.

Meanwhile, up in the press box, the boys were slashing at their typewriters. From the red-hot keyboards rolled stories of the "greatest World Series thriller ever played." Henry McLemore wrote, "When you give the Yankees a reprieve, they get up out of the electric chair and electrocute the warden."

He was right. All of MacPhail's inspiring speeches couldn't put us together again. In the fifth game the Yankees beat Wyatt easily, 3-1. We were a dead team. We had clawed and scratched and fought all year, and our antics had attracted

1,200,000 fans at home and a million more on the road. But that last day, facing Ernie Bonham, we were as mild as tabby cats.

The Brooklyn fans faced a new kind of winter. For the first time they did not have to wait for that "next year" which had taken twenty-one years to arrive. Now they had something to get their teeth into. They could make a perfect case to show we would have been world's champions in five games—except for the Russo line drive off Fitzsimmons' knee, and the Owen muff, and a lot of bad breaks.

Chapter 14

THE NATIONAL LEAGUE CHAMPIONS

WE SHOULD HAVE SEEN THE HANDWRITING ON THE WALL. BUT MacPhail was not smart in such things, and I had not been around long enough to recognize the symptoms.

The team that had died on us in the 1941 World Series might reasonably have been expected to run out of gas a little earlier in 1942 than it had in 1941. However, we were the National League champions, and we were proud and complacent. So we did not rip and tear and rebuild, and we did not give the club a transfusion of youth. Instead, MacPhail added Arky Vaughan, still a great ballplayer, but even older than Walker and Camilli and Medwick and Herman, who had folded up on us in the World Series.

As I look back, I can see now that the signs showed up early. We had to send Herman and Camilli to Johns Hopkins Hospital for examinations even before the season opened. Herman, who had been knocked out of the World Series, was in bad shape. He said he felt as though his hip was out of joint.

Then Wyatt, who had been the difference between the pennant and second place for us the year before, went into a holdout battle with MacPhail, and reported late.

Again we trained in Havana, and there was another crop of rhubarbs.

One of the players was doing a rhumba on the dance floor of the Nacional Hotel. He was giving it everything he had and what he thought it needed when a Buenos Aires publisher gave vent to a *low* "Hisssss!"

Of course, that's only a Latin's way of attracting attention. But the ballplayer thought it was a criticism of his dance-floor technique. So he promptly hauled off and flattened the publisher. That caused what might be described as "a mild furor."

Much has been made of the fact that the Dodgers were puzzled by Cuban customs. We puzzled the Islanders even more. I am thinking of the affable desk clerk at the Nacional who said to Kirby Higbe one day, "You like Havana, no?"

"No!" said Hig, quite firmly, and walked away.

We were the champions, and it went to our heads. Especially when we came home and the veterans, in better shape than the rest of the league because of the fine Havana weather, got off to a good start. They were to run out of gallop later, as the sun-baked diamonds of July and August took their toll, but in the first weeks they kicked up their heels in great style.

We became a gambling ball club. The stakes at poker were high, and a lot of the players bet on the horses. But so did almost everybody in the organization, beginning at the top with MacPhail, so who was there to apply the brakes?

One day MacPhail, starting for Belmont Park at the last minute, phoned Willie Gibson, the auditor, for some cash. That was nothing new. Larry could blow through the box office like a gust of wind, screaming for cash, and for the next month the boys would have to chase him with vouchers to sign, so they could balance their accounts.

Now he crammed his hat on his head as he dashed in. He did not want to miss the first race.

"I want five hundred dollar bills!" he had bellowed to Gibson on the phone. "I'll be in your office in a minute."

Gibson had the money ready. He handed MacPhail five packages of dollar bills, one hundred singles in each.

Without another word, Larry flung the five packages at Gibson and hit him between the eyes. The bands broke, and dollar bills fluttered everywhere.

"Idiot!" screamed MacPhail, stomping out into Montague Street. What he had wanted was five one-hundred-dollar bills!

Night or day, there was always a seven-card stud poker game going at the club. The bets became bigger, starting with a quarter, then a half, and finally as much as a dollar on a card.

As the last card went face down, I can still hear the dealer saying, "Down the river of golden dream—"

That was it: a golden dream! We were all rich. We were heading for another golden World Series, and we were moving as in a dream.

I sat in on these contests of skill and chance. Often the players owed me money—a fact that Branch Rickey was to lecture me about long and loudly when he appeared to run the show. But now MacPhail was running it, and the sky was the limit, with no holds barred.

I usually had Higbe on the hip for a couple of hundred bucks. If he was to start a tough ball game, I would go to him and say: "Win this one, Hig, and I'll take off two hundred dollars!" They were paper debts, and I didn't collect my winnings in cash anyway. I thought it was great stuff. Now I can see that it was not good for the ball club.

But that was the kind of club we were: cocky, riding high, probably not as careful of training rules as we should have been.

Yet, we got off fast. Lavagetto had gone into service during the winter, but we had been lucky and acquired Vaughan, one of the game's really great hitters—for a collection that included Phelps, Hamlin, Wasdell, and Petey Coscarart, the only pretty good ballplayer in the lot.

One day in mid-May, with Les Webber, a new kid from the Coast, pitching against the Cubs, we were six and a half games in front. In 1941, we had never been more than four games ahead.

The Cubs were tough as usual. They were leading this day, 1-0, when Billy Herman came to bat.

"Turn his cap around," said Jimmy Wilson, loud enough to be heard on our bench.

"Oho!" muttered Webber. "So they play like that up here! We'll see how they like a little of that themselves!"

The way he said it made me like the kid. The look in his eye let you know he wasn't going to be pushed around, or let his team get a pushing around. Webber was always like that. It kept him in the majors even when he did not really have big-league stuff.

Anyway, now he went in to pitch. Lenny Merullo, their first hitter, had hardly gone to bat before he sat down. Webber had almost taken the button off his cap.

Merullo was white as a sheet. He starter to holler. I hollered back that this was no ladies' auxiliary meeting. "If you can't take it, go get yourself a broom, instead of a bat!"

Then I hollered over to their dugout that since they had started this beanball stuff, we would keep it going for the rest of the afternoon.

The whole Cub bench hollered back at me. Paul Erickson, their big pitcher whom we had beaten in the first game that day, screamed: "Just wait till I get a chance to throw at you guys again!"

I told Erickson he had a strong arm but a cement head, which was pretty nearly true. The boys called him "Li'l Abner."

Anyway, even Jimmy Wilson fell for it. In the last of the sixth, he said to Johnny Schmitz, loud enough so I could tell it was for my benefit: "—And the first Dodger that comes up there, stick the ball in his ear!"

I gave him the horselaugh. "If you do, you bum," I said, "Vaughan will turn and catch the ball in his teeth. You're not fast enough to dust anybody off!"

Anyway, Schmitz walked Vaughan, and then threw three dusters at Pete Reiser, who also walked. Bordagaray went up and sacrificed them along. One man came in on a fly, and that left Reiser on third. Pete took a run at the plate and stole home easily. That gave us a 2-1 lead—two runs without a hit or an error! That put us out in front 2-1, and eventually we won the ball game, 4-3.

In Flatbush, with the boys at the head of the National League, all was carnival. Every sports writer in the business assured me again and again: "The pennant's a breeze, Leo!"

We poked fun at everybody. Even Gladys Gooding, goddess of the Hammond organ that MacPhail had installed at the field, became gay one day when Umpires Stewart, Magerkurth, and Dunn strolled out to start a game. She struck up, "Three Blind Mice"! The crowd roared. MacPhail chuckled. Ford Frick burned when he heard about it.

Then a gent named S. Reid Spencer, not an umpire, went to court for an injunction to restrain MacPhail from having the organ played. Spencer claimed that the music disturbed his afternoon nap in his near-by Lefferts Avenue apartment.

Immediately, from unsuspected quarters, music lovers rallied to defend MacPhail's electric calliope. Fans in the fifty-five-cent seats at Ebbets Field signed a petition asking that Spencer, rather than the musical notes, be removed from the vicinity of the Dodger park. Ebbets Field had become the poor man's Carnegie Hall!

When the case came up in court, the magistrate looked down his nose at Spencer and asked: "Are you a Bill Terry man?"

Had he said, "Are you a spy?" or, "Are you a traitor?" the implication couldn't have been plainer.

Spencer's chin dropped. So did his law suit.

One day late in May, MacPhail walked over to a typewriter in the press box and, with two fingers, punched out an announcement: "Fred Fitzsimmons has been given his unconditional release as a player. He has been offered a position as coach. He will confer with MacPhail tomorrow!"

So Fitzsimmons, whether he wanted to admit it or not, was through at forty-one. He had won twenty-two games for us in the past two years, and had lost only five, but now his arm was as crooked up as a corkscrew.

With or without Freddy, we galloped on. In mid-June Reiser was belting .356. We were four games ahead of our 1941 pennant-winning pace, noted the statisticians.

We played the Giants. Mize, who only had to step on first base for the third out in one big inning, threw home. His catcher missed the tag. Then we pulled a triple steal.

Mize was hooted by the Dodger fans. How smart Mac-Phail had been, they shouted, not to have taken him. Actually, Larry had bid high for Johnny Mize, but instead he had acquired Don Padgett—who had gone into the Navy before he played a single game for us.

The Giants, like the rest of the league, began to burn at us. Eddie Brannick, the dapper New York secretary who likes to dress à la Jimmy Walker, arrived at Ebbets Field. He looked for his box seats, and got the brush-off. He blasted everyone in the Brooklyn organization. When he spied John McDonald, Brannick's voice became louder than his own sport coat.

"Who is Durocher's assistant manager today?" screamed Eddie. "Is it Danny Kaye? What are you running here in Brooklyn, a ball team or a musical comedy?"

McDonald mumbled something about second-division clubs being jealous. Brannick almost blew a fuse.

"You have no infield!" he ranted. "Herman is through. So is Vaughan. You have one outfielder, Reiser. I told Horace Stoneham not to buy Medwick when Rickey was peddling him, that he was washed up. You got stung!"

Ducky Medwick overheard it. He let loose a blast at Brannick that appeared in the papers. He did more than that. A day or so later he made a sliding catch on Bartell. Three were on, one was out, and everybody was running. "As soon as I had that ball in my mitt," Medwick chortled later, "I looked around for Brannick. But he had disappeared. Probably into a hole in the ground."

McDonald, too, got his revenge. He went on the air with Jimmy Powers, of the *News*, and poked fun at the flashily dressed Giant secretary. Asked for a rejoinder, Broadway Eddie snorted, "I never listen to those small stations!"

The irony of it was that Brannick, who had knocked Medwick's brains out talking to McDonald, and said he was washed up, all through, was to have Ducky on his Giants a year later, when we released him!

We continued to gallop out in front. We rode special trains and ate double-thick steaks. On August 5, we were ten full games in front—our biggest lead. As late as August 16, we were nine and a half games ahead, and there was only one man in America who dared say that we would not take the pennant. That was Eddie Brannick. In our plush-lined splendor, we felt sorry for second-division Eddie. He was blinded by anger and envy.

But wait a minute. There was one other man who said we wouldn't win.

One day after we'd won a big one, I said to this fellow, "We've got great spirit on this club. Everybody's happy!"

He scowled. "That's the trouble, Durocher. Everybody's happy, and complacent. Nobody's hustling. You have a fat, overconfident club. This time I don't think you'll win!"

"You're crazy!" I said. I'd told him that before. This time, I thought I was sure.

So it came out, I was sure wrong.

He—MacPhail—was right. How very, very right!

Chapter 15

WE START TO SKID

WE WERE STILL EIGHT GAMES AHEAD OF THE LEAGUE WHEN MacPhail called the whole team up to the Press Club one August evening. Before all the newspapermen, he hit us right between the eyes. He declared we would not win the pennant.

As usual, Larry pulled no punches. "You are not hustling," he accused us. "You should be twenty games in front of the Cardinals, instead of only eight. Right now, only six men on this club are carrying their gloves out there every day: Reiser, Reese, Medwick, Owen, Casey, and Davis."

By "carrying their gloves," MacPhail meant pulling their own weight, and not taking it easy.

Some of the columnists made sport of his blow-up. One remarked that it must have made Larry French feel great to hear himself classified as a non-hustler, when that very afternoon he had pitched a four-hit shutout to beat the Phillies, 1-0.

A few days later another columnist took a blast at MacPhail. Larry answered him and showed us his letter. "You copy all your facts from Dan Parker's column," he had written. "The only difference between your column and his is that Parker's is interesting!"

MacPhail feuded with everybody. One night he telephoned Parker every hour until dawn; between calls he thought up new insults. In his column Parker printed a salvo at MacPhail nearly every day. In these blasts, he furnished a new handle for MacPhail's first two initials, "L. S." Once it was "Lucifer Sulphurious" MacPhail. Another time, after Larry had sold more tickets than there were seats in Ebbets Field, Parker called him "Letemall Standup" MacPhail.

But Larry was also feuding with his own players. If Larry

French felt badly, he did not show it. But Dixie Walker, also classified among the non-hustlers, spoke up. When MacPhail said the club wouldn't win the pennant, Walker blurted out, "I'll bet we will!"

Ordinarily, Walker would not have bet that dawn would break the next day. Now, however, he was so mad he waved his money and challenged MacPhail, before the newspapermen.

Larry backed off. He would not bet against his own team. The boys thought his bluff had been called.

But he had sensed, or guessed, something.

Perhaps he attached more importance to Pete Reiser's troubles than the rest of us did. In mid-July, Reiser had cracked himself up against the outfield wall in St. Louis, after chasing a long shot off the bat of Enos Slaughter. Pete had caught the ball, hit the wall and then, as he went down limp, let the ball roll out of his glove. Slaughter had spun around the bases for a home run that beat us.

"So what?" was the general feeling at the time. Reiser would be all right in a little while, and while Pete was taking a rest, other good outfielders would work.

But it was not to be that way. On August 1, when he snould have been ready to bound back, Pete still suffered headaches and muscular pains. He would play one day and be sick the next. Something was always going wrong. He was not the free-swinging hitter who had led us to a pennant the year before and paced us to our ten-game lead this season. We hoped he would snap out of it, but he couldn't. His batting average, which had reached .353 the first day of August, fell like a barometer in a hurricane. By the end of August, he was down to .328. Then when the battle really got bitter in September and we had our backs to the wall, poor Pete got worse. During the last two months, in the forty-one games he was barely able to drag himself into, he was a .220 hitter. He did end at .310.

However, it was more likely that the reason for MacPhail's

current was a talk he had with Rickey. When his Cardinals were eight games behind, Branch had told Brooklyn newspapermen, "This team of mine is playing great ball now that it has jelled. I don't know about the Dodgers. But I do know that *we* will go on winning right down to the finish line. If the Dodgers stub their toes, it will be too bad for them."

Rickey had said that much to the writers. It was likely that he had said much more to MacPhail in private. At any rate, Larry had studied long enough under Rickey to know that Cardinal clubs, young and inexperienced and bewildered in the first half of the season, had a way of pulling themselves together in August and September.

MacPhail knew that the 1930 Cardinals had trailed the Cubs by six and a half games on Labor Day morning—and had gone on to win twenty of their next twenty-three games.

He must have remembered many things. That the 1934 Cardinals, with whom I played, had lost two games to the Pirates on Labor Day, and were six and a half behind the Giants as we started an Eastern trip; that Dizzy and Paul started us off in Brooklyn with a double-header sweep; that we went on to take twenty games out of twenty-five to cop the pennant.

MacPhail had seen the 1939 Reds lead the league by twelve and a half games on August 1. He had seen the Cards put on a great spurt and come within two games of the lead before time ran out on them. And, he had seen the 1941 Redbirds come up from behind and almost nip us in the last week of the season.

Now he knew, and Rickey knew and was telling everyone, that the 1942 Cardinal team was better than any of the others. Branch was quoted in the papers with, "Brooklyn had better win the pennant this year, for the Dodgers are going down, and we are coming up. This Cardinal club will win the pennant next year with ease, and the year after that, too."

Rickey was right, and MacPhail was right. The St. Louis club was to streak through the last month and a half of the season like a bunch of Supermen. They won thirty-seven of their last forty-three games.

During the streak they started August 16, when they were nine and one-half back of us the Cards beat us five out of six. Aside from those beatings—every one a close game—we did pretty well ourselves. For instance, we won fifteen and lost nine in September, a pennant pace ordinarily.

But "pretty well" and "ordinarily" just didn't mean anything once the Cardinals got hot. After they had whizzed past us, we won our last eight games of the season, and actually *lost* half a game in the standings. When Mr. Redbird got his foot on our neck, he wasn't letting up!

Despite the fact that it was this great Cardinal outburst of power that was responsible, we will always be known as the Dodger club that "blew" the 1942 pennant. The experts say we folded like a Japanese lantern in a rainstorm. I don't agree. I do agree that we weren't the team we were in 1941, and early in 1942. Baseball historians debate the reasons.

What were those reasons?

Some say the Number One reason was Whitlow Wyatt. He had been what the boys call "the difference" the year before, the margin between the pennant and second place. He won the big ones, the money games—like the 1–0 game over Mort Cooper in St. Louis.

This year, Wyatt was again quite a pitcher. He has been quoted as blaming himself, saying his holdout battle had got him off to a slow start. True, he did not win the twenty-two he had won the year before, but nineteen is not to be sneezed at. And the fact remains that on July 4 his record was: eight won and two lost. At that point Cooper, who was having a red-hot year, had won eleven and lost three.

Whit was not winning the big ones as he had the year before. One of his two losses was to the Cardinals, 1–0. In that game we got only two hits off Mort Cooper. The run came in because Pete Reiser was out of action and Walker, playing center field, let a ball he should have caught sail over his head. The year before it had been Billy Herman's ball, in St. Louis, which fell safe because Terry Moore was not in center. Baseball has a way of squaring things up in time.

We began our last Western trip seven and one-half games in front. After Lanier had beaten us the first game in St. Louis, Mort Cooper and Wyatt went at it again. This time Cooper again won, 2–1, in fourteen innings. We actually had the lead when we made the first run in this game, in the top of the thirteenth inning. Then, instead of charging out there with fire in his eyes, as he had the year before when he struck out Slaughter with the pennant in the balance, Wyatt told me he did not want to continue.

"Whit," I argued, "we're ahead, 1–0. If you can get three more Cardinals out, this may mean the pennant."

"I'm tired," he said. "My arm hurts."

The moment Wyatt indicated he wanted out, Larry French had begun to warm up furiously in our bull pen. I motioned to French to sit down. I made up my mind that we would sink or swim with our ace. I let Whit know it.

How much of Wyatt's trouble was in his arm and how much in his head, I never found out. Eventually, I had to take Whit out of there in the bottom of the thirteenth, for he all but bounced the ball up to the plate, and put the first two men on. They got one run to tie us in that inning, and finally beat us in the last of the fourteenth.

The next day Johnny Beazley beat Max Macon, and cut our lead to four and one-half games. We were desperate. We had won only two of our ten games in St. Louis all year.

But Curt Davis stopped the slide—momentarily. He beat the Cards, 4–1, in the final game of the series. We escaped from St. Louis with a five and one-half game lead, and a fat check— the fattest Sam Breadon had ever signed, they said. Our four-game series had drawn 91,028 fans. Not so long before that, a pennant-winning Cardinal team had drawn no more than 400,000 all year in St. Louis!

The game that Davis pitched marked the last we were to see of the Cardinals for a while. But we were to hear about them plenty. They won eleven of the thirteen games they played before they met us again—in Brooklyn. By then, our lead had shrunk to two games. We were due to play two with the Red-birds. If we could win *one*, we'd be all right.

We couldn't even do that

We had been leading the league since April 21. Whitey Ku-rowski hit the homer that won the second game and finally pulled the Cardinals up to us on Saturday, September 12. That was after Wyatt had failed us again. Cooper beat him in the opener of that series.

Whatever the reason, our ace pitcher was not the Wyatt of 1941.

After the Cards pulled up even with us MacPhail dashed into the clubhouse. "I feel better than I have for weeks," he declared breezily. "Now we'll start fresh. The breaks will change." "Sure, boys," I said, "now it's a new season!" I said it loudly enough, but I didn't feel it. Larry and I were both whistling in a graveyard.

We had been a tough, hard-riding ball club when we had been up there in the lead. Now we didn't have a friend out-side of Brooklyn. Everybody was happy to see us in trouble.

Baseball historians point to that as another reason for our 1942 failure. We had been involved in beanball wars on several fronts, and all the other clubs were mad at us. John McGraw used to claim that it was fatal to get clubs that were out of the race peeved at you. He insisted they would play over their heads to beat you. "Let sleeping dogs lie" was his motto. Maybe he was right.

But no dogs were sleeping when we were around, no matter

who we played. They were all up in arms against us. In Chicago, in a battle of dusters, Hi Bithorn, the Puerto Rican player, fired a ball into our dugout as he left the game. He missed me, and I lost no time telling him about his lousy control.

Wherever we went, cries of "Stick it in his ear" and "Turn his cap around" resounded. When Wyatt and Manny Salvo threw bats as well as baseballs at each other in Boston, Ford Frick stepped in. He made the managers responsible, and threatened to fine them two hundred dollars for anything that even looked like an intentional beanball.

MacPhail screamed at this "luxury tax" on dusters. He called a meeting and defied Frick. He told our players he would pay their fines. If we were dusted off, he hollered, we were to give the beanballs back, two for one. The Brooklyn club hadn't started this beanball war, he vowed, and nobody was going to tell the Dodgers to hold their fire in self-defense! What was really eating Larry was that Frick had fined Wyatt seventy-five dollars for the Boston ruckus, and had nicked Salvo for only fifty dollars. That made it seem that we were more to blame than the other side. As a final shot, MacPhail had the writers listen in on extension phones while he called the National League offices and blistered Ford Frick's ears!

Now we were to reap the troubles we had sown the year before. The day after the Cards beat us to tie up the pennant race, who should come into Ebbets Field but the Cincinnati Reds. The year before . . . Johnny Allen had mowed them down. . . . Held over was the bitterness of that long game in which we finally beat Derringer in the dark. Now Bill McKechnie and the Reds gave it back to us in spades. They beat us twice. The Cardinals divided a double-header, and thus passed us—for good.

In that Sunday twin bill with the Reds I started Pitcher Bobo Newsom, one of the biggest windbags the game has ever known. Bobo was a disturbing influence on the club from the moment he reported to us, late in August.

When we bought him and his big salary from the Washington Senators, Eddie Murphy wrote in the *Sun*, "Road Map Newsom, the man who put the forwarding address in baseball, now stops a while with the Dodgers."

Gus Steiger in the *Mirror* said, "The Dodgers were two-toned with Durocher and MacPhail. Now they acquire another strident note, Bobo Newsom."

When MacPhail bought him for $45,000 as pennant "insurance," Rickey was called to task by Cardinal rooters. They demanded to know why he had not bid for the talkative Newsom and kept the Dodgers from getting help.

"I didn't bid for Newsom," Rickey said dryly, "because I was afraid I'd get him!"

How right Branch was! From the very first moment Bobo walked into our clubhouse in Cincinnati, he was popping off. "You guys got nothing to worry about now!" he cracked, "Ol' Bobo's here." That did not sit well with some of our older players. After all, in 1941 they had won the pennant without his help.

Actually, Newsom won his first start in Red territory. But he was to lose the big one, September 13, and he was not much help, all in all, winning two and losing two. His purchase touched off a chain of events that was to affect Dodger history.

The high-stake card games that were nearly always in session on our club have been cited as a factor in our "collapse." The claim has been made that some of our players lost heavily and, therefore, had the jitters; that others were much more worried about filling a flush than getting a base hit. Personally, I do not think the cardplaying was nearly as important as it has been made out to be. The poker games got a lot of publicity because Bill Klem, who was through as an umpire then, got into the game one night, with a lot of newspapermen looking on, and won three hundred bucks. "Soft touches," he laughed. "I'd be a rich man if I could travel with this Dodger club."

Editorials were written pro and con. In a New York paper the charge was flung that "ballplayers as a class are not overly free with their dimes. It is inconceivable that enough of them could be found on the same team who would play for stakes large enough to be alarming."

This brought a sharp rebuttal from a columnist in the *Eagle*. He jumped in to defend his Dodgers' reputations. He quoted a Ring Lardner story in which manager Frank Chance, who gambled with his players, lost forty dollars in less than an hour. The stakes on the Brooklyn club, this writer insisted, were much higher. He quoted a ballplayer named Tom Needham as asking to stay on the Cubs in Chance's day for nothing, if he could just play poker with the other players! He said that Durocher was twice *that* good, and could live on what he won from his athletes.

Other disturbing things happened. Medwick, a cocky gent when he was hitting, and morose and ill-tempered when he wasn't, had just about worn out his welcome on the club. A lot of the boys had begun to growl at him. Joe had had fist fights on the Cardinal team. When things went bad, I had to step in several times to avert them on our club. I still had faith in Joe, but perhaps I humored him too much. Anyway, one day when Joe had made a display at Ebbets Field, MacPhail sent me a pencil-written message in the dugout. He was livid when he wrote it, and the writers near him knew he was exploding about something. They were not long finding out. Larry had borne down so hard on the pencil that it had pressed through the paper and into the mahogany surface of the bar in the pressroom! There, after MacPhail had stomped off, they were able to piece together the note he had sent me: *"Leo: Medwick is a nice fellow* (this was sarcasm because we were pals) *but why let him run the club? Larry."*

As I look back now, I think we would have won the pennant that year if I had yanked Medwick sooner, and gone along with Augie Galan in left. But that's second-guessing. Medwick fell from .325 to .310. But in the last forty games his decline was nowhere near as sharp as Reiser's.

It was true that we were pretty tight and jumpy as the St. Louis bunch breathed down our necks, inching up toward the pennant. Why wouldn't I have been irritable? MacPhail was already tossing the harpoon into me, talking about his "next manager." On top of that the Army was calling me and I felt that this might be my last chance. I might be in khaki before another season rolled around.

One day, late in the game, as we were blowing a lead, and the scoreboard already shouted the news that the Cardinals had won another, Pete Reiser dropped a scrap of paper in my lap as he went to bat.

As I unfolded it, I read: "Casey looks tired. Better get somebody warmed up!"

What was this? Weren't 20,000 managers in the grandstand and one in the front office enough? Did I need one more on the bench?

I called Reiser over, my eyes smoldering. "Who will you pitch tomorrow? Now that you've decided to take Casey out today," I asked.

"Casey?" repeated Pete, with a bewildered look. "What about Casey?"

"You said in your note that I should get him out of there!" I snapped.

"Oh, the note," mumbled Pete. "I didn't read it. Hilda tossed it to me. It was addressed to you, so I stuck it in my shirt, and gave it to you as soon as I could."

"Hilda!" I said, knocking my head on the roof of the dugout. "Where in blazes is she?"

"In her usual seat," replied Pete, "in the center-field bleachers. She scaled the note down to me."

I cooled off then. Hilda can do no wrong—or hardly any, in my opinion.

The last put-out, which the Cardinals plastered on us the afternoon of September 12, when they beat us to pull even at last, was the final out for Larry MacPhail, too, practically speaking. He had sprayed money around in such a golden stream that a few of the men behind the club began to wonder where they were heading—

Strangely enough, the finale revolved about the globular figure of Bobo Newsom.

When this picture was taken, Leo Durocher and Branch Rickey had got over one of their few rough spots, and everything was O.K.

Conference on a bench. Rickey gives Leo a few words of wise advice.

A return bout is about to start as the aftermath of the previous day's historic 1946 brawl between the Cubs and the Dodgers.

New York policemen and special cops were assigned to guard the Cubs' dugout after a pre-game slugging match in 1946.

Chapter 16

END OF THE MacPHAIL ERA

EARLY IN MACPHAIL'S APPRENTICESHIP, BRANCH RICKEY HAD recognized the streak of promotional genius in his man. Ford Frick had also played a major part in bringing Larry to Brooklyn.

Both men, however, had pointed out that genius sometimes has its drawbacks. Frick had been fairly specific in his warning to the Board of Directors of the Brooklyn club. "He will do a major job of building up in three years," the National League president said. "But after that, watch out. MacPhail will stand up and start to rock the boat."

That was the perfect analysis of MacPhail. He had to be ripping and tearing all the time. Even when he had built something that was running smoothly, he had a strong urge to make it over. For that reason he never stayed long in one place.

MacPhail had been in Brooklyn more than five years, and he had worked wonders. He had made the Dodgers a power in baseball. He had pulled, pushed, and driven them into their first World Series in twenty-one years. But the directors were on the alert for signs of that change about which Frick had spoken. They fancied they detected symptoms in the "desperation" purchase of Newsom.

Larry knew the directors did not approve of the $45,000 price he had paid for Bobo. One of them called this plan for saving the pennant evidence aplenty that "MacPhail had gone haywire." It was still in the planning stages then, but the determined MacPhail went through with it anyway.

When Newsom failed and the plan failed, MacPhail had failed. He knew it. It was like a house of cards. Had the move helped to win another pennant, and Larry's next fantastic scheme had also worked, the entire history of the Brooklyn club might have been different.

MacPhail planned to go into the Army. He probably could have gotten a high commission without much difficulty, and have left John McDonald, his traveling secretary, in charge as nominal general manager of the Dodgers. MacPhail, of course, would actually direct the club from Washington, or Germany, or wherever he happened to be. McDonald, sitting in Montague Street, would keep the seat warm till Larry's return.

But this proposition had no appeal for the Board of Directors. Jim Mulvey was most outspoken. He did not like the idea of a "fill-in." "I think we should get the best man we can," he declared, "and let him build the club soundly during these war years. Then we can jump into competition as soon as peace is signed. All we would ask of a new man is to keep our heads above water."

It is not generally known that Mulvey had nursed the idea for years that the man for the Dodgers' helm was Rickey. He did not approach Branch directly. He spoke to Ford Frick and to Sam Breadon, the Cardinal president. As a result of those conversations, Breadon had quickly signed Branch Rickey to a new five-year contract in St. Louis.

Now, however, Mulvey and his confreres went after Rickey with real intensity. When MacPhail announced that he would resign in September to accept a commission as lieutenant colonel, his resignation was accepted. It was no surprise to Larry. Years later he told Mulvey, "You did the right thing. I was just making a play to keep my job open. But I'm glad you didn't see it that way. Otherwise I would never have gotten into the Yankee proposition."

During the fall of 1942 there was plenty of speculation about MacPhail's successor. Actually, George Weiss, the brains behind the Yankee empire, was the only other candidate to receive serious consideration in the council room of the Brooklyn club. To show how earnest Mulvey and his friends were, they gave Rickey a contract that would pay him a fine salary even if baseball had to be suspended "for the duration."

In *PM*, Tom Meany, emphasizing the horsy atmosphere that had crept into the Dodger offices during the lush MacPhailian era, used this amusing "chart" as his announcement when Rickey got the Brooklyn plum:

And the Winnah!.. BRANCH RICKEY!

THE MacPHAIL HANDICAP, $65,000 added (all to winner). For 30-year-olds and upward. Start good, won easily, place driving.

Starter Owner	Wt.	PP.	¼	½	¾	Str.	Fin.
Rickey, Cardinal Farms	200	1	1 ¹	1 ¹	1 ¹	1 ¹	1 ³
McGrew, Hoosier Stables	240	4	4 ⁴	4 ²	3½	2 ¹	2 ¹
McDonald, MacPhail S.	180	3	3 hd	3½	5 ²	4 ²	3 ⁵
Mann, Atlanta Club	185	5	2 ²	5 ³	4 ²	3 hd	4 ⁴
Terry, Coogan's Bluff	200	6	6 ²	6 ¹	6 ¹	5 ¹	5 ¹
Shaughnessy, Int'l	195	7	7	7	7	6	6
Weiss, Yankee Crown	205	2	5 ³	2 ³	2 ³	br.	dn.

Mutuel Prices—

Rickey	$2.20	$2.20	$2.20
McGrew		4.10	3.20
McDonald			10.60

Rickey broke in front, was held in restraint for a mile and opened gap when boy gave him his head. McGrew closed some ground in stretch but weight impost hurt. McDonald ran evenly but had no speed. Mann shut off at first turn and thrown off stride. Terry never a factor. Shaughnessy over his head in this company. Weiss an early contender but bled.

All during the fall of 1942, when the rumor factory was grinding out stories that Branch Rickey might come to Brooklyn, B.R. had insisted that Ebbets Field, in 1943, would be a "baseball graveyard" for any man who attempted to revitalize the Dodgers.

When, as early as August 24, Harold Parrott prophesied in the *Eagle* that Rickey was coming to Brooklyn to join his son, Branch Senior held up his hands in horror. We thought it was simulated, but as events proved, the feeling was quite genuine.

"The Brooklyn club is sitting on a volcano of complete and sudden disintegration," he boomed. Then, turning to Parrott with a smile, he added, "You Dodgers had better win the pennant this year. If you don't you will never win it from the Cards in 1943."

We thought Branch was being properly coy. After all, wasn't he taking over an organization that had won the pennant in 1941, and had missed in 1942 by the slimmest of margins? Were our prospects that terrible?

But he looked at us with a critical eye. What he saw was a team that had run down, and was as burned out as an old jalopy. He saw that the age-ridden club was great on name and reputation and short on performance, agility, and speed. He recognized that what we needed was new, young blood.

Of course, when Rickey looks at a team, or at a single player, he sees much more than I, or any of the rest of us, do. He foresaw that he had some real purging to do. The digging had to be started in this "graveyard," as he had called us.

He was inheriting a tough job, and I was part of it. He liked me, yet I was part of a situation he was determined to change. We had all played the horses. Charley Dressen and I had set no example that would inspire the others.

Branch hated betting, and the tight-lipped guys who hung around race tracks. Tom Meany wrote, "Rickey thinks Satan sits behind every pari-mutuel window."

Actually, Branch was not against race tracks. I know that he used to take Mrs. Rickey to the Kentucky Derby. But no man is more jealous of baseball's fair name, and he understood how dangerous the association with those questionable characters on the fringes of the gambling fraternity, with their connections in the racing world, could be. He detested the price-fixers, the odds-makers, the tip-givers, the sure-thing guys. How right he was! College basketball, with the Brooklyn College "fix," and later, professional football, was rocked by scandals that grew out of friendships with such gamblers.

Rickey entered the Brooklyn picture loaded with information which Landis had provided. He had the lowdown—and I do mean lowdown—on who was betting the races, and how much. Nothing made all the lights on the Judge's internal switchboard flash like the mention of a race track. His notion was that if you had ever been seen even *talking* to a horse, you did not belong in baseball. Rickey's own convictions, always antigambling, were backed by Landis himself in his cleanup crusade in Brooklyn.

It was common knowledge that scratch sheets and racing forms were scanned as avidly as box scores in MacPhail's flamboyant days with the Dodgers. In fact, the 1943 New York Baseball Writers' Show, in February, included a hilariously funny skit about what Rickey had found when he walked into the Brooklyn office for the first time. When "Rickey"—Arthur Mann made up as B.R.—asked an office helper for "scratch paper," he was handed "Armstrong's," the "Green Sheet," and other racing-information rags. When the phone rang and "Branch" answered it, a bookmaker answered. A ballplayer who had lost both his shirt and his pants, evidently in a poker game, wandered around in a barrel.

Part of the script read:

RICKEY: Leo, I called you in to ask the reason for that queer blackboard in this office. What's the meaning of those strange, cabalistic inscriptions?

DUROCHER: Holy Cow! I thought MacPhail took that into the Army with him! Why—well, it's like this, Branch— Those are the scores of some ball games we played last year.

RICKEY: Baseball games? (*Studies board.*) Leo, exactly when did the Dodgers beat Alsab?

DUROCHER (*in double talk*): Why, that was a cammer nudent sturse on the frammis—

RICKEY: It was? Really? Well, when on earth did you win a baseball game by five-and-a-half to two?

DUROCHER (*peering at board*): Well, that was one of those days when we had special ground rules. Balls hit into the stands counted only half a run.

RICKEY: I see. (*Aside.*) Frankly, five-and-a-half to two on Alsab is an overlay. Now, Leo, it comes to my ears that there was not only betting on horse races among the

Dodgers last year, but that they also gambled at cards.

DUROCHER (*quick to cover, and breaking into doubletalk*): You mean a sort of patternating cammer with the keen and quins for ammolay moolah? Say, that reminds me, Mr. Rickey— When I was with the Yankees, Miller Huggins let us play hearts. But on the Dodgers, why, you can ask any of the players, Wyatt, Reiser, Higbe—

HIGBE (*entering in a barrel and shuffling a deck of cards*): Someone call me? Hy-ya, boss. Hello, Leo! Gimme a chance to get even? How about a little beer-barrel pokah?

DUROCHER: Ix-nay, ixnay—ixnay on the ardscay!

RICKEY (*turning to look at Higbe*): Judas Priest, Higbe, what happened to your clothes?

HIGBE: They took me to the cleaners.

DUROCHER: Yeah, yeah, Mr. Rickey. One of those places where they press your clothes while you wait.

HIGBE: Well, come on, how about a little gin rummy?

RICKEY: Please, Mr. Higbe. I'll have you understand that the terms gin and rummy are both reprehensible to me. You know what the good book says—

HIGBE: My good bookmaker says, "Astounded is he who has bet upon a horse when it runneth last."

RICKEY: In other words, you have been gambling!

DUROCHER: The way he plays, boss, it's not gambling.

LOUDSPEAKER: Coming out at the Fairgrounds . . . So Fast is sixth . . . Broiler is twelfth . . . Whistling Dick is ten . . .

RICKEY: What's this?

DUROCHER: That's doubletalk, boss. Ain't it a scream?

At that, the "Horsehide Messiah," as they called Branch in that show, finally got a pledge of no gambling from his Dodger family. With a great sigh of relief he boomed, "Praise the Lord!" To which the loudspeaker replied with, "They're off at Narragansett." Rickey said, "Praise the Lord" again, and the speaker echoed, "They're off at Saratoga!" Then they swung into a parody, one of the best the Writers' Show had ever had.

Indeed, the strangle hold that gambling had on the Brooklyn club was no secret. Naturally, Rickey appreciated that there would have to be some changes if he was to break up what he regarded as hurtful to the team. But every move he made was greeted by heavy criticism in the press. Some of the boys pictured him as a fuddy-duddy, a psalm-singing temperance leader who classed Broadway and Brooklyn with Sodom and Gomorrah. This was not true at all. Branch had to do his job as he saw it.

B.R. never liked to fire people. It had been his boast that he had discharged only two in his twenty-odd years as a Cardinal executive. Yet, when he let Charley Dressen go, on the gambling count, he was criticized for making Charley the "goat." Branch told Charley that if he could stay away from the race track and revamp his habits, his old job would be waiting for him. After a few months Dressen did return—and it was Rickey who gladly called him back.

Meanwhile Branch kept me, too, on the anxious seat. We had countless conversations about cardplaying and gambling. He hoped his ideas would sink into my head. I guess it was a slow business.

One day, in his home at Country Life Acres in St. Louis, he told me of his plans to release Charley Dressen.

"You can't do that, Branch," I complained. "He's my right arm. I couldn't manage without Charley!"

"Oh!" he shrugged, leaning forward in his chair. "And what leads you to believe YOU are the manager . . . ?"

For once I was caught without words. They stuck in my throat. Branch had tossed me back behind my own goal line!

John McDonald, the big, ambling, amiable traveling secretary, was another in the "circle" Rickey wanted to break up. He gave John the general managership of the Dodgers' Montreal farm team. This is perhaps the best job in minor-league baseball, for the farm is a million-dollar property, and Rickey had always sent top men there: Mel Jones and Buzzi Bavasi, for example. McDonald, however, always a bright-lights guy, chose to regard anything away from Broadway as banishment. At once, he and his many friends began to take pot shots at Rickey. Tom Meany carried on a running campaign in *PM*, scourging Rickey for that action.

Ironically enough, McDonald went to MacPhail for a job during the 1947 World Series. John made one remark that blew all of Larry's fuses. "Rickey," John declared, "takes care of his own!"

MacPhail's reply was typical: a punch that blacked the McDonald eye, and made all the front pages the next day.

Few who were not on the inside could understand that. But MacPhail was bitter at McDonald because his old right-hand man in 1945, while working for Rickey, had co-authored a national-magazine piece entitled "The Fall of the House of MacPhail." The article had recited a few items that Larry thought should have been kept secret. He rushed to a telegraph office and sent McDonald a cryptic wire, which stated only, "St. Matthew, Chapter 26, verses 14 to 16." Wondering if his old boss was trying to steal Rickey's trick of quoting the Good Book, John rushed to a Bible. What he found made him blush. "Chapter 26, verses 14 to 16" was the passage about Judas betraying his Master for thirty pieces of silver!

At the time I remarked to Rickey that it was a brutal wire for MacPhail to send his old confidant. "There's no answer to a thing like that," I said. "How could you possibly have a comeback?"

"Easy," said Branch. "Leo, don't you see, if MacPhail is making out that McDonald is Judas . . . don't you see how he is casting himself in that little parallel? He's calling himself Jesus!"

Hoping that his lessons had been driven home, Rickey finally gave me the job. My relief was great. The salary, $25,000, wasn't so bad, either.

I had hurdled that one. Now it appeared that I would miss out anyway. Uncle Sam was calling me. It seemed likely that I'd be in the Army before spring training began. I was going for thirty-eight, but I was in better shape than I'd been for five years. I had been playing golf in Florida, and I was lean and tanned.

I was on my way up to Grand Central Palace in New York to be inducted, and the newspapermen were hounding the Brooklyn offices, badgering Rickey to name my successor.

"I honestly don't know," said Branch. "I haven't given it any thought."

"Suppose you give it some thought right now," one writer proposed. "If Leo goes in the Army, will it be Billy Herman? Leo recommended him to you, didn't he?"

"I don't know," repeated Rickey. "There's time, gentlemen. Time is my ally!"

That was Rickey's watchword. The writers were to hear it often in the coming years: "Time is my ally." Branch waited for events to ripen. His timing on big deals we made was perfect. When he placed Jackie Robinson, the first Negro to go into big-league baseball, on the Dodger roster, proper timing was essential to success. He had always figured on time as his ally.

First, he waited to see what my draft board would say. It seemed a cinch that I would be in khaki, but he gave me every chance to hold my job.

I was rejected because of a punctured eardrum.

I really was unhappy. Not unhappy at the prospect of keeping my high-salaried Dodger job, of course, but unhappy at the thought of the riding I would get. I knew what to expect. The columnists would use me for journalistic target practice. "The Lip," they would say, "is getting by on his ear."

I had no wish to be painted in the unflattering colors that had been used on some athletes in World War I. People did not stop to inquire whether you had wanted to serve. They just asked, "Did he do his bit, this big, strong athlete, or is he still out there on the nice green grass, chasing that little white ball around while others are being wounded or killed?"

With mixed feelings I went back to Branch, and told him I was still free to manage his club. He gave me a warm welcome.

"My boy," he said, "you and I face the toughest job of our lives."

Chapter 17

ON THE ELEVATOR—GOING DOWN!

BRANCH NEVER MADE A TRUER STATEMENT IN HIS LIFE.
Here he was stuck with the oldest ball club in the National
League and shackled by the war. He had always talked about
youth, and banked on youth, and won with youth. Now, instead of cutting out the deadwood and importing the younger
men he would have liked to train, he had to load up with more
oldsters.

When else would Rickey have picked up Johnny Cooney,
forty-two years old, one of the men he had taken from Mac-
Phail in the deal that originally sent me to Brooklyn? He had
to take free-agent Paul Waner, who was the very type of ballplayer he had never liked to have on his club because Paul dis-
regarded training rules. When he netted Lloyd Waner and
Alban Glossop from the Phils in a trade for Babe Dahlgren,
the writers joked about the grandpas in the Brooklyn outfield.
They pointed out that the two Waners, reunited after galloping around in the Pirate outfield for fourteen years, and Johnny
Cooney, made up an outfield combination that totaled 118
years!

They said "Arsenic" and the "Old Face" were together
again, "Arsenic" being "Little Poison" Waner and "Old Face"
being "Big Poison," who had been a Dodger once before, in
the MacPhailian era.

It was good for laughs in the press, but it was no joke to
Rickey. The young athletes he had hoped to build around
were going fast. Reese and Reiser had already departed into the
Service, and those who were left either creaked at the joints or
had their "greetings" in the mail.

Rickey, worried about Owen, signed thirty-eight-year-old Ray Hayworth as reserve catcher.

Shades of Pepper Martin and Terry Moore and Walker Cooper, and the galloping, hell-for-leather clubs he had built in St. Louis! This Brooklyn team couldn't move out of its own way in the field. Nobody realized it better than Rickey.

Every time he signed a "spav" which was what he called an overaged player, Branch would give me another lecture on the evils of the very same thing he was forced to do. Quietly he was educating me in the building of a team, an education that was to continue through many years. I had never dreamed there was so much to learn about the game of baseball.

For my money Rickey is the best in the business. He can "put a dollar sign on a muscle," as he himself phrases it, more accurately than anyone else. If that isn't the most important trick in building a team from raw material, then I don't savvy baseball.

His record when he was with the Cardinals speaks for itself. When he had two great "prospects" coming up out of the St. Louis farm system, he invariably kept the boy who was "going all the way," which is the Rickey term for major-league stardom. The year Johnny Rizzo and Enos Slaughter hit within a few points of each other in the Cardinal chain—both had terrific records—he sold Rizzo to the Pirates and for himself kept the greatest outfielder the National League has seen in the past ten years. When he had Slats Marion and Bobby Sturgeon, and they were saying Marion wouldn't hit enough to make it, he sold Sturgeon to Jim Gallagher for a suitcase of cash, and kept Marion and proved he was right.

How does he arrive at his decisions? By seeing more than anyone else when he watches a boy hit, run, or throw. He sees form at the plate: short stride, for the over-strider can never be made into a good hitter; bat motionless before the swing, and no hitch in the swing itself. He sees stride, not apparent swiftness, but actual speed; the boy who may seem to lope, but actually outruns the short-stepping man. He watches body control, how the boy breaks after the batted ball, or leads off the bases. In appraising young pitchers, Rickey's in a class by himself.

Judge Landis had ordered the ball clubs to train in the North to keep them out of the way of the armed services mobilizing and training in the South, and taxing transportation to the limit.

Through the ingenuity of John Martin, proprietor of Bear Mountain Inn, we made a contact which resulted in an offer from the Army of the indoor training facilities for certain hours each day of the West Point fieldhouse. Meanwhile, we lived in fine style at Martin's inn, forty miles up the Hudson from New York.

John, who has since become one of the best-known restaurateurs in the business, offered this idea to both the Yankees and the Giants before he saw Rickey. The other clubs passed up the chance, but our boss jumped at it.

At Bear Mountain we laid the foundation for the later successes of the Brooklyn club. Here Rickey brought in bright-eyed, beardless boys who were still too young to be called to the colors.

That was all future stuff, of course. To be truthful, I wondered if any of them could possibly make big-league material. They looked so young, so inexperienced, so bewildered.

Some of our grown players didn't act exactly like college professors, either. Take Rube Melton. Take him? The Dodgers had taken him twice from the Phillies, the first time because Judge Landis found out that MacPhail had induced the Philadelphia club, in last place as usual, to draft the Rube from Columbus on the promise that Brooklyn would buy him. That gave Gerry Nugent and the Phillies a nice profit, and gave us Melton.

Landis had made MacPhail return this six-foot-three-inch giant with the big feet and the fast ball, to the Phillies. But not permanently. For Melton had a zany streak that made him a Dodger born and bred.

Now Rickey, who had owned Melton at Columbus, took him back. It was his first big Dodger purchase. Branch should have known better—a $30,000 headache!

Rickey bought Melton to pitch, but the first thing Rube did was to hold out. Rickey reached him on the telephone at Victory Station, North Carolina.

"I ain't gonna pitch for what you're offering me," declared Rube. "I'm gonna stay on my farm."

"Wonderful!" said Rickey. "You will help solve the food shortage. How big is your farm?"

"I don't know," admitted Rube. "I hain't got it yet."

"I see," went on Rickey, a farmer himself and a pretty good hand with guys like Melton. "Where is the farm?"

"Well," evaded Rube, "it's about fifty, maybe a hunnert miles from here—"

"Hmmmm," said Branch, "tell me more. Is it in North Carolina, or in South Carolina?"

"It's—it's right on the border," Melton stammered.

"I think you had better come in and see me, Rube," B.R. urged.

"I think so, too," admitted the big guy.

When Melton's huge frame moved through Rickey's doorway, it was listing noticeably to port. The Rube had a limp.

"What's wrong?" Branch inquired.

"It's nothing," scoffed Rube. "It'll go away. It might be rheumatism—or a broken bone I had in that ankle a couple of years ago."

Wondering if he'd paid all that money for a one-legged pitcher, Rickey put the big fellow in a cab and hustled him to Caledonian Hospital. An hour later he got the diagnosis. Melton was a sick man. The sulfa drugs they pumped into him would have felled a horse.

A week later Rube, weak as a cat, called Rickey from the hospital.

"They won't let me out of here," he complained. "They say I ain't all cured yet. But I can walk, Mr. Rickey, I can walk fine. Tell them to let me out, will you?"

"Young man," declared Branch, "I did not buy you to walk, I bought you to pitch. Durocher and I are not in charge of you now. The doctors are. When they say you're ready to pitch, I'll talk to you."

When Melton got out of the hospital, he continued his campaign for more money. He insisted that he had received $5,300 for pitching for the Phillies the year before. Rickey, who had a copy of Rube's 1942 contract, was positive the wage was $3,500.

"But there was all that extra money," insisted Rube.

"Extra money?" Rickey hoisted his eyebrows. "For what?"

"For being good," returned Rube innocently. "They fined me five hundred dollars in the spring. Then when I behaved, a few months later, Gerry Nugent handed it to me—five hundred bucks, cash. That made it $4,000. Then another time—"

"Wait a minute," said Rickey. "That five hundred dollars wasn't extra pay. They were only giving back what they had already taken away from you—"

Melton looked at Branch suspiciously. "That's what you say," he blurted out. "All I know is that I got the money!"

On top of it all, Rube was an inventor. He had an idea for a radio that could be wound up, instead of being plugged into an electric socket. He had built a house of his own, too. When it was all finished he found he had forgotten to install a chimney.

His mind was always darting off in several directions at once. When he lay in the Caledonian Hospital, he had thought up arguments to toss at Rickey. He was full of them when he headed for Bear Mountain to challenge the boss.

John Martin spotted Rube near the Inn. The big guy seemed

to be stowing his suitcases underneath a scrub-pine bush. Martin asked, "What're you doing?"

"I'm hiding these until after I see Rickey," Melton confided. "I want to walk in empty-handed, like I didn't intend to stay, see? I want Rickey to think I'm a tough holdout."

Thousands of ballplayers have tried to fool Rickey, only to find, too late, that they were outmatched. I have always told him the truth, no matter what he asked me. That is one reason we get along so well.

The truth is powerful medicine. It is the only thing that has ever cooled me off and abruptly stopped me from charging an umpire. When an ump has kicked a decision and I run out there screaming, and he says "I am sorry, but I booted that one," I know I might as well turn back to the bench. What more is there to say? You can't gripe at straight-from-the-shoulder stuff.

At Bear Mountain, as we groomed the first club to carry the colors of the Rickey-run Dodgers, everybody was feeling sorry for himself.

The baseball writers, missing their usual Florida or Cuba vacations, were a sad lot. They looked back on those good years in the South as though the war had wiped them out forever. Tommy Holmes, the *Eagle*'s veteran baseball writer, put together a long lament in which he listed all the things he wanted to do once more.

Like the rest of us, Holmes had squawked about the bumpy bus rides between towns in Florida, when we went to play an exhibition game. But now, freezing up on Bear Mountain he went whimsical on us.

"I want to ride in a Florida bus," Holmes wrote, "when the warm evening breeze is filled with orange blossoms—and Dixie Walker is leading a quartet through the old favorites. I want to listen once more to Roscoe McGowen talking to God from the bottom of a sand trap. I want to drink another Sazerac cocktail at Monteleone's bar in New Orleans. I want to hear Bill Klem singing 'Roll Out the Barrel' as we roll up to the Nacional Casino in Havana. I want to see a bald eagle hover over a Florida swamp. I want to eat fried chicken and fish chowder at Dazzy Vance's place in Homosassa. I want to bowl once more for the Elite Barber Shop team in the Clearwater City Championship. I want to sail a boat once more off beautiful La Playa in Cuba and see that spray breaking over the Malecon."

Rickey's worries were tougher to take. He missed the young, dashing ballplayers he had hoped for. The average age of the men on the team worried him stiff. I don't know how many times he pointed out to me that we had eleven men who had each been in baseball ten years!

I listened, but was not too worried. I thought we were going to do all right. Only Rickey realized how bad our team really was.

"The elevator is going down, Leo," Branch said to me one day, early in 1943, at the Bear Mountain Inn, "and we are both on it."

I asked him if he felt all right. There are no elevators at Bear Mountain.

"I mean this club we have," he explained. "It's going to drop because it's too old. It hasn't a chance. A newspaperman asked me today where I thought we would finish. I told him, 'Trying to tell where the Dodgers will land this year is a scramble in the field of prophecy.' He scolded me for giving him doubletalk. I had to give him doubletalk, Leo. If I had been honest, I'd have said, 'Sixth or maybe seventh.'"

Branch pulled another thought out of the big cigar he had stuck in his face and tossed it over to me in a cloud of smoke. "My inclination is to pull the whole thing apart right now," he said, "and start new, with young fellows. I would like to fire all the ten-year men: Medwick, Camilli, Wyatt, Allen—"

What is the man going to do, I wondered, yank the club out from under me?

"There's only one difficulty, Leo," Rickey went on. "There's one chance I may be wrong. Starting in a new job like this, I can't afford to be wrong. So we'll stay in the elevator a while longer. We'll give it everything we've got. Maybe we can get it going up, instead of down."

When Branch said he'd give it everything, he really meant it. He got me Dolf Camilli when it seemed that Dolf was going to stay out of baseball and run his ranch. I doubt if any other man would have gone so far to lure Camilli to Bear Mountain.

Camilli wrote Rickey that he had a 2700-acre ranch, and had to ride herd on his cattle. He was shorthanded, for his men had gone off to war. There was nobody else to handle the cattle, so he would have to stay there himself and do the job. He was not holding out, he explained, just telling the truth.

In Brooklyn, where the strong-armed Italian was a hero, this was a catastrophe. Camilli got hundreds of letters from people offering to do the work on his ranch, if only he would come and cover first base for the Dodgers.

One Italian barber wrote to Dolf: "I will lay down my scissors and learn to ride a horse and do your work, if you will come here and hit home runs for the team."

Rickey found a man to handle Camilli's chores for him. Then he promised he'd find a house in Brooklyn for Camilli, his wife, and his five children. He paid a couple of thousand bucks in rent on the house in Belle Harbor. He paid the train fare East for Camilli's family, and rented a car for Camilli to get over from Belle Harbor to Ebbets Field every day. Rickey, who usually bargained with ballplayers, handed Camilli everything on a silver platter. He would try to win with these old guys first, even though he was convinced they were washed up.

Bobo Newsom held out. "I think the team would be better

off without him, Leo," said Branch. "I wish he would stay down there in Carolina where he is. But if you want him, you shall have him."

I took Bobo. Soon I was to have too much of him.

To get Arky Vaughan, Rickey had to do everything but roll out a red carpet to Potter Valley, California. Finally Arky, like Camilli, agreed to report by April 5. With Reese gone, we needed Arky to share the shortstop job with me.

With Reiser gone, we had to look for an outfielder, too. We thought of Luis Rodriguez Olmo, a Puerto Rican we had bought from the Piedmont League. "Chico," as we called Olmo, could hit with power and run like a rabbit, and he had a good arm.

Rickey had quite a job signing even Chico. "It takes me a week to get a proposition to him in Caguas, Puerto Rico," Branch complained. "After Chico says no, or maybe, it takes another week for me to find it out."

Eventually, Chico said yes, and set out from sunny Puerto Rico for Bear Mountain. They had told him we had a pool table, and he fancied himself quite a pool player.

Chico must have thought he was dreaming. The first thing on his arrival in New York he ran into a big snowstorm. He had never seen snow before. Then we put him on a ferryboat for New Jersey, where we were to get the train on the west bank of the river. He had never seen a ferryboat before. All he could say was *"Frio!"* which meant "Brr, it's cold."

After he got warm at Bear Mountain, Chico began to brag about his skill with a cue. That was one thing he thought he had on these *Americanos*.

Naturally the boys rigged up a match between Chico and me. Some folks have heard that I know how to coax the one ball into the side pocket.

Chico missed a shot, and I said, "That's all, brother!"

"What you mean?" Chico stammered and gawked as I ran twenty or twenty-five.

Every time I said "That's all, brother," he lost his shirt. How was Chico to know that I had been invited to play in the 1928 and 1929 world's pocket-billiard championship? I had done well against the best of them.

After awhile he groaned every time he heard me say, "That's all, brother, rack 'em up!"

Another day I came up unnoticed when Chico was playing some of the other boys. One of them missed a shot. Chico cracked, "Thass all, brudder, rack 'em up!"

That became our war cry on the ball club.

After his education at the billiard table, the next thing Chico had to do was let a doctor stick a needle into him and take a pint of his blood! We were all selling bonds, giving blood, doing our bit for the war effort.

Before Chico even had a chance to wonder "What next?" we asked him to change his Dodger suit for one that had "Battling Beavers" written across the front, and put on a beard! Like the rest of us he was about to become part of a moving picture, *Whistling in Brooklyn*, which starred Red Skelton. They were shooting the movie at Ebbets Field in April, just before the season opened. We were all in the cast.

Skelton learned more from us than we did from the movie makers. "You are the funniest bunch I ever met," he told me.

He carried a big, black book in which he wrote all the funny cracks made while we worked on the picture. I wonder if his notes saved him the price of a gagman.

Ballplayers have many superstitions. One is that a new pair of spiked shoes must be sprayed with tobacco juice. Everybody helps.

Each time Skelton stopped to write in his book, two or three of the boys used his nice new shoes as a target. It got so that he was afraid to stand still and he moved gingerly among us.

True, we rode Skelton hard. He was certainly no athlete,

although he was supposed to be a star pitcher in the movie.

When they first saw Red throw from the pitcher's box, the boys let out a roar. As the ball crossed the plate on the first bounce, Bordagaray cracked, "When did Gertrude join the club?"

"Where did the guy learn to throw like that?" growled Newsom. "Didn't he never have no boyhood?"

Skelton's legs were painfully thin; they seemed to have no muscles. "Bird legs" the boys called them.

"Hey, Skelton," cracked Dixie Walker, "where did you get that pair of fungo sticks you use for legs?"

"Yeah," added Higbe, "do they always swell up like that in the spring?"

Before we would do any acting, we made Skelton run around the ball park three times. We insisted he must get in shape. Then Charley Dressen hit him grounders that rattled like castanets off his shins, and raised lumps all over him.

Red limped over to the dugout. "How do I look, fellas?" he asked hopefully.

"I don't wanna say the word," replied Walker.

Then we sent him to the outfield and John Corriden made him chase flies. Back and forth he ran, his tongue hanging out.

"Careful, you guys," said Higbe, "or we'll need a stretcher to get this athlete off the field!"

At last we pulled our favorite gag. I called him in and hit some pop flies right in front of the plate. He caught a few, and became overconfident.

"Bet you five bucks you can't catch the next one," I offered.

"It's a bet," accepted Red, "if you promise not to hit it any higher than the grandstand."

Skelton was standing at the plate as I popped that ball up. At that moment, every ballplayer on the field, who had secretly armed himself with a ball, let it fly, right above the comedian. We had forty players on the squad, and forty handmade pop-ups went into the air. They showered Red.

He could no more have picked out the ball I had hit than I could pick out one particular grain of sand on the beach. He ran around desperately, pelted on the head, arms, and shoulders by the cascade of baseballs.

"Hey, wait a minute!" said the director, thumbing through his book. In vain he tried to find that scene in his script. He was afraid his star would get killed.

It was cold at Ebbets Field in April. After devoting perhaps an hour to the movie we had our regular practice workout. We usually played against the Montreal club, managed by Fresco Thompson. Thompson is a fast one with a wisecrack, and not far behind him was Eddie Morgan, an outfielder we had sent to the Phillies in the Camilli deal, but whom they had now shipped to Montreal.

One day Rickey was watching the workout. Everybody knew Branch was antialcohol. I nearly died when I heard Morgan say to him, "Well, Senator, a shot of Old Grand-Dad would warm you up today, wouldn't it?"

Not to be outdone, Branch cracked back: "Two shots wouldn't do it, son!"

Because of his reputation as a nondrinker and a religious man, the writing boys took Branch over the jumps every chance they got. When he traded Tex Kraus and Schoolboy Rowe off the Montreal roster to the Phils for Bobby Bragan, one of the scribes, knowing that Bragan had studied for the ministry, jibed, "If Rickey calls up Bragan, would you say it was a parson-to-parson call?"

However, Branch's great Cardinal record made the brighter writers go slow. They knew he could spot a good ballplayer quicker than anyone else in the business, and that he rarely got stung in trades. Tom Meany, veteran wit of the Ebbets Field press box, meant it as a tribute when he hung the tag "Mahatma" on Rickey.

I asked Meany what "Mahatma" really meant.

"John Gunther in his book *Inside Asia* described Mahatma Gandhi as a combination of God, his own father, and Tammany Hall," said Tom. "I think it fits Rickey."

We hadn't found much at Bear Mountain. I thought we would develop Roy Sanner, a left-handed pitcher whom Thompson had on his Montreal team. But Sanner had too much to learn. In fact, he had everything to learn.

Roy was from some fork in the road in Arkansas. He had pitched pretty well at Topeka in the Western League. But he insisted on wearing his hat all the time. He even sat down to meals in the Inn dining room in his toppiece. Pretty soon the boys were wagering that he wore it to bed and Bordagaray had to peek in Roy's transom to settle the dispute.

Maybe Sanner clung to his hat; he did not own much else. He had no underclothes and no socks. He explained that no one wore those things in his part of Arkansas.

Rickey was afraid the boy would freeze to death in Bear Mountain. He sent Buzzie Bavasi to New York with Sanner to buy him some clothes—and a suitcase to put them in. All he had fetched from home was a paper bag!

"Not me," protested Roy, when informed of the trip to New York. "I ain't a-goin' down to that city."

"Why?" Bavasi asked.

"No room to walk," explained the hillbilly. "Them sidewalks is so crowded somebody will run right into me."

Bavasi induced Sanner to accompany him to Brooklyn on the subway. He was all right until Buzzie, without thinking, told him they were under the river.

"Lemme out!" Roy screamed, pulling at the door. "How can we live down hyar with all that there water pressin' down on us?"

Since Rickey's teaching had made me talent-conscious, I kept an eye on the Montreal club, which was training with us. Thompson, the Montreal manager, was having his own troubles. From the start he was afraid I would latch on to Hal Gregg, a big, good-looking pitcher dug up by our scouts in an orange grove in California.

Gregg had great stuff, but every time Thompson started him, he walked a lot of batters. Each time Gregg issued a pass, the Frenchmen in the Montreal stands shouted "*Chou!*" Finally it became a refrain: "*Chou!*" they chanted, "*Chou! Chou!*"

"What's eating them?" Thompson asked his Canadian bat-boy. "Do they think Gregg is the Big Train?"

"No, M'sieu," said the youngster. "*Chou* is, what you call heem, head of cabbage. They call your pitcher head of cabbage because he no good, walk so veree many."

It looked as though Walker, Galan, and Medwick would open in our outfield, with Herman at third, Vaughan at short, Glossop at second, and Camilli at first. The catching would be all right, in the hands of Owen, Bragan, and Dee Moore. But the pitching, especially with Wyatt's arm doubtful, looked shaky: Higbe, Curt Davis, who had broken a finger on a line drive and was now pitching himself into shape with a catcher's glove, Allen, Newsom, Max Macon, and Ed Head looked like our best bets.

We played an exhibition game against Yale, at New Haven. Kirby started.

"That's the only way you'd ever get into Yale, Higbe," cracked Newsom.

Higbe, flexing his muscles, boasted he'd win thirty games.

Hig looked good and won, 5 to 1. That night he raised his estimate. He said he'd win thirty-five.

We got off fast. We won five of our first six. Counting the fall of 1942—and I do mean *fall*—when we had won our last eight games, and counting the exhibition series in the spring, when we had won eleven out of twelve, we were really on a streak: twenty-four victories in twenty-six starts.

I wondered, the way things were going, if Rickey could be

completely wrong. Perhaps our club was a challenge for the pennant. With the war on, every team in the league had lost players, and was weakened.

The first of our key men to melt was Medwick. He looked sick at bat. In one stretch he got only two hits in thirty-two trips.

Then we lost Johnny Allen. He went crazy mad and mauled George Barr, the umpire, who had called a balk on him. I got Johnny off Barr once, but he broke away and went at him again. Finally, six of us had to sit on Johnny on the grass back of second, practically had to carry him to the clubhouse, still frothing.

Allen was suspended for a month. But he was really out for good, as far as Brooklyn was concerned: Rickey, who had seen the game, said to me, "That was a disgraceful episode today. He is a bad man for your club, Leo. He'll have to go!"

Next we gave up on Kampouris, and brought in Boyd Bartley, a youngster from the University of Illinois campus. We tried him at short, where Vaughan could not move any more. We were only a half a game out of first place on July 1, but the Cardinals whipped us three straight. The Cards, it became apparent, were moving upward and we were going down, on that "elevator" Rickey had talked about. How they booed us *in St. Louis!* Medwick, Rickey and myself, all former Cardinals playing against their near-championship club.

Yet, it never occurred to me to give up. I kept on hoping that Wyatt and Higbe would deliver. Still, the figures showed that the former had completed two games in eleven starts, and the latter had gone the route only once in twelve tries.

An infant could see that Medwick had lost his wallop. He had had only nine extra-base wallops among his forty-five hits; these nine were doubles.

But Camilli's case was the most startling. The year before he had hit twenty-five home runs. Now, up to July 4, he had hit only four.

Branch Rickey summoned me into his office. He opened up those famous blackboards on which every player owned by Brooklyn is listed, and said, "If we let it go, Leo, this elevator is going to hit bottom. But if we rip it apart at once we may get it started upward again sooner. There's only one force that will turn that control around: youth! We have to get rid of the older men, and do our best with the promising kids from the minor leagues. They'll make the mistakes that all kids make, because they'll be learning here instead of in the minors. But we'll just have to grin and bear it."

We shook hands on it. We agreed it would be a tough job. But before we could get going on this assignment, one of our veterans was removed in a way we had hardly expected.

Chapter 18

THE NEWSOM MUTINY

I HADN'T BEEN EXACTLY PALSY WITH BOBO NEWSOM. HE HAD his own ways, as older players sometimes do, and he also had a way of sounding off that his way was the best.

In a clubhouse meeting before a game, I might say, "We pitch Musial high inside."

Bobo would mumble, "I pitch him low outside, an' he never hurts me!"

"As long as you get him out," I'd say, although I didn't like it much, "I don't care if you throw an old shoe up there."

Of course, the younger players wondered, as Newsom continued to buck me. The question in their minds was naturally, whose methods were better, Durocher's or Newsom's?

What made it harder to take was that Bobo was our leading pitcher. He had won nine games, and he boomed around our clubhouse as though he was John McGraw and Judge Landis rolled into one. He would sit down with a young pitcher and whisper, "Do it my way, kid—what does Durocher know about pitchin'?" Early in a game against the Pirates at Ebbets Field, Bobo threw a ball that seemed to dip.

It got away from Bobby Bragan, who was catching, and a run came in from third.

"What was that, a spitter?" I asked, jumping up, and realizing that spitballs are outlawed.

"It seemed to do something at the last minute," said Fred Fitzsimmons, who was on the bench next to me. "I think it was a spitter." Curt Davis nodded. Charley Dressen thought so, too.

As Bragan scampered after the passed ball, I looked at Newsom, who was doing a Barrymore out there on the mound, with his hands on his hips, as much as to say, "How can a great pitcher like me be expected to win with support like that?"

I thought that poor Bragan had been crossed up, as well as shown up, by the big show-off on the mound. So, when the inning was over, I questioned the catcher.

"I called for a fast ball, Skipper," he said earnestly, "but I think there was something extra on the ball. It did something funny."

At the close of the inning, Newsom scaled his glove from the pitcher's box right to our bench, in a supreme gesture of disgust. As he stalked into our dugout, he heard us talking about the "spitter."

"It was no such thing!" he roared. "It was just an ordinary fast ball, an' whoever says it was a spitter—"

"Take it easy," I warned. "Don't get on your high horse."

It was a close ball game, and Vince DiMaggio came to bat in a jam, with men on. We always pitched him high and tight. You could strike him out there, because he had a blind spot. Everybody knew it, and Vince had led the league in strike-outs.

Now DiMaggio got the meat of his bat on a Newsom pitch, and singled to left field. A run came in, and Pittsburgh was ahead.

It was a seesaw game, and I relieved Bobo with Higbe. We tied it up again. Then they got two off Higbe in the top of the ninth, but in our turn we made three to win.

Afterward, in the clubhouse, I said to Higbe, "That was a bad pitch you made to Fletcher in the ninth."

"I know it, Skipper," Kirby replied. "The ball got away on me."

Then I saw Newsom, already dressed, sitting on a trunk at the back of the room. "You too, Bobo," I said. "You made a bad pitch to DiMaggio. You should keep it high and inside on him."

"It was a perfect pitch," he retorted, without batting an eye. "It was right in on him."

"I saw the ball," I said. "It was out over the plate, where DiMaggio could get his bat on it."

"You're wrong," he glowered. He got up off the trunk and walked toward me in a challenging way. "That was a perfect pitch, high inside, and my catcher came out to the mound and told me so."

Now I was hot under the collar. We went at it hot and heavy in front of all the players. Newsom talked back. He said he wasn't so keen on pitching for me, anyway.

"Okay if that's the way you feel about it!" I barked, "you're suspended, without pay."

"That's all right with me," huffed Bobo. "I don't care if I never pitch on this —— —— club again."

"You won't," I said. "If I have my way, this suspension will be for the rest of the year."

I went into my office to take off my uniform. Hugh Casey, who was in the Service at the time, was sitting there. As one of my older players, I told him my troubles.

"Did you see the pitch that got away from Bragan?" I asked.

"Sure," Hugh shrugged, "it looked to me like a spitter!"

"It was," I said. "An' the big showboat made the poor kid catcher look sick, because it got away from him. That's one thing I won't stand for—showing a youngster up, out there on the field. Newsom is through on this ball club, as far as I'm concerned."

Just then I turned. Tim Cohane, a reporter from the New York *World-Telegram*, stood in the half-opened doorway of my office. I didn't know how long he had been there, or how much he had heard.

The next day I was in the same office with Roscoe Mc-Gowen, of the *Times*, when Arky Vaughan, of all people, came in, all agitated. He had read the story Cohane had printed after overhearing my outburst to Casey and now he plucked at the front of his uniform shirt and said ". . . and here's another uniform you can have—"

I was stunned. I hadn't read the story.

But I said to Vaughan, "Okay, if that's the way you feel, take it off. But remember, Arky—you're suspending yourself, I'm not suspending you!"

Roscoe McGowen, the dean of the Dodger reporters, who labors for the *New York Times*, has always taken secret pride in the fact that he got this nearly scandalous quote in the front-page story he wrote for that staid newspaper. Said Roscoe, quoting me: " 'He quit,' said the manager. 'He turned in his uniform and told me what I could do with it!' "

Some time passed before the rest of the players learned about the rhubarb. Vaughan had peeled off his uniform and taken a shower before I cleared the clubhouse of visitors and made my speech.

I assured the players that I had not given Cohane the stuff he put in the paper.

"That whole story about Newsom showing up Bragan is there in print," said Walker, "and if you've suspended Vaughan, I'm not going to play either!"

It was a dramatic moment. There wasn't a sound in the clubhouse.

"Wait a minute, Dixie," I objected. "I haven't suspended Vaughan. You can ask him, he's right over there. Ask him, and he'll tell you he took himself out of this game. And as far as I'm concerned, he can get right back into it now, if he wants to!"

Walker thought it over a minute and returned, "In that case, I'll play!"

"Well," I said, "we gotta have nine men. Will *you* play? Will you?" And I went around the room, polling each man.

As usual the players all went along with Walker. Then our "disorganized" team went out and beat the ears off the Pirates, 23 to 6. By the sixth inning Vaughan was in our dugout in uniform. Branch Rickey, hearing about the trouble, had dashed to the park in a cab. He had gone to the clubhouse while we were on the field, and persuaded Vaughan he had made a mistake, and that he should get back into uniform.

Up in the press box, the writers took different views of the situation. "This mutiny," said one, "will make the French Revolution look like a basket picnic, before it's over!"

Some of the boys predicted that it was the end of me, and that Rickey had only been looking for an excuse to fire me, anyway. Others, like Tommy Holmes, declared that Rickey was a man who insisted upon respect for authority. They forecast that Branch would back me up because I was the manager, and I represented him.

Saturday, the day of the big rhubarb, Cohane had not been at the park, because his paper did not publish Sundays. But we called him on the phone, and he promised he would surely show up at Ebbets Field Sunday. We would straighten the whole thing out before the players.

They were all there Sunday, the team, and all the writers.

I had told the players that I hadn't given Cohane the "interview."

Now Cohane backed me up. He declared that he had heard me say those things, but not to him, and that he had only printed what he had heard.

"I can't help it if somebody overheard me," I explained. "I was talking to Casey. I didn't say those things for publication."

Everybody, including Cohane, was satisfied. Everybody, that is, except Newsom, who remained suspended.

After the meeting, I cleared the clubhouse of everybody except the players and the coaches. I had a talk of a different kind to make, and I really choked up.

"It's been a shock to me," I began, "the way you fellows let me down. You left me on the spot with that reporter . . . after all the things I've done for you.

"You, Camilli," I asked, "did I fight your battles for you with MacPhail? Did I get you the dough you wanted? When you needed a friend, wasn't I always on your side?"

Camilli's voice was husky. "You've always been great to me, Skipper," he said.

I continued. "Walker—Wyatt—Owen—" I was crying as I talked to them. It was the first of the two times I was to cry openly in front of my men.

I left the clubhouse, retreated into my office, and closed the door. I felt terrible.

In a moment there was a knock. Arky Vaughan walked in. "I made a mistake, Leo," he muttered in his quiet way. "I made some trouble for you yesterday, and I'm sorry."

He was a real fellow, and that proved it to me right then.

Other knocks at the door followed as other players dropped in. They knew I was under terrific pressure, that the papers were saying I would be fired on account of this rhubarb, and they all wanted to let me know how badly they felt, and that they were behind me.

It was a great response, and it gave me a new grip on myself.

Rickey, Bobo, and I met in the boss's office. Rickey told Newsom he would get rid of him, and was trying to make a trade.

Newsom said he felt different now, that he wanted to stay and pitch for the Dodgers.

"Don't talk to me about that," Rickey returned coldly. He pointed my way. "There's the man you should have made your peace with. But it's a little late now."

Branch tried to ship Newsom somewhere, anywhere. It took him three days to do it, and by the time he held a conference beside his sickbed in his downtown Brooklyn apartment, and announced that Newsom had been traded to the

Browns for a couple of left-handed pitchers, some of the boys had big, black headlines predicting that Billy Herman would be the next manager. This was tough on Herman. They made it seem that he was tunneling underneath me. Actually he wasn't, but how could he stop those stories?

As Rickey announced the departure of Newsom in the deal which was to bring Fritz Ostermueller and Archie McKain to Brooklyn, he cited the piece Holmes had written about upholding authority. "You took that story right out of my mind, Tommy," said Branch. "I back my manager to the limit, always. He is entitled to that."

The storm died down, but some of the boys thought it was only a temporary lull. "Peace, it's wonderful," wrote Holmes. "Or is it? Is it peace, I mean?"

There was harmony, but not exactly peace. The big purge was on in earnest. Rickey had made up his mind to halt the downward drop of the Brooklyn elevator.

Medwick was the next to pack his bag. He was hitting only .269, and he was sent to the Polo Grounds to join Eddie Brannick, the "pal" he loved so dearly.

Now the boss wanted to begin to move in some of the brighter boys we had in the minors. The first one he thought of was "Chico," or to use his right name, "Olmo," who had looked good all spring, but who had been sent to Montreal, to learn how to hit an inside pitch, and how to talk English.

It wasn't so easy to get Olmo. Rickey ran his farm clubs on the promise that once the teams were "set" in the spring the fans could root for their heroes with the full assurance that none of the players would be kidnapped by the parent Dodgers. Only twice in twenty-five years of running the Cardinal farm system had he tapped his minor-league teams to snatch key men: Heinie Mueller from Houston, and Heinie Schuble from Danville. Olmo's name was not Heinie, but Rickey wanted him just as badly. The Latin Boy was larruping .310.

So, apologetically, Rickey approached a meeting of ten

Montreal baseball writers and stated his case. Such was his eloquence that all ten agreed "Chico" should get his chance in the major leagues.

Just about this time another player "arrived" on the Royals. But he was something. This boy, Rex Barney, was younger than even Gregg or Olmo. Four years later, after he had been through plenty of rugged warfare, driving a tank destroyer in Germany, Burt Shotton dropped him into a tough spot as the starter in the sixth game of the 1947 World Series. With bases full and no one out he struck out DiMaggio and Johnson and got McQuinn to tap to the box. Johnson was quoted as saying that Rex was "faster than Feller."

The first look we had at Barney was one afternoon in the fieldhouse at West Point. The place was overrun with the Dodger "youth movement," as some of the writers called it derisively. I was hitting grounders to an infield composed of four Andy Hardys, and Charley Dressen was looking over a couple of red-hot phenoms who were going to pitch in the game that was to start in a few moments. Mr. Rickey had a perch high on the wall. There he sat with Jane Ann Jones, his secretary, and made notes. We thought he was watching us. Instead, he was watching the seventeen-year-old boy warm up directly below him.

When Rickey watches a pitcher, you might say that he sees a double-header in one glance. He watches the rotation of the ball: grip and spin are what make the fast ball either "alive," which is tough for the hitters, or straight as a string. He watches the boys spin their curves. To test their aptitude he will tell them to throw an entirely new pitch. I have never seen anyone come close to him in appraising a boy. Sometimes a promising one is a humpty—i.e., an athlete with little ability. Then again in a cubbish, awkward kid he may see the stuff that will take him "all the way."

Whatever it was he saw in Rex Barney that afternoon, he forgot the rest of us. He sent for more information about the boy.

"Just a kid out of Omaha," reported Scout Tom Green-wade. "Mr. Rickey, we brought the boy in on his Easter va-cation from school. He's not signed yet, but I think this trip will help us land him. He's going back to school tomorrow."

Rickey's orders were unusual. "Go back with him," he commanded Greenwade. "Go back to Omaha. If you can, get a room in the boy's house and live with the family. If you can't do that, get a room across the street. Stay after him. And if you let him get away, you better not show up around me for a long, long time!"

Greenwade did land Barney. When his school term ended, he was sent to pitch for our Durham team in the Piedmont League. The kid struck out ten or more men almost every game he started. But Durham was a cellar club. They kicked the ball around behind him—and once they made eight errors in seven innings and never got any runs. Another time, he fanned twelve and gave only two hits, but still they lost, 1-0.

Barney looked so good they moved him up to Montreal. There Fresco Thompson pitched him with misgivings because he was so young. After a while, all the misgivings were in the other dugout, and Thompson was crowing that Barney was the best pitching prospect he had seen in twenty years.

Meanwhile, we were dropping as rapidly as the 1929 stock market. I jiggled all the controls, but still couldn't get the elevator to brake its downward glide. In July we won only ten out of twenty-eight games. By the end of the month we were in third place, ten behind the leading Cardinals.

The baseball writers composed a song about my troubles:

> Once he was happy, but now he's forlorn
> Wishes his pitchers had never been born
> So let's all chime in and help Leo mourn . . .
> While the ball games go slipping away.
> There was Wyatt and Melton and Higbe and Fitz
> Expected to do rather well
> But goshawful wildness and line drive hits
> Exploded our chances to Hell!

As the Cardinals began to stretch their legs and gallop away, the second-division pit yawned before us. Our attendance fell off. One Sunday at home we drew only 6,000 fans!

Branch looked at it darkly. "Only God, fortune, time, and fate can bring the Cardinals back to the field," he sighed.

However, I had reason to believe that he wasn't relying on fortune, time, or fate to pull the Cardinals back to where they could hear us shouting. He was taking after them, as fast as he could and with every bit of skill and generalship at his command.

Chapter 19

BRANCH RICKEY'S "GRAVEYARD"

"WE HAVE AN ANESTHETIC BALL CLUB, LEO," SAID B. R. ONE evening. We had blown another that day.

I wasn't sure I knew what he meant, but I said I didn't think we were too badly off. Newsom and Medwick had left, and we had our youth program. That made things brighter.

I began to catalogue what we had. First, Camilli.

"Camilli is through!" Rickey said, sadly. "He's an anesthetic to you, Leo. Don't you see what I mean?"

I didn't see.

"You think you're all right at first base," he explained patiently, "because you have a big-name player there who has done better in his day. You keep hoping he'll do better again. At any rate, you think he'll do well enough. Oh, the anesthetics are the dangerous ones. The bad ballplayers don't hurt you so much, because you know they're bad, and you take steps to replace them. But the anesthetic players, the 'good enough' boys, kill you."

I was all ears now, as he went on with the lecture. "Leo, you're like the fellow who has just come out of the operating room. He's sitting up in bed, and the anesthetic has not completely worn off. Ask him how he feels, and he says, 'Fine.' What he doesn't know is that his leg is off at the knee!"

Rickey took a drag on one of his blockbuster cigars. "You are like the fellow with the leg off, Leo. You have Camilli at first base, and you think you're all right. But he is only half the player you think he is."

I was unconvinced. "Camilli is only thirty-four!"

"I see all the signs," replied Rickey. "He has lost his power. He's hitting to the opposite field. I saw Cobb go that way, play for a whole season after he was through, with everybody thinking he could come back. Frisch went the same way. I can name half-a-dozen others. Camilli is through."

He insisted that I was cheating myself if I decided to keep Camilli and hope for a comeback. "You'll get by this year," he continued, "and he won't hurt you so badly. But next year and the year after— The youngster you could be breaking in right now for later service is being deprived of that experience because of Camilli. You'll be a year late with your whole program."

Rickey stated boldly that holding on to a fading star too long was the most frequent mistake made in baseball. "I would rather trade a star a year too soon than a year too late."

It sunk in. Camilli would have to go. We knew it would arouse criticism. It would be a blow to the club, too, for it was an admission that we were surrendering for the 1943 season.

"I want to announce Camilli's departure," said Rickey, "when our new first baseman comes in."

Who was the new first sacker? It developed that Branch had looked at a six-foot, six-inch youngster named Schultz at the American Association in St. Paul. Bob Tarleton, an old admirer of Rickey's, was general manager of the St. Paul club, and was trying to induce Walter Seeger, the owner, to make a working agreement with the Dodgers, and profit on some of the young playing material that Rickey owned.

When the Schultz matter first came up, Rickey decided to go another year with Camilli and the other veterans to have one last fling at the pennant. So he rejected Schultz.

Now that we had decided to let Camilli go, Rickey telephoned Seeger and asked for Schultz. "I'm on my way to the Polo Grounds to sell Schultz to Horace Stoneham," replied the St. Paul owner. "You said you weren't interested."

"But I am now!" declared Rickey, biting off the end of his cigar.

Seeger never reached the Polo Grounds. Rickey intercepted him and started talking. Once that happened, Stoneham never had a look-in. While Horace sat and waited for the Minnesota man to deliver his new first baseman, Rickey concluded the bargain on a Sunday morning. Seeger got $55,000 and a working agreement through which the Brooklyn club would stock his team with fresh young players.

Now, Rickey was ready to shoot the works. He hoped to synchronize the departure of Camilli with the majestic entrance of Schultz. But he could not deliver Jack Bolling, the replacement first baseman he had promised Seeger, to St. Paul in time. So Schultz had to remain in St. Paul for a while.

Meanwhile, the Camilli storm broke over Rickey's head. On August 1, Branch let Camilli and Allen go to the Giants in a waiver deal in which we picked up Bill Sayles, a pretty fair young pitcher with arm troubles; uppercut hitter Joe Orengo, whom Rickey had sold Stoneham years before; and the veteran Bill Lohrman. Lohrman had been a good pitcher with a slider, a fast ball that spins, but does not break like a curve; but now he was about through.

Brooklyn was less disturbed by those who had come in than by those who had been sent out.

On the corner of Flatbush Avenue and Empire Boulevard, Roy Richard, the sixty-year-old newsboy who sing-songs the Dodger news as he hawks his late editions, wailed: "Oh, Branch Rickeeee, what you done to us!"

Next he moaned for the ears of all the fans: "Cameeeley was our hero-oh! You sent him home wit' a broken heart!"

And the final, ominous note he sounded was: "Durocher is the next to go-oh!"

Had Rickey burned down Ebbets Field, the reaction could have been no more bitter. The "letters-to-the-editors" columns of the papers were packed with protests, and the *Eagle* sports page was jammed with pleas that this man Rickey be stopped before he gave away any more of the Dodger standbys.

Of course, hardly anyone noticed what Dolf Camilli said when the news hit him: "There isn't much use kidding myself. I can't pull the ball any more."

That is, nobody noticed it except Horace Stoneham. Stoneham couldn't get Camilli to report. Dolf said even those handy home-run targets provided by the Polo Grounds foul lines wouldn't help him. "I'm through," he insisted. "Earlier I was thinking of quitting myself. If we had been in the pennant race, I would have because I would have hurt the team. When I saw we didn't have a chance, I just went along."

So Stoneham, who had lost Higbe to MacPhail, and lost Schultz, got a Dodger first baseman who never reported.

Four of our ten-year men were gone: Newsom, Allen, Medwick, and Camilli. But the elevator was still going down. We dropped four straight to the flying Cardinals in St. Louis. We fell thirteen and a half games off the pace, and were in danger of plummeting into fourth place.

We were all upset as we saw the floor coming up to meet us. We scrapped and we fought, and we bled inside, but it didn't do any good. The stuff just wasn't there.

During that humiliation in St. Louis, the games became a little rough. One day Walker Cooper spiked Augie Galan, who was filling in at first base. Promptly Mickey Owen, with all his catching paraphernalia on, dashed into the fray. He jumped on Cooper's back, and wound up on the ground, under the big fellow.

In his first time at bat the next day, Mickey brought the house down by sticking out his paw and shaking hands with Walker Cooper, who was again catching.

Later in the game Morton Cooper, Walker's brother, tapped Mickey on the shoulder. "I had to laugh at you hoppin' on Walker yestiddy," two-hundred-pound Morton said. "A little guy like you, Mickey! Why, I bin tryin' all my life to whup my brother, an' I ain't done it yet!"

We were not bringing much of a team back from the West. We had given up 107 runs on the trip, and made only 47. Now we came home to play to a crowd of less than 7,000 *on a Sunday*. I thought nearly half of the fans carried placards accusing Rickey of ruining the team!

In the midst of this hue and cry, when it was fashionable to blame everything on Rickey, Tommy Holmes wrote: "Rickey has not ruined the team. Time and old age have done that. He is trying to correct the condition."

We lost ten in a row and dropped to fourth. Then Schultz arrived. He broke in spectacularly, and helped Wyatt win a game. Then on August 17, Thompson in Montreal got news that could not have made him very happy. We were taking away Gregg and Barney, his two best young pitchers, for the Dodgers' roster.

On a Saturday, Branch called me into his office and said he had Gregg and Barney. "They're babies, Leo," he said. "Just babies. They're scared to death, coming up here. If you use them, they'll walk everybody in the ball park. My advice is to let them sit around a week or two, until they get used to things."

I promised I would. But with a ball club like Brooklyn, I never knew what I would have to do next.

That Sunday Ebbets Field was crammed. Down at the end of the bench sat my two teen-age giants, gaping like a couple of yokels.

I was pretty fed up with the pitching we had been getting. I thought to myself, "If we're going with the kids, we'll go with them. Why not use them right now, today? The longer they sit and think about pitching here, the more scared they'll get, like kids on a high springboard. I'll just shove them in, right now!"

Gregg went two and a third innings, and Barney lasted four. They were fast, blinding fast. But they could not tell where the ball was going when they threw it.

Yet, they weren't so bad. Not after veteran Higbe relieved that same day and had to face eleven men in one inning!

I worked the kids. Soon they weren't stomping and scratching and sweating from nervousness on the mound. Six days later, Barney went nine innings against the Pirates, and actually beat them.

Then Barney pitched a corker against the Giants. He had them licked 2-1, with two out in the ninth and two strikes on Sid Gordon, when he delivered a pitch in the wrong spot, and Sid swatted into the seats. Rex had to go seventeen innings to win that one, quite a chore for anyone. He fanned eight and gave up only seven hits. The fans and the writers, too, sat up and took notice of our youngsters.

Suddenly Wyatt, too, began to get something out of his arm. He won ten straight, and the team started to gallop. In one winning streak we took seven in a row. We jumped from fourth to second place in this flurry. But the Cardinals, as is their habit in September, were also flying. We had been fifteen games behind them at the end of August; now, after they put in their special effort, we landed sixteen behind them.

We finished a hopeful third in 1943.

Rickey's first year had been a rough one. He had known what he was talking about when he said Ebbets Field might be a "graveyard" for the man who took the job, and that "Brooklyn was sitting on a volcano of complete and sudden disintegration."

Most of the press had been frankly hostile. Every time he got rid of a fading star, the writers howled that Branch was lopping off another fat salary, or that he wanted to operate his club with youngsters who would play for peon wages.

On his handling of the Newsom revolt Rickey had received a bale of mail. "Fifty per cent of it took me to task for firing Newsom," he sighed. "The other 50 per cent criticized me for backing up Durocher!"

However, several of the thinking boys in the press box began to put the facts together. Holmes and Frankie Graham, of the *Sun*, said Rickey had done it before, and he could and would do it again. "Rickey knows more about this baseball business than any of us," warned Graham. "Would you tell the pilot how to fly the plane?"

Yet in those dark days the man who really outlined the whole Rickey program, with its mass production of playing talent through an expanded minor-league farm system, and who even predicted the pennant fruit it would bear, was Jim McCulley of the *Daily News*. A photostat of McCulley's column, which was then derided, hangs today in the office of Branch Rickey, Jr. It is, in a sense, a monument to baseball prophecy.

But what about Durocher? I had had a rough year, too—in baseball and in my personal life. The manner in which this team, which we had thought so good, had fallen apart was bad enough. The Newsom "strike" incident was worse. In September, my wife and I decided we couldn't get along together. Grace was a wonderful woman, and for me, this decision looked like the dead end of a road.

When I thought that about everything bad had happened to me, Rickey himself let me have it, right between the eyes.

He announced to the writers: "Leo Durocher is released outright, both as a player and manager."

"What's the idea?" asked Roscoe McGowen. "I must conclude from this that you don't want Durocher to manage the Dodgers next year, Branch."

Rickey said quickly, "No, no, I don't think you can come to such a conclusion. It's just that I want to leave the boy free to accept other positions. He may want to go on the stage, he may want to take a job in Hollywood . . . or in radio."

That blow was intended to make me think. But I was so stunned I couldn't think!

Chapter 20

PILOT WITHOUT PORTFOLIO

So it started again. The newspapermen wrote that Rickey was not announcing me as his manager, but was *denouncing* me. They said I was a "pilot without portfolio," that Rickey was riffling through my papers, while I was left holding the bag.

A few new indictments were invented. One typewriter detective wrote that some of my players were peeved at me because I hadn't gone "all out" in September, 1943, to clinch second-place money, which would have been about $1,200. Imagine that! The story was that I had experimented with youngsters, when the veterans—if we had stuck with them—could have nailed the cash. This fellow added that I wasn't too interested because I was "wealthy." What a laugh that one was—I always spent more than I made!

Rickey himself told one writer I had become "despondent" about the time that Camilli was traded, and the whole team had slumped. "But then," he added, "we got Schultz and outfielder Gene Hermanski, who looked so good before he went into the Service. Leo began to see a brighter future and pepped things up."

The next story had me reconciled with my wife, who had always been a big favorite with Rickey. Branch told the writers that I had been "affected more than anybody could imagine" by the breakup, that he had asked me to the World Series, and I had refused to go to St. Louis because I did not care to revive painful memories. So the writers went to work on that one. "If Leo goes back to Grace," they ruminated, "he can have his job back as Dodger manager."

It became so bad that I was afraid to read the newspapers.

I couldn't figure whether I was in or out. Finally, I stopped trying to outguess the boys.

Of the barrage of criticism that was thrown at me the *Eagle* stated, "Most of Durocher's critics write for the newspapers, it seems. So do Roosevelt's, but F.D.R. hasn't been fired yet either."

Perhaps if I had known what was ahead, how far the elevator was to go down in 1944, I would have cared less.

About mid-October I got myself calmed down. "Why worry?" I thought. "If Branch wants me, he'll call me. If he doesn't—" I shrugged. So, although I knew that Charley Dressen had been bounced for just that, I went off to the race track.

On October 25, Branch summoned me to his office. He talked about the Newsom incident, and I contended that I had regained the confidence of the players. He said he had checked with them all, except one man, and was convinced I was right in that respect.

Then he offered me a contract. First I signed it, then I read it. To my amazement I discovered that it was the fattest document I had ever had. Rickey started me with a base pay of $20,000, and, for every 100,000 attendance we drew over the 600,000 mark, he provided another $5,000.

What is 600,000 at Ebbets Field through a season? That many fans would attend if the only attraction was a meeting of the Ladies' Auxiliary at home plate. I would make a lot of money.

If I needed a lift—and I sure did—this furnished it. I knew that Rickey was behind me with his bank roll as well as his brains.

As soon as Rickey announced me as his 1944 manager, one of the writers cracked, "Did you know Leo has been at the race track?"

If Branch was surprised or hurt or annoyed, he didn't show it. He puffed on his cigar, and said, "If the boy's heart is right, and I know it is, it doesn't make much difference where his legs carry him."

Then they fired questions at him about the "revolt." He leaned back and declared that that was all over. He had polled twenty-four players, all but one key man. I was okay in their book.

"The twenty-fifth man?" Rickey repeated. "We didn't talk to him."

"Durocher loves twenty-four Dodgers!" cried the sports pages. "But the twenty-fifth is in the doghouse."

There was more guessing about Number Twenty-five than there was about Miss Hush. I wouldn't say who it was—except that it wasn't Arky Vaughan. Vaughan and I were pals. Branch wouldn't say who it was—except to insist that it wasn't Billy Herman. It wasn't Herman and it wasn't Vaughan. Who was it?

Rickey gave the writers a great talk. He convinced me that he knew more about my inner workings than I did myself.

"You noticed that Durocher never came to me this October, to ask for his job, one of the richest in baseball," he said. "Maybe he had made a few mistakes during the year. Maybe most people would have apologized and pleaded for another chance. If Durocher had come crawling, I probably wouldn't have hired him. I'd have known that he'd lost his drive, that he had changed.

"Leo wouldn't know how to apologize," chuckled Rickey. "He wouldn't know how to put words like that together!

"The same things holds on this club," he went on. "If there's a player he says he doesn't want, that man will have to go. I don't expect to change Durocher, so I'll have to change the club!"

The identity of the twenty-fifth Dodger became a subject for coast-to-coast discussion. "He must go!" Rickey had stated. Every day, sports writers queried him and badgered me for news of a firing. They were eaten up with curiosity about the identity of this mystery man. But the twenty-fifth Dodger was a pretty good ballplayer, and Rickey did not want to let him go. Although his name has never been revealed in this connection, I can now say that it was Dixie Walker.

I was bitter at Walker for the way he had sided with Newsom and Vaughan. He hadn't bothered to find out the facts or to think them through. I was also peeved at Dixie because of other, if minor, incidents.

Of course, Rickey played his cards slowly and carefully. Again, he made time his ally in dealing with me and this fellow I didn't care for.

One day, quite unexpectedly, Branch mentioned the subject to me. A month had passed since I had told him I could get along with every Dodger but one. I had cooled off considerably.

"If this player walked into the room right now," he asked, "would you say 'Hello!' to him?"

I said, "Yeah, sure!"

"Would he say 'Hello!' to you?"

My answer was the same.

"Then, my boy," he advised. "a chasm has not been riven between you two. We can straighten it out!"

That had been in his mind all along. Walker was one of the really fine hitters in baseball. Rickey knew that his popularity in Brooklyn was such that my own position with the fans would be weakened if I insisted on trading him.

The way things turned out, I was mighty glad I did not insist on getting rid of Walker. Dixie hit .357 for me that year, and was voted the National League's Most Valuable Player.

We always got along well after that, although the rumor persisted that we were not pals. That Dixie was traded to Pittsburgh just about the time I came back to manage the club in 1948 was only a coincidence, nothing more.

That what I say is absolutely true can be supported by one little-known fact. In 1948, when news of my reinstatement by Commissioner Chandler hit the sports pages, the very first telegram of congratulations I received was signed, "Dixie Walker!"

The writers warmed up to Rickey. He was talking their language. Sometimes he even dropped a cussword into the conversation. It startled them, but they liked it. He had seemed too perfect and far away before.

J. G. Taylor Spink, the powerhouse publisher of the *Sporting News*, came to interview Rickey about the baseball outlook for 1944. Spink phrased his questions carefully. After all, Rickey was respected as a perfectionist in phraseology, a meticulous precisionist on whose tongue each word was carefully rolled for the pastel shades of meaning. Gosh, what words I learned in Brooklyn!

Spink asked whether the Cardinals, because of the loss of several key men, would not be weakened in 1944, even to the point of mediocrity.

"Nuts, Taylor!" replied the old perfectionist. "The Cards will win easier than they did in 1943!"

Spink was startled, but he said nothing. Rickey observed that he was taken aback and decided to have some fun.

"Leave us face the facts," snapped Branch, without cracking a smile, "the Jints got no chance this year." He said it in real Brooklyn style: "Jints."

When Spink asked another question and Rickey replied, "You got me there, Kid," the editor nearly fell off his chair.

Now Rickey roared and asked, "Do I sound as though I belonged in Brooklyn, Taylor?"

Branch used the episode for an illuminating discussion of how he had figured out the Newsom case. "I just discovered the other day," he confided to Spink, "that the word 'needle,' which in all my unenlightened days in Ohio and Missouri I had always supposed was a noun, can be a verb. In Brooklyn 'to needle' means 'to irritate, to provoke, by a continuous series of incidents.' "

Spink listened. What else could he do? When the boss goes off on one of those intellectual tangents, everybody listens.

I was happier because Spink couldn't or wouldn't interrupt, for Rickey put on the record a complete explanation of the whole Newsom incident. As I have said, he knows me better than I know myself. Although he wasn't there, he had pieced the whole thing together and was able to clarify it in a way that had never occurred to me.

"Let us consider a manager, Taylor," said Rickey to Spink. "He is the aggressive, hard-driving type. He has positive ideas and methods for winning. He calls a clubhouse meeting before the game and with all the players, particularly the younger ones, listening, he says, 'We pitch Doakes high and inside.'

"On the fringe of the gathering," Rickey went on, lowering his voice, "is a veteran pitcher who murmurs, 'I dunno, I pitch the guy low an' outside, an' I get him out.'

"This goes on and on. One small thing after another, to be sure. But if the manager says one thing, this big know-it-all says another. The important thing is that the big blowhard keeps winning and winning, and is, in fact, the team's leading pitcher!

"Now, Taylor," pursued Rickey, pulling his chair up closer, "the manager is suddenly not so sure of himself. He is not as aggressive, as positive in his statements as he once was. He cannot say in front of the younger players 'Do it this way' because he knows that they have noticed that the other methods work pretty well for Old-Know-It-All. So instead of being as sure as he once was, he decides to give himself a way out in anything he says, just in case his own method doesn't work. But Old-Know-It-All never lets up. He is in a fine position because he is a winning ace. He needles the manager in his subtle way, until the manager finally begins to seek for a way to discredit this disturbing influence and so regain his authority.

"What happens, then, Taylor?" Rickey asked, waving his cigar.

Spink, being a good straight man, blinked and said, "I dunno."

"Well, the manager seizes on some little incident, in which Old-Know-It-All is wrong. It may be a bad pitch, say to Vince DiMaggio. DiMaggio gets a base hit that hurts the club. Now the manager has Old-Know-It-All, he thinks, and he jumps on him with both feet!

"Say Durocher is this manager," Rickey went on calmly. "Durocher leaps in and pursues his advantage. Old-Know-It-All, whom we will call Newsom, is wrong, sure. But what Durocher doesn't appreciate is that he is also wrong himself, for making a mountain out of a molehill. Pretty soon he is in hot water with his players, his press, and his public, for being 'unfair' to Newsom.

"Of course, what they do not figure, because they do not know the facts, is that Newsom has been wrong, *all wrong*, right along, for needling the manager, for making his job tough and for making his authority shaky."

Yet, in the minds of some newspapermen and a lot of the fans, I was still in a bad position.

I was in Florida, waiting to embark with Danny Kaye for a U.S.O. camp tour overseas—it never did get clearance, and we played the camps in this country, instead—when a story broke in Brooklyn that Max Meyer, a Brooklyn manufacturer of artificial pearls, was about to buy control of the Dodgers. He was dickering with the Brooklyn Trust Company for 75 per cent of the stock, which had belonged to the Ebbets heirs and the descendants of Ed McKeever.

At once some of the boys broad-jumped to a conclusion that was interesting, to say the least: Durocher would be fired. Here Rickey had just signed me, but because Meyer might come in, they were confident he would make his pal, Casey Stengel, the manager again.

However, I wasn't worrying. A pretty good pal of mine was still running the Brooklyn club, and he, Branch Rickey, and I were still on the elevator together. We had already thrown off some of the old ballast.

But we were destined to go down to some of the lower floors in the National League. Rickey might well have said, "Hold your hat, Leo, here we go again!"

Chapter 21

WE HEAD FOR THE CELLAR

MIDWAY IN THE 1944 SEASON, WE MADE A DEAL FOR A SO-SO outfielder named Goody Rosen.

He had been a Dodger back in 1938 under Grimes; now that the war was on he looked like a great ballplayer. To get him we sent Ostermueller and Lohrman and $20,000 to Syracuse. "Flatnose," as I always called him, had hit .340 in Syracuse.

Ostermueller squawked about going to the minors. "It doesn't add up," he complained to Rickey.

"My boy," returned B.R., "not only does it add up, but it subtracts, too. And you are the one who is subtracted from the Dodgers."

The Pirates, who had refused to make a deal for him with Rickey, snatched him from Syracuse, and sometimes Ostermueller was pretty tough for us after that.

Rosen did not get into the line-up at once. While he was a substitute, he had to ride in an upper berth. We were due to leave St. Louis one night for Cincinnati. On the list that was pasted on the clubhouse mirror, Rosen was slated for an upper berth.

Suddenly, I had a hunch. So I played Goody in the first game of the double-header the next day. He promptly got three hits. I announced him for center field for the second game, too.

The next thing I knew, Harold Parrott, whom Branch had made traveling secretary late in 1943, when Mel Jones went into the Navy, came to me in a state of agitation.

"Rosen," Parrott spluttered, "Rosen says he's a regular now, Leo, and I have no more lower berths. They're all assigned. He's squawking about his upper. I don't know what to do."

Today, that would not bother Parrott. But it was his first problem, and he was anxious not to muff it.

I said, "Leave it to me, Harold, I'll fix everything. I'll take Rosen out of there right now."

"Out of the upper, Leo?" asked Harold, in astonishment.

"No," I replied. "Out of the line-up!"

And I did, too. It was that kind of team. We had about a dozen humpty-dumpties, and it didn't much matter which of them played. Most of the lads were just props, so to speak, for a few promising kids we wanted to keep for the great days we thought we could see a year, or two, or three ahead.

When spring training opened in Bear Mountain, we realized that we weren't going to have much talent to help us out. We had a second baseman named Frank Drews, who had been at St. Paul. Drews could make all the plays, but he could not get to the ball. He could run about as fast as your Aunt Kate.

We had a "whatsit" named Smut Aderholt, a left-handed hitter who looked great, and could really powder the ball. My eyes lit up when I saw him hit. The others quickly warned me, "You can't play him anyplace, Leo."

"We'll worry about that later," I declared, as I watched Aderholt peel off those line drives in the West Point field-house. "I'll put him where he won't have many chances. In right field, maybe, or at third base. You say he's a poor fielder?"

"It's worse than that," reported one of our scouts. "He just can't pick up the ball. When it comes to him, it sort of —well, hypnotizes him. He breaks into a cold sweat, and the ball goes right by him."

I couldn't believe that. But two weeks later, I was repeating those same words myself.

In two weeks, I had other stories to tell, all of them sad.

That spring at Bear Mountain we had the quaintest-looking ballplayers I have ever seen.

Buck Tanner was a rookie pitcher who might have walked out of the pages of Ring Lardner. He told terrific stories of his accomplishments: so many that Arthur Paterson could not get them all into one story in the *New York Herald Tribune*. I doubt whether either Joe DiMaggio or Bob Feller got more news space when they came up to the big-league clubs as rookies. This eighteen-year-old from Rattlesnake, Florida, was even the subject of a serial story in the *Herald Tribune!*

Tanner towered six feet, six inches. On top of his lanky frame was perched a head not much bigger than a large grapefruit. He claimed he had won sixteen letters in various sports in high school, and had hit .416. "But I have a brother," he swore, "who can hit better than me."

"How much did your brother hit?"

"Well," drawled Buck, "they never really did git him out!"

We decided to start the season with Gene Mauch at second base. Mauch was one of the bright young men in camp. In fact, he had been president of the student body at his Fremont, California, high school.

About the first thing Mauch did was to break my finger as he tossed me a double-play ball in an exhibition game against the Red Sox at Ebbets Field.

By May, Mauch was gone, farmed to Montreal. Eddie Murphy wrote in the *Sun:* "He was a nice boy, but they asked him to play a man's game."

When Rickey finds himself overstocked in one position, his favorite remark is: "Let's do some cocoanut-snatching," which means, "Let's see if we cannot get, for example, a shortstop to do the job for us at first base." "Aptitude" is one of the top words in Rickey's book, and if a boy has aptitude, he says, he can play where you need him most.

He explains his theory by the story of a team of cocoanut-gatherers. Half-a-dozen cocoanut-gatherers were assigned to climb a tree to toss the nuts down, and another six were to pick up the nuts and throw them in a cart. One day two of the boys who climbed the trees got sick. Rather than slow down the work, the foreman took one of the nut-gatherers and made him a cocoanut-snatcher up in the trees, and so the business could go on.

Rickey worked like that himself, except that his cocoanut boys were ballplayers. He transformed George Sisler from a pitcher into one of the all-time greats as a first baseman. He developed two of the greatest modern-day hitters in the National League by taking them off the mound—though they wanted to pitch—and insisting that they stay in the outfield, where they could play and hit every day. Chick Hafey was one of these. He had led a minor league in strike-outs his first year, but he wanted to quit the game when Rickey insisted that he play the outfield. The other, also a pitcher, was Stan Musial, who later proved his aptitude by taking over in great style at first base for the Cardinals. Both Hafey and Musial led the National League in hitting.

(Perhaps Rickey's outstanding job of "cocoanut-snatching" came with his insistence that Jackie Robinson play first base for Brooklyn in the 1947 pennant race. Jackie had never played first base, even in spring training. Everyone, including the other players, was openly skeptical. But it worked, and the Dodgers won the pennant.)

Now Rickey was doing more cocoanut-snatching, but for a different reason. He was so short of manpower that he was desperate.

Billy Herman was in the Navy. Vaughan wired that he would have to stay on his ranch. Then when Bordagaray held out, we tried Dixie Walker on third. People said I was trying to get Walker killed. Dixie looked so unhappy that we moved him back to the outfield.

Next we tried Mickey Owen, the catcher, at second base. Then we used Luis Olmo, the outfielder who had looked so good, and hit over .300 in his 1943 trial. At that position neither of them was a Napoleon Lajoie.

In Boston, in April, we ran into a no-hit game. It was pitched by, of all people, Jim Tobin. Jim was what we called a rocking-chair pitcher. With an effortless motion, he could throw one knuckle ball after another. On a good day, when the wind or the air currents were right, the knucklers danced and dipped, and made black-and-blue marks all over Phil Masi, Tobin's catcher, who had to block them because he couldn't catch them. You can't hit something you can't catch. My hitters looked like old ladies trying to swat flies.

Naturally, I was not happy. You don't mind being shown up by a world-beater—but Tobin was something else!

A Boston reporter asked me if I thought Tobin had a lot of stuff.

"Stuff?" I screamed. "Why, if Tobin's fast ball hit you right between the eyes it wouldn't make a red spot!" But he got a no-hitter.

We lost five of our first nine games, one by the tight score of twenty-six to eight. That day I got the gate for folding my arms. Umpire Tom Dunn said I was imitating him, making fun of him. If I was, that was about all the fun I had that afternoon.

Dunn did not understand me as George Magerkurth did. Mage and I have been pictured as archenemies, which is not true. Some of the run-ins we had started rather badly, but they ended in chuckles. Once, in St. Louis, Mage gave me the heave-ho, and I refused to leave. Our argument had been bitter and had already held up the game for more than five minutes. So he passed the final sentence. When the umpire "pulls the watch on you" and you don't leave, he can "throw the book" at you, and your club will catch a heavy fine.

This day Mage strode toward our dugout; his lips were

quivering, he was so angry. "I'll give you one minute to get out of here, Durocher!" he stormed.

"Oh, yeah?" I jeered. "Why, you big meathead, I'll bet you haven't even got a watch!

"Oh, no?" he growled, madder than ever. He reached into his pocket, and fumbled around. A peculiar look came over his chubby face. He tried to smother a smile, and couldn't. "Leo," he confessed, "you got me. *You're* right, for once!" Then he added, "Now get out of here right away and I won't slap a fine on you!"

"Right!" I ducked out of sight. He kept his word.

The next series we met the same trio, Mage, Dunn, and Bill Stewart. Again Mage booted me out of the game. Again I lingered, near the mouth of the runway. Again Mage "pulled the watch" on me. "An' we got one this time!" chirped Stewart, waving a shiny new "onion."

Another time, Mage and I had ourselves a chuckle with 35,000 people roaring at us. That was the day he reversed Bill Klem, the "Old Arbitrator"—never a healthy thing to do. Klem had called a Cincinnati runner out at second on a double play we attempted. Then Bill had turned toward first. What Klem had not seen—according to Magerkurth—was that after he turned his back our shortstop had juggled the ball.

So Mage called all hands safe, and the crowd yelled for me, as they always do in Brooklyn. "Leo, Leo!" I heard them screaming. They wanted me to go after the hated umpires.

I wasn't exactly chained to the bench. By then I was well on my way out there. I had tried every method—even the dignified Deacon McKechnie approach, with the quiet conversation, and the gentle nod of the head. But that had got me canned, too. So now I ran out normally, unrestrained.

Magerkurth was in retreat along the third-base line. He seemed to want to put as much distance between us as possible. "I reversed the decision, the man is safe," he barked

I kept my hands in my pockets—because if you lay a finger on an umpire, you may get life. Now, the only way I could slow him up was to get in front of him and try to trip him a bit. Even then he put his head down and barged straight ahead, like a tank.

"Keep plowing," I said. "And if you butt that cement head of yours into that left-field wall, you'll break a new entrance through it!"

That brought him up short.

"One more crack like that and I'll put you out of here," he threatened. But it was the way he said it that counted. He had been chewing tobacco, and the word "put" exploded and sprayed me with juice.

I made as if to spit back. As a matter of fact, in a celebrated rhubarb, Billy Jurges, the Giant shortstop, had done that once.

When Mage saw me puckering, he roared, "Spitting is punishable by a two-hundred-dollar fine!"

I pulled out my handkerchief, carefully wiped my face clean of the juice and showed him the evidence. "What do you think I have here?" I shouted. "The measles?"

Mage had to smile in spite of himself. Again he told me to forget about it, and get out of there.

I've had more than my share of rhubarbs with the umpires, but they haven't all been the result of frustration or anger. Occasionally, I have had a definite purpose in mind for challenging an ump. Believe it or not, there is a National League umpire who could tell you how I saved his job. He admitted it himself.

We had a rather poor club and were not fighting for the pennant at the time, although we battle just as hard to stay out of last place as we do to get into first. This night we were beating the Cards in St. Louis. They had a runner on second with none out when a fly ball was hit to Augie Galan, who was playing left field.

Augie's arm is not especially strong. The Redbird on second, like so many of the Cardinals, could run like a deer. So when the ball was hit in the air he prepared to dash for third.

But he left second base a split second before the catch, and after he had taken maybe ten steps toward third, the umpire, who shall remain nameless, called, "You left too soon!"

Naturally, the Card runner, realizing he would be called out if he went to third, retreated to second. One of our infielders heard the umpire's remark, which, of course, was out of order. Our boy really put on a scene. He threw his cap and his glove, and screamed. Normally, he would have been banished from the game, but the unhappy umpire realized that he had pulled a terrific boner. He did not dare compound the injustice by yanking our player. So the umpire just stood there, red-necked and red-eared, and took it.

When I charged out to learn what was going on, the ump stopped me. "I just kicked one, Leo!" he confessed.

I felt sorry for him. He came to me after the game, which fortunately we managed to win, with tears in his eyes. "Your player will tell the newspapermen," he said, "and if this gets in the New York papers, it will mean my job—the end of me!"

I told Harold Parrott to go to the press box after the game and ask the writers to drop any mention of the umpire's mistake. Everyone cooperated and nothing on that episode went out over the wires. The umpire was grateful. Still, as might be expected in a job like his, he called a couple of rough ones against us from time to time.

It's easy to get off on the subject of umpires. But it was not poor umpiring, but poor ballplaying that got us into hot water early in the 1944 season.

Chapter 22

"LOSE 'EM ALL—LOSE 'EM ALL!"

On our first western trip of 1944, we lost ten out of fourteen games. The last one in Cincinnati we lost because Bill Hart, our shortstop at the moment, dropped a pop fly your Aunt Emma could have got.

That night in the station, waiting for the rattler to take us back to New York, I sounded off. "I am going to send Bill Hart so far away a Pinkerton man could not find him," I swore.

In New York, Hart's wife read the early editions and became alarmed at my threats. She telephoned Branch Rickey and asked his help. Somewhat amazed by the whole thing, Branch promised he would prevent violence.

When Branch spoke to me the next day, I had cooled off and could hardly remember the harsh things I had said. Bill was just a fair ballplayer doing his best. I had become impatient with him because I wanted him to play like a Reese.

In desperation, we signed a semi-pro named Eddie Basinski in Buffalo. He turned out to be another high-class violin player. He could make the double play, something these other fellows couldn't do, and he started all right at bat. But by fall he was back in the minors.

Three of the old guard played great ball for us. At the end of May, we were under .500, and in fifth place. Walker was hitting .431, Bordagaray was clouting .354, and Galan was playing first, third, and the outfield, and was also hitting very well.

Rickey had been generous with these men. He had dickered with Galan. Yet, when they agreed on $13,000, Branch offered to give Augie another $1,000 if he would agree to fill any position he was asked to play.

Walker had been painting his house in Birmingham while he held out, but he finally dropped the paintbrush and came a-running at Rickey's lavish offer.

Early in spring it had looked as though we wouldn't get Bordagaray at all, and for a reason that had nothing to do with baseball. Branch Rickey is a student of checkers and chess. I think he has read all the books on both games. One afternoon in training camp, when he was beating somebody's ears off, he made a statement about a certain combination on the checkerboard.

"I'm sorry, Mr. Rickey, but you're wrong," said a spectator.

We all looked up. Tom Greenwade, the veteran scout, was challenging the Boss.

"Young man, would you like to play?" asked Branch, figuring he'd teach this upstart a lesson.

The crowd made way. Greenwade moved in and sat down. We all pitied the poor victim. Of course, a hick like Tom couldn't know all the big-city angles on checkers. But Tom was from Willard, Missouri, where they undoubtedly play checkers all winter long on a crackerbarrel in the general store.

He beat Rickey once, then twice. He casually mentioned something about a tournament he had won in the West. Rickey bore down, calculating every move, but he lost again.

I quickly dubbed Greenwade the "crackerbarrel champ." I was kidding Branch plenty.

That was the moment Bordagaray picked to arrive and talk terms with Branch. It wasn't exactly the best time to hit the boss for a raise. Frenchy announced breezily that he had been declared 4F and was therefore more valuable.

"Not to me!" snapped Rickey, and Bordagaray was soon on his way back to New York—unsigned.

Eventually, after a long holdout and another fruitless trip to Bear Mountain, Frenchy compromised and agreed to accept $9,500.

"You will be happy playing at that salary?" asked Rickey.

"It's great," said Frenchy.

"All right," Rickey beamed. "Then we'll make it $10,000."

Bordagaray was so happy he hustled his head off all year, even when the sports writers accused the rest of our club of not hustling. We called Frenchy our "alley cat." He was always yammering, always scampering and sliding, always figuring ways to beat the opposition.

In one game at Ebbets Field, Bill Voiselle of the Giants had us on our knees, 2-1, with two out in the ninth. Hal Gregg was on second and Frenchy was jumping up and down on first. Lloyd Waner, whom we had finally lured from Oklahoma, was the pinch hitter. Lloyd lifted an easy fly to right field, and the crowd headed for the exits. Even I had one foot on the dugout stairs.

Bordagaray, however, did not give up. It was 1000 to 1 that the ball would drop safely into Charley Mead's glove in right field. But Frenchy put his head down and ran as fast as his speedy little pins would push him. He could not have gone faster had there been $1,000 to be picked up on home plate.

Johnny Rucker bumped into Mead and the ball dropped to the ground. Gregg came in to tie the score, and pounding behind him came Frenchy, sliding in to win the "hopelessly lost" contest, 3-2. That feat made a great hit with me. Rickey talked for a week about the way his "alley cat" had come through.

We had a bad team, but the white silk uniforms we wore for our night games made glamour boys out of "Dem Bums." We swished when we walked. As I came out to coach when we played Pittsburgh, Frankie Frisch sang out, "Dearie, can I have the next dance?"

Frisch's Pirates knocked Cal McLish out. McLish was an Indian boy from Oklahoma whom we had signed as a prospect. He had a lot of ability, but he was only eighteen and scared, and the big leagues were no place for him yet.

"McLish is half Choctaw," wrote one of the scribes, "and half pitcher."

That month the long-expected invasion of Europe was under way. That operation made our own plight seem pretty insignificant, of course. All sports events were temporarily called off. On June 8, we traded Bob Chipman, our left-handed pitcher, for Eddie Stanky, a reserve infielder on the Cubs. The same day we made two other notable acquisitions which were to play a big part in clinching the 1947 pennant. We obtained Ralph Branca and Eddie Miksis.

Branca was a big, shy youngster who had been given the brush-off at the Polo Grounds where he had gone first for a tryout because he had always been a Giant fan.

Miksis was a prodigy we fetched from Trenton.

"The way this boy can hit, run, and throw, Leo," said Rickey, "he is worth five times as much as the Trenton franchise."

Miksis was given an unusual guarantee. He would not be used in a game for two weeks. He was inexperienced and shy. I was dying to get him into the line-up, but I had to let him sit on the bench. No kid with a package marked "Do not open until Xmas" ever was more impatient that I was.

However, I could use Branca, and I did. At the Polo Grounds I stuck him in as a relief pitcher against the Giants who had given him the bum's rush. A nice, quiet rhubarb resulted.

When Branca began to unfold his huge frame and warm up, he was as awkward as the average eighteen-year-old, and twice as big.

Eddie Brannick, the Giant secretary, took one look at

Ralph, and popped off like a string of Chinese firecrackers.

"What is Rickey trying to do, get by with sem-eye-pros?" Eddie needled Parrott. "Does he think a clown like that will ever make a big leaguer?"

"From what they tell me, Eddie, the boy has a great chance," replied Harold. "He's fast, and has a good overhand curve. All he needs is control—"

"That's ignorance talking," sniffed Eddie, the expert. "You're hypnotized by Rickey. I feel sorry for you. Anything Rickey says, you believe. Why, I'll bet you a hundred-dollar suit of clothes that Branca never develops into a star pitcher in the big leagues."

"Okay," Parrott agreed. "We'll shake on that bet. I have fifteen years to win it. But we have to agree on one thing, Eddie. What do you mean by 'star pitcher'?"

"He must win twenty games in one season in the majors," said Eddie, "for you to win your suit of clothes."

Branca pitched against the Giants that day and did all right. He fanned Buddy Kerr, Bill Voiselle, and Johnny Rucker, the first three men he faced in the major league.

After the game, Parrott told Gus Steiger of the *Mirror* about the bet. Gus printed the details. This was regarded as a breach of secretarial protocol, or something. Brannick would not talk to Parrott for more than a year. In fact, Eddie has not talked to Parrott yet about the hundred-dollar suit, although Branca won twenty-one games in 1947.

Winning the suit came to be a Dodger project. When Branca won a game, he would say to Parrott, "Well, we got the vest today. Now we will start after the pants."

We continued to shuffle the line-up. This inspired a lot of criticism of me in the press. The boys said I lacked patience with the youngsters. By the end of June we had used eight different shortstops, seven third basemen, and six second basemen. Even Schultz had to be benched, and we tried Jack Bolling at first base.

We hoped that Wyatt, resting his arm, would come back strong and lift us out of fifth place. When we won five straight and got over the .500 mark, with thirty-three won and thirty lost, we had new dreams. Then something snapped, and we went into the worst tailspin I've ever experienced.

Walker was hitting .378. He backslid to .351. As Mickey Owen said, "It wasn't the kids, but us older players who couldn't do anything right in the West."

Whatever the reason, we lost fifteen in a row, and Roscoe McGowen, poet laureate of our bunch, composed the now-famous epic "Lose 'Em All," sung to the tune of "Bless 'Em All." Each day as we dropped another, Roscoe and his newspaper pals composed an additional stanza. It was already deep into July when the writers sang:

"The Dodgers won five in a row and went West,
Ev'ryone feelin' swell.
Hope and high confidence filled ev'ry breast
They'd give those Western clubs hell!
But O! what a slip 'twixt the Cubs and The Lip!
(Even Toledo brought gall).
So weep with the Dodgers, those young and old codgers,
Whose slogan became: 'Lose 'em all.' "

CHORUS:

'Lose 'em all! Lose 'em all!
In Chicago they started to fall.
John Whitlow Wyatt was first to go in,
Then came Les Webber and oh, what a din!
Bad Bill Nicholson blasted the ball
From Times Square to Carnegie Hall!
And meanwhile Bob Chipman was giving The Lip-man
A pain in the neck . . . Lose 'em all!"

It was endless. Every loss brought another chorus. I don't know which was worse, losing the game or listening to the new lyric:

"Lose 'em all! Lose 'em all!
'Twas like a Lake Michigan squall.
Next game Durocher sent Gregg to the mound
But by the eighth poor Hal wasn't around.
Cavaretta had emptied with ease
The bases Hal filled by degrees,
And Grimm had a Wyse guy who turned out a prize guy
In beatin' Dem Bums . . . Lose 'em all!"

There was more—and more—

"Lose 'em all! Lose 'em all!
The next one was bitter as gall.
Ed Head had 'em scoreless with one out to go
And then came a Bruin, one Andy Pafko.
Andy whacked one right out of the park,
Making Grimm just as gay as a lark,
For his Leslie Fleming with skill had been stemming
The Bums with three hits . . . Lose 'em all!"

Some of them I wish I could forget:

"Lose 'em all! Lose 'em all!
They answered the Cardinal call
Down in Saint Louis with Ol' Dan'l Boone—
Marion played 'em a triple play tune!
Oh, so charming in Alice blue pants
Were they all—but they hadn't a chance.
Before those fierce Redbirds the Dodgers were dead birds . . .
Four down, ten to go! . . . Lose 'em all!"

When we reached Number Fifteen it ran like this:

"Lose 'em all! Lose 'em all!
A jinx truly held 'em in thrall.
Andrews beat Melton in Saturday's fray,
Tobin topped Gregg in the first one next day,
And that loss ran the string to fifteen—
A new Brooklyn record, I mean.
And the Dodgers were tossed on their fannies by Boston,
A cellar place team! . . . Lose 'em all!"

But at last—

"Lose 'em all! Lose 'em all!
Our Bums had their backs to the wall.
Groggy and reeling, they swung without aim—
And damned if they didn't come through with the game!
For Ol' Dan'l, while belted for five,
Emerged from the carnage alive.
And thanks to Al Javery, they came out of slavery—
They're free men again! BLESS 'EM ALL!"

It was worth breaking that losing streak to have them stop singing those choruses!

When they sang "Can this go on until Fall?" I was beginning to wonder myself how far it would go. We couldn't do anything right; Gregg, who had won six by Decoration Day and seemed headed for a great year, now lost eight in a row. Wyatt was in St. Louis having his sore arm examined.

Back in Brooklyn, the "Flock Boosters" a society of Dodger rooters, decided to do something about it. They held a solemn meeting in the DeWitt Clinton Hotel and shipped us a carton of vitamin pills to pep us up.

Finally, on July 16 (Roscoe McGowen's birthday, incidentally), we won a game on eight unearned runs. Pretty soon we dropped five more in a row. I never knew there were so many ways to lose a game. How bad can you get? We lost twenty-one out of twenty-three starts and hit the cellar with a thump.

Rickey called Jack Pitler, who was managing our Newport News farm team in the Piedmont League. He asked Jake if he had anyone on his club who could be of help.

Rickey never knew in advance how Pitler would react. Once before, the boss had gone through the Newport News roster until they came to the fifteenth and last man on the team. According to Jake the first fourteen were all promising ballplayers.

Rickey asked, "Is Number Fifteen a good hitter?"

"He can't hit at all, Mr. Rickey."

"Can he run and throw?" prodded Rickey, envisioning a possible defensive genius.

"He can't run," admitted Jake, "and he can't throw!"

"Judas Priest!" exploded Branch, "why do you keep him?"

"He's the only one old enough to drive our bus," Pitler replied.

Jake was—and still is—highly regarded by the Brooklyn organization. Once he had a pitching prospect at Newport News who had arm trouble. Rickey inquired about the boy.

"It's his elbow, Mr. Rickey," vowed Jake. "The poor kid can't bend it."

"Ossified?" asked Branch.

"Not at all, sir," returned Pitler. "He doesn't touch a drop."

Now, as Rickey called for help, Jake declared he had a shortstop whose throwing was so wild that for a rib some of the fans behind first base in Newport News had worn first-basemen's gloves to the park to catch his "overthrows."

"We can't use him," Rickey decided. "He might kill somebody at Ebbets Field. Anybody else?"

No, said Pitler, nobody else worthwhile, but he thought this boy Brown could help the Dodgers, anyway.

"How old is he?"

"Sixteen," said Jake. "But he can run, and he can hit, and he will really show you something."

"Put him on the next train," was Rickey's order.

That was how Tommy Brown came to join us. The boys christened him "Barbasol" because he didn't shave yet. At sixteen he played forty games at shortstop for us that year. A child shall lead them!

One day, off Preacher Roe—who came to Brooklyn later in the Walker trade—"Barbasol" hit a ball that carried into the upper deck in left field.

As the youngster circled the bases, Red Barber rolled the customary carton of Old Golds down the screen behind home plate. That was the reward for hitting a homer. I stepped in quickly to intercept the cigarettes. I waved a stern "No!" at Brownie. The kid was too young to smoke! The crowd got a big kick out of that.

Young as he was, Tommy Brown could not make any mistakes our club had not already made. We were in the cellar, thirty-one and one-half games back of the Cardinals. During the month of July we won only five games. Strangely enough, in four of those five we beat ace pitchers Mort Cooper, Rip Sewell, Bucky Walters, and Alva Javery.

Rickey received criticism from every quarter. The newspapers had dubbed us "Goats of the Gowanus" and anybody who could tap a typewriter was taking a hand at making armchair deals and laboring at second-guess management of our club. *They* had fun.

One of the anchors we had dragged all year was Whitlow Wyatt. He had been a great pitcher when we won the pennant in 1941, but now he just could not throw. It was pitiful to see him shot-put the ball up to the plate. He had won only two games all year.

Lou Niss, sports editor of the *Eagle*, had a notion he could help.

"Give Wyatt to me for two weeks," pleaded Lou.

"I will give him to you for good," snorted Rickey. "I think he should go home, anyway. The poor fellow is through."

"No, he isn't," Niss insisted. "I will make him as good as new in two weeks."

So Wyatt became an *Eagle*-Niss project. Lou put the big fellow through a course under "Doc" Gallagher, who is not a magician, although some ballplayers think he can restore dead arms.

Gallagher pulled and yanked and kneaded. He had Wyatt

bouncing the ball off the right-field wall at Ebbets Field, twenty minutes at a stretch.

Finally came the big unveiling in Pittsburgh. Wyatt said he felt great, and there wasn't one of us who didn't hope the big fellow would stage a comeback.

However, the Pirates teed off, five hits in two innings. Wyatt walked from the mound, hanging his head. Soon after that, he went home. He never rejoined us.

We pitched the wild youngsters again and again. Columnists, fans, and radio experts pasted Rickey right and left as a "team-wrecker." Branch continued to say to me, "When this war ends, we'll have a running start on those other National League clubs that haven't rebuilt!"

It wasn't so rough on me. As we finished at Ebbets Field that final Sunday, and shoved the Phillies into the cellar by half a game, all Brooklyn turned out to say good-by with a kind word—and bushels of presents. I got so many gifts I couldn't carry half of them to my car.

"They sympathize with me," I thought. "Because if Rickey keeps me, I'm facing another year as manager of a rag-bag team!"

During the dismal 1944 season, I received bales of letters from our boys in the Service all over the world. When we went into that fifteen-game losing streak, the mail doubled.

"What goes on, Leo?" was the burden of the missives. "What's wrong? Can we help?"

In November, I left on a U.S.O. winter tour of the European Theater, and got those queries in person. They asked the same questions as the letter writers, but there was one big difference: I had to face them.

Tom Meany, the columnist, Joe Medwick, then with the Giants, and Nick Etten, big Yankee first baseman, made the tour with me. We all learned something.

The first thing Meany discovered was that a traveling secretary's life is not all peaches and cream. We landed at a big airport in Italy. It was cold and dark, and we were miles from nowhere. Medwick sat on his bag and asked Meany: "When are our cabs getting here?"

Nothing bothered Ducky Medwick very much. He was granted an audience with His Holiness the Pope. On another occasion, a general invited us to dinner in the officers' mess. Medwick was hungry. He sat down at the nearest table and began to stoke up. The general said, "Mr. Medwick, your seat is at this table, with us."

"I'm all right here, General," replied Joe, hardly missing a forkful. The general frowned and said snappily, "Mr. Medwick, that is an order!" Joe quickly dropped his knife and fork and joined us!

I learned plenty, too. I found out what it was like to eat Spam and shave without water, and live in cold hotels where you had to walk maybe ten or twelve flights to get to your room, because there was no electric power to run an elevator.

It amazed me that our boys, enduring every hardship, followed baseball avidly. Copies of overseas editions of the *Sporting News*, which is the bible of baseball, were worn so thin from handling that they looked like lace handkerchiefs.

We talked in tents near the front, where we could hear the shells going off. We talked in opera houses. We talked outdoors, where the G.I.'s climbed into the trees, and their lighted cigarettes winked eerily in the dark. Our largest audience was about 9,500, as large a crowd as could quickly be assembled under the circumstances. We traveled 20,000 miles. Everywhere we were asked the same questions, and we in turn asked the same stickers we had prepared for a baseball quiz that was part of our act.

It was impressive, wherever we went, to find youngsters who knew every detail of baseball history. "How many games did the Deans together win in the 1934 Cardinal pennant-winning year?"

"Forty-nine!" came the answer, quick as a flash. Baseball was one of the things they were coming home to, you could be sure of that.

In Florence, Italy, one night, I had slumped into a chair in the lobby of the broken-down hotel where we were staying. We had been on the go since seven o'clock that morning, up close to the front lines. I was trying to catch my breath before hitting the long trail of stairs that led up to the nook where I was supposed to sleep.

The dirtiest, muddiest human being I have ever laid eyes on, appeared. He shuffled to the desk. He was a young lieutenant. As he turned he saw me. He rubbed his hand over his eyes.

"You're Durocher!" he said softly. "Or I've gone nuts!"

"You're okay," I reassured him. "I'm Durocher!"

He began to babble excitedly. "I live three blocks from Ebbets Field! I see every game there—been twenty-eight days in the foxholes—will you wait right here while I wash up? Don't leave, promise me you won't leave!"

I would have waited a week for that youngster. He was back in ten minutes, and for the next five days he stayed with us wherever we went, until his pass was up. Every moment he was awake, he talked baseball. It was the longest conversation even I had ever had.

Tom Meany, a real wit, quick with the answers, was our master of ceremonies. He introduced Etten and Medwick, who spoke ten or fifteen minutes each. Then I came on. Most of the time they would not let me get off the platform. Sometimes I gabbed and answered questions for at least an hour.

In one place, a G.I. from up a tree hollered to Meany, "How is Mike Smith, the Brooklyn undertaker?"

Smith is a great Dodger fan, and a pal of Charley Dressen's.

"I saw Mike just before I left the States," replied Tom, "and he was fine!"

"Thank you," called the G.I. "He's my uncle."

Etten, a real humorist, wowed the boys when he came out. On the stages of those big Italian opera houses he yodeled "Mi-fa-sol-la-ti-do-oh-oh! How'm I doin', fellas?"

Nick got off the best gag of the trip. We were close to the front lines one night. We were so close we couldn't show the World Series movies, as we usually did, because the Germans had captured this unit's projector—along with the film, *Guadalcanal Diary*—the night before. We were going on with our show, and I was right in the middle of the story that always wows the boys—the one where I tell about a run-in I had with George Magerkurth—when there was a noise that sounded like *gr-rrr-umpppp!* At first I thought it was Mage growling back at me, but I knew he couldn't be there.

I stopped talking and looked at the major in charge.

He said, "Don't worry, Leo. The only time to worry about the Germans being close is when your audience starts to run out on you. Then you follow them."

I said, "Major, you are slightly in error. When the first man leaves this tent, I will be right *in front of him!*"

We were pretty well blacked out that night. The lights became dimmer and dimmer, and the shells seemed to be dropping closer and closer. It became so dark in the tent that when we handed out the autographed balls we gave as prizes on our quiz, the winners seemed like shadows.

On the way back to our quarters, Etten said, "Leo, I didn't want to say anything at the time, but that last guy you handed a ball to was Field Marshal von Kesselring!"

Once, for the benefit of a lot of G.I. Joes, we even ribbed a major general. They loved it, of course—and so did he.

The major general came in as we were about to start our show. All the G.I.'s stood up. When I came on, nobody stood up.

I let out a yell. "What's the matter with me?" I asked indignantly. "Do a couple of stars on your shoulder make that much difference?"

The G.I.'s roared. So did the general. As he laughed, he pulled out a cigar. There was a strict "No Smoking" order in this building, but it did not count for generals. I was right in the middle of my Magerkurth story when the general struck his match.

I said, "And by the way, General, don't go lighting one of those nickel cigars in here!"

It brought down the house.

Later the general said, "That was great stuff, Leo. That's the stuff that makes the boys feel good, gives them something to talk about!"

I worried about getting back for spring training. We went down to the transportation headquarters. They had a backlog of requests from six hundred performers, officers, diplomats, and what not. It looked to me as though we would be Numbers 601, 602, 603, and 604 on the list.

Then the phone rang. The Navy was calling; the admiral wanted us to give a show for his lads at the near-by naval base. They never got any shows, he complained: the Army got everything.

I said it was against the rules. But Medwick and I agreed to go, anyway; we could not find Meany or Etten. We were in no hurry; it seemed as though we weren't going anywhere for a long time.

We talked to the Navy bunch an hour or so, and showed our pictures. The admiral then treated us to the best meal we had ever had over there. He invited us to his club. When the right time came, I popped our troubles. I said we'd be stuck for weeks.

"I can do something about that," he said. "Have your bags in the hotel lobby Friday morning at seven."

We said we couldn't very well leave Etten and Meany behind.

"They're going, too," he nodded. "Don't worry!"

That Friday a full commander flew us to Casablanca in the admiral's own plane. The admiral had cabled ahead to have the United States-bound plane wait for us. We were home quicker than you could make it in peacetime!

But when I got to spring training at Bear Mountain and looked over our club, I grumbled to myself, "Leo, what was your big hurry?"

Chapter 23

THE ELEVATOR STARTS TO GO UP

WHITLOW WYATT'S 1945 "COMEBACK" WAS NEVER GOING TO reach Ebbets Field. Branch offered him a contract under which he'd have to show some results before he'd get big money. Whit held out. Finally we shipped him to the Phillies.

Again the howls arose! Again the fans loudly accused Rickey of wrecking the team. We had to put on the earmuffs and go ahead with our work.

A half-pint youngster named Vic Lombardi came home from the Service, and was signed to a Montreal contract. Vic had never pitched better than Class B ball at Johnstown and Santa Barbara. Branch took a look at his stuff, and declared, "He can win in the majors today. He's got a smooth delivery with three different pitches off the same motion. He reminds me of Willie Sherdel."

In the infield, we were also in trouble. We figured Brown could go in at short, but he made so many mistakes we knew he'd need another year in the minors. At last Branch begged me to get into shape. He told the newspapermen he'd give me $1,000 to play the first fifteen games.

I tried it. But after the first two games I played, I offered Rickey $2,000 to call off the deal!

Bill Hart, who had been so upset when I criticized his short-stopping the year before, would play third this season. Stanky seemed best at second base. He had played some short in 1944, but his arm was not strong enough to make plays from the hole, nor could he cover enough ground.

But we did not have too wide a choice. On March 15, we had only fifteen ballplayers in uniform at Bear Mountain; even some of those were not really ballplayers, just guys wearing uniforms. This against the forty who had formerly made up our squad!

One day Rickey had a phone call from Joe Bostic, a Negro sports writer, and Nat Low, sports editor of the Communist *Daily Worker*. They proposed to bring him two red-hot ballplayers, both Negroes.

They did not ask permission to bring them up to try out; they just told Rickey they were coming. I got a chuckle out of that, and sat back to see Branch handle them.

The two promoters came up with their "prospects" trailing behind them reluctantly. All day Rickey either forgot them or purposely let them cool their heels. He went about his business of appraising pitchers, and looking over young players.

"We do things up here by appointment," he told Bostic and Low. "It's the same for everybody. Do you want more privileges for these Negro boys than the white boys get?"

Bostic and Low had hoped to put Rickey on the spot, of course. As they were about to blast him for "ignoring" their men, Branch asked suavely, "When would you like me to look at them?"

They made a date. Rickey spent an hour and a half "looking" at the two players, Showboat Thomas and Terris McDuffie. At the end of the test he knew more about Showboat, who was a first baseman, and Terris, who was a pitcher, than they knew about themselves. Throughout the routine he spouted comments to Jane Ann Jones, his secretary. When the document was typed it looked as imposing as the Declaration of Independence, it was that long.

Meanwhile Bostic told Rickey off. "These two boys can put Brooklyn in the first division. With that bunch of clowns out there"—he waved at the youngsters who were to help us win the pennant a few years later—"you'll finish last."

"Indeed!" said Rickey. "That's an interesting observation!" Finally he gave copies of his comments to the press. He criticized the two players kindly and with real consideration. I

made it short and loud. In my opinion, Thomas, the first baseman, couldn't hit a curve ball with a paddle, and McDuffie,
the pitcher, was nearer forty than thirty, and could hardly be
considered a "prospect."

"Old Coonskin" Davis was back. So was Frenchy Bordagaray, whom we had resolved to move to the outfield for 1945.

During the off season, Davis had turned quite gray, and the
boys kidded him.

"But remember," he retorted, "while I was pitching I had
to watch Bordagaray playing third last year!"

We had a new left-hander from the Coast named Tom Seats.
Rickey had owned Seats in the Cardinal chain; at that time
Tom had been a pitcher with no control. But in the Pacific
Coast League, in 1944, he had walked only a handful of men.
He held a war job and pitched between shifts. He had won
twenty-five games; we gave him another look.

We were expecting big things from Gregg, who had won
nine and lost sixteen after his great start the year before: Rex
Barney had been called into the Service.

I thought Les Webber would help us, too, but Rickey never
liked him because, as he said, he was a "back-door" pitcher.
"He's always coming up from behind, pitching at two balls,
no strikes, or three and one," explained Branch. "He just hasn't
got enough stuff to get by that way. They'll be laying for that
'cripple' he has to put in there, and they'll kill him. I can't
understand why he doesn't start off with a strike, and get
ahead of the hitter. Why does he pitch strikes only when he's
behind the hitter?"

Eventually, Webber went down to Montreal. Pitching in the
International League, where he could get the first or second
pitch over for a strike without worrying too much that it
would go flying over the wall, he was almost unbeatable. I
think he won his first nine games, and returned to us before
the season was over.

At this time the sports pages crackled with news that was a sign of things to come. Rickey, with Walter O'Malley and Andrew Schmitz as his partners, had acquired 25 per cent of the club stock. O'Malley was a well-known Brooklyn lawyer who had done the legal work for the club. Schmitz was in insurance.

That left 25 per cent of the stock in the hands of the Mulveys, and 50 per cent with the Brooklyn Trust Company, as trustees for the Ebbets heirs. During 1945, Rickey, O'Malley, Schmitz, and John L. Smith, head man of Pfizer and Company, the chemists, made a bid for the Ebbets half. Surrogate McGarey shelved this bid temporarily.

The club must have looked attractive, because everybody tried to buy in. The Army nine beat us; Branca was the loser.

Dixie Walker still held out, and that was no help. At last Dixie made a great play. He announced from down in Alabama, where, his story went, he was painting his house, that he would take the $21,000 salary he was demanding in war bonds instead of cash.

It took no rapid calculations to get Rickey to agree—because $21,000 in war bonds—maturity value—was only $15,750 cash.

Someone must have coached Dixie, for he quickly corrected the figures. He meant, he said, $21,000 in *cash* value.

Offering to take his pay in bonds was a smart move. Because he always used his head to think up unusual notions, Dixie was a favorite with the fans.

A writer once asked Walker how come he got to be the "Peepul's Cherse." Dixie ascribed his success to a three-point program which he had followed since he had joined the club. First, he answered every question the fans shouted to him when he was playing the outfield. Second, when they rode him, he dropped his head and made no reply; when they applauded, he tipped his hat. Third, he was generous with autographs.

I could not spend time figuring angles the way Dixie did; I had other things to do. After our drill sessions, I hopped into my car and raced down the Hudson shore to a rehearsal for a radio show. I appeared with Milton Berle, with Fred Allen, and with Ed Gardner in "Duffy's Tavern."

Rickey worked long and hard trying to bring our club along. He gave blackboard lectures in the cafeteria of the Inn at night, drawing on his vast store of baseball knowledge. Those were terrific talks. The older players marveled at Branch's range of information, and the thoroughness with which he covered every aspect of the game, from the break a base runner must get to steal, to the moves a pitcher has to make to hold a man close on base.

Once in awhile Rickey would ask about me. Too often, I was gone.

One night, when he heard I had left for a radio rehearsal, he popped off to the writers. "That boy," he said, "will have to make an election of professions."

When I heard that, it brought me back to Bear Mountain in a hurry. I had been so anxious to pick up that easy cash on the radio: First it had been $500 an appearance, but now I received more than $1,000 a show. Temporarily, I had lost sight of the fact that it was my work with the Dodgers that had made me "somebody."

Quickly I called off the rest of my radio work. My agent, Mark Hanna, would book me when we were in the city, and only when Rickey approved.

Strangely enough, once I decided to quit radio and settle down to managing, I got ten times as many offers as I had had before. The publicity did it, also the hoopla kicked up when Rickey declared I must make an "election of professions."

"The election is over," I assured Rickey, "and, Boss, I voted for you over Milton Berle."

The Army ball club had almost as many good players as our draft-shot team. The year before, I had raved about Josey, their shortstop. Eddie Murphy wrote, "With the Services taking all the Dodger players, Durocher thinks he can turn things around and steal one from the Army!"

Now, the lad who looked especially good against us was Glenn Davis, who later became a football star. He had had no spring training to speak of, for he had been out with the track team, but one afternoon he spit on his hands, picked up a bat, and whacked four hits against us. How that boy can run!

Mike Sandlock came to us from a war job. We had formerly taken Mike from the Braves in a deal; now he won out over Brown for shortstop, and the latter was sent to St. Paul.

I began the season at second base. My Charley horse let me last a game and a half. Then Eddie Stanky took over.

Eddie developed a new technique in leading off. He perfected a hunched-up stance that seemed to make him hard to pitch to, and he talked back to the pitchers, and got them mad. As a result, he got a lot of bases on balls. He later became a first-class pest. Murphy, in the *Sun*, christened him "The Brat." Eddie lived up to the name.

Stanky delighted Rickey, who paid little attention to the statistics which the fans and the experts usually feed on. For instance, Branch always scoffed at "runs-batted-in" as a useless column. "The player's position in the batting order alters his chance to drive in runs," he insisted. "And the men up ahead of him, by getting on continually, earn more of the honors than he does by driving them in." So, for the first time the guy reaching base was getting notice, too.

There was no doubt that Stanky was getting there. He was dropping his bat on the catcher's toes, making pitchers so mad they "aimed" the ball and still missed the plate. Managers ranted and raved, and commanded their pitchers, under threat of fine, to get the ball over to the little pest. But Eddie hunched himself into a heap at the plate, glared at the pitcher, fouled off the good pitches, and "took" balls that were a fraction off the plate, or high, or low.

Rickey raved about his aggressive little second baseman.

Stanky was to set a new National League record with 148 bases on balls in 1945. However, Dixie Walker's admirers regarded it all as a plot to discredit their idol. For Walker kept driving Stanky across so frequently that Dixie led the league with 124 runs batted in. It was the first time Dixie had been near 100 in this department. Instead of praising Dixie, Rickey raved about the guy who was getting by with hardly a swing of his bat!

We started slowly. We won five and lost five in April. Our old pal Mungo turned up as the Giants' great pitching hope. One day, when it seemed Mungo had us beaten at the Polo Grounds, Goody Rosen belted a hit with three on in the ninth to win the game and return us to normalcy. Somehow Mungo was always on the verge of being a good pitcher, but he never made it.

He hadn't changed. Neither did Wyatt, who didn't have a thing when the Phillies unveiled him against us. The Phils got five in the first off Ben Chapman, but we made seven off Wyatt and beat their ears off. That was a hooperdo of a series: twenty-five errors in four games!

We had a St. Paul pitcher named Otho Nitcholas, who looked distinguished with his white mane, and lent dignity to the club, but he had no fast ball. The teams facing us did not respect his gray hairs enough to strike out.

I had another pitcher who could throw strike after strike in batting practice, but could not come close to the plate in a game. In fact, he became so nervous and so wild he even missed the catcher.

I pondered how could I make this pussycat, who didn't like pressure on the mound, into a lion? I tried something that Rickey might have fired me for had he caught me. Before he warmed up I gave my nervous pitcher a big shot of brandy.

The transformation was amazing. "Gimme that ball, Skipper," he said. "I'll go out there and beat their ears off."

He did, too. As a matter of fact, he shut the Cardinals out that time.

The St. Louis club, which had lost Musial, Litwhiler, and Walker Cooper, did not look so hot. The Giants were leading the league, but none of us thought they could stay up there.

Olmo was hot and got hits in thirteen straight games. Walker and Rosen belted the ball, too, so hard that I had to put Galan at first base to keep him in the game.

We ripped off eleven straight wins, the longest winning streak the club had had since 1924, and all Brooklyn asked two questions:

(1) Can the Dodgers keep it up?

(2) When will the Japs be beaten to their knees?

We got all the breaks. In that eleven-game streak, we had won eight in a row, and trailed in the ninth game, when a storm came up and washed us out.

Voiselle had us on the run in a night game at the Polo Grounds. The score was 2–1, Schultz was on first, with two out, and there were two strikes on Sukeforth. Voiselle threw over to first, trying to catch Schultz off, and hit him on the head. The ball bounced to the stands. Schultz went to second. Voiselle then walked Sukeforth. Hart drew a pass as Voiselle blew up. Then Chapman, pinch hitting, blooped a hit just over the second baseman, and in front of Mel Ott. Two runs came in, and we won that game, 3–2.

Goody Rosen had been a fine investment. He was hitting .355, but Rickey complained that we would never win a pennant with an outfield full of Rosens. "Watch how he times the ball. He just reaches there as it drops into his glove. The good outfielders run as fast as they can, and get there with time to spare, so a gust of wind can't beat them out of the play, even if they don't figure it in advance. Rosen is a 'timing' outfielder. Some day he will lose a big game for you that way. And, Leo, he does not run hard when he hits the ball. He gapes at it, to see where it is going to fall. He loses a lot of two-base hits that way. He's still standing between the plate and first, when he should be rounding the sack and tearing on toward second. He often gets thrown out at second base because he doesn't get away from the plate fast enough."

I learned more Rickey baseball every day. I checked up on what Branch said about Rosen and every word was true.

At a Saturday night game on June 11, I had a run-in with a particularly noisy fan named John Christian. It seemed unimportant, but the story was messy in the papers because Christian happened to be a veteran.

During that trying period Rickey tried to take some of the heat off me. He told the writers he wanted his players to be "ferocious gentlemen," and that the club had erred in not providing the players with protection from obnoxious "riding" by a certain few in the stands.

The "ferocious gentlemen" handle stuck. Asked to define one, Rickey declared, "I mean by that a player of the Pepper Martin stripe, who will break both your legs if you happen to be standing in his path to second base. But after he breaks your legs, he will politely pick you up and dust you off—and then break them again, if you stand there the next time he comes your way."

We ripped off one seven-game streak and then another. Late in June, we led the league by three and one-half games. Of our thirty-six victories, twenty-five had been racked up on streaks of eleven, seven, and seven. Truly, we were a "streak" ball club.

How different the club was from the previous year's dismal outfit. The extra punch came from Stanky, and Olmo and Gregg. The latter, who had not won ten all during 1944, was gunning for his tenth win by mid-June.

Meanwhile, the Cubs, who were to gallop through to the flag, were in the second division in June. They worried no one but Charley Grimm, their manager.

Suddenly, who should appear back on the Brooklyn scene but Kirby Higbe. We thought he had served his hitch in the war under Generals Patton, Hodges, and Patch, at Cologne, in the Ruhr, and at the mop-up of Berchtesgaden.

"I closed out that war over in Europe," said Hig, with a grin. "Now they're sending me into the Pacific to finish those Japs!"

It was curious that Higbe, who had gone into the Army with no inhibitions, had become thoroughly regimented. However, when a general asked him if he would pitch for a camp team when he first went in, Kirby said: "Okay, buddy, give me the ball." The other G.I.'s almost passed out when they heard him address the general so familiarly.

I have never encountered a spirit so blithe or carefree as Higbe's. A pretty nurse wrote him from overseas after the war, and the letter fell into the hands of Anne, his own lovely wife.

"Omigosh," I said. "What did you tell Anne?"

"Oh, I just told her it wasn't written to me," he grinned. "I told her it must have been meant for some other Kirby Higbe!"

How we would have liked to keep Higbe! But he went his way, into the Pacific Theater, and we rattled along.

Ed Basinski could make the double play, but none of us thought he could really play the fiddle. He talked a good concert. He said he was a classical player and claimed he practiced in private. I made up my mind to find out. I bet him a one-hundred-dollar suit of clothes he couldn't give a "concert" in the clubhouse.

The first day he brought the fiddle, we lost a tough game and he didn't play. The next day he gave out with the long-hair stuff. Eddie wasn't kidding, because he could really play classical music. When he was with the Pirates, and later, he played off-season violin with the Buffalo Symphony Orchestra. We sat there greatly impressed, as Eddie poured his soul out in music.

As he was about halfway through, Frenchy Bordagaray cried: "Gimme that thing, I'll really show you how to fiddle!"

Amazed, Basinski handed over the violin and Frenchy broke out with "Turkey in the Straw!" and all the boys started to jig. When the jig was over I conceded the bet and agreed to buy Basinski his suit.

Speaking of jigs, the jig was up with our club, too, although we didn't know it yet.

Chapter 24

FIRED AGAIN–ALMOST

Perhaps a trip we took to Cherry Point, North Carolina, early in July, set the pattern for our nose dive. Certainly, the whole club almost dropped out of the sky that night after we had played an exhibition game with the Marines.

We took off from Cherry Point and headed home in two Navy transport planes—the type with bucket seats. Over Washington and Philadelphia we ran into terrific storms and were tossed about like corks in a washing machine. The radio in our plane went out of commission, and we could not communicate with either the other plane or with the ground. Besides, no flight plan had apparently been sent through to Floyd Bennett Field, where we were supposed to land, and nobody knew where we were.

At one point, our plane dropped several hundred feet, and I found myself on the ceiling, looking down. What I saw was not a happy sight. Everyone was sick. Eventually, we landed in Norfolk, Virginia.

Meanwhile, the players in the other plane, with Harold Parrott, had been forced back to Cherry Point. Roscoe McGowen of the *Times*, who was also on the plane, did not know they had turned around. When he stepped out at the airport, he asked a mechanic for the Flatbush Avenue bus. Since Roscoe was in North Carolina at the moment, the man thought he was nuts.

Back home, Branch Rickey was nearly distracted. Where were his two plane loads of Dodgers?

Meanwhile we took off from Norfolk in a new plane. This time, the motor began to spout oil, and we had to turn back.

Parrott, stranded with the other half of the team in Cherry

Point, finally reached the boss on the phone. Time was growing short. The Dodgers were due to play that night at Ebbets Field.

"The Captain here at Cherry Point is all upset about this mix-up," Parrott told Rickey. "He says it wouldn't happen again in the next hundred times we made the trip!"

"Next hundred times!" thundered Rickey. "Harold, this is the LAST time!"

We all landed in Brooklyn in late afternoon. We were shaky, and several of the boys were green for a week.

That night we played the Reds, the visitors on this occasion, like the married men's team at a church picnic. They beat us. So did almost everybody else during that month of July. We ended up with a record of fourteen won, fifteen lost.

Meanwhile, the Cubs, who had been in fourth place at the end of June—we had led the league at that time, two and a half games in front of the Cardinals—went on a terrific winning spurt. In July, they won twenty-six and lost five. They jumped into first place, we dropped to third. Pitching did it for Chicago; the steady hurling of Derringer, Passeau, Wyse, and Prim, with spot work by Erickson.

I had been moaning for a left-handed pinch hitter. Branch got me one in Babe Herman, who could still swing that bat. When we made the first attempt to get him, we thought we had a great chance to win the pennant. That was in July, before the bottom dropped out of our plane ride, our stomachs, and our pennant bid.

I had heard so much about the Babe as a Dodger that it was really a thrill to see him in action again. He had played with Brooklyn last in 1931, the windup year of Uncle Robbie's eighteen years as manager; he had hit .393 in 1930. He was traded to the Reds, for whom I was then playing shortstop, in the spring of 1931.

I used him almost as soon as he appeared in Brooklyn. He was in good shape. He had played with Hollywood in the

Coast League the past six seasons and seemed always to have a bat in his hands. The first clutch that came up gave me a chance to put him in. At once he pulled a ball to right field for a clean base hit. Then, running like mad, he tripped over first base and fell flat on his face, while thirty thousand fans roared. It was just like the Herman of old. He came up with not one Charley horse in his legs, but two!

The Babe did all right at the plate, and he didn't hurt us at the gate, either. In our first forty-five games at home, we drew 711,000 people, topping our entire 1944 attendance by 100,000!

During August we continued to go sour. Olmo was a flop at third. I rode him hard because he did not like to be pitched tight, and the pitchers, discovering that, knocked him down again and again, and sidearmed him to death. When his hitting fell off, he lost his hustle in the field, and I really went after him.

Instead of trying harder, the Puerto Rican folded up. I pitched batting practice. Although my fast ball wouldn't dent a cream puff, he went white and backed up when I sidearmed him like the pitchers did in a regular game. He moaned that I was "showing him up."

We had scheduled an exhibition game up at Kingston to try out a few more youngsters. But I was fed up with seeing kids make mistakes and blow ball games. I decided, on the quiet, to skip the game.

It didn't stay "on the quiet" very long. Unexpectedly, Rickey showed up at Kingston and found Dressen running the team. The next morning Rickey was still hopping mad. He told Dressen to take charge of the team "until further notice."

As Rickey rode back to Brooklyn with Harold Parrott at the wheel, my fate hung in the balance. Branch Rickey, Jr., was in the front seat. Mrs. Rickey was in the back with her husband.

"Durocher has no interest in what we're trying to do here in Brooklyn!" B.R. stormed. "Here we are, trying to find players so we can win a pennant, and he won't even look them over! I'm through with him!"

"Now, Branch," said Mrs. Rickey, "don't say things you don't mean!"

"I do mean it!" he thundered. "Branch, Harold, do you think Dressen can do the job for us?"

"Remember," offered Parrott, "it's a tough time to fire Leo. The writers and the fans are going to say you waited until you stuck him with a bad club, and then bounced him. They'll say you fired Wyatt and Camilli and the rest just to make Leo vulnerable."

"I don't care!" Rickey retorted. "What's right is right. If it's the right thing to do, I'll take the criticism—"

"Why talk about firing Durocher," put in Branch, Jr. "You know you're not going to do it, Dad."

"What do you mean, I'm not going to do it? Don't you think I'm mad enough to do it, Son?"

"You'll never do it," insisted Junior. "Because then you'd have to admit defeat. You know Leo is your favorite reclamation project!"

"Harrrrumph!" was about all the boss replied, as he bit through his cigar.

The next day when he came in to see me he didn't say much. I was dressing for the game.

Before I had arrived, Dressen didn't know what to do. Was he the manager, or not? Then, just as Charley called a clubhouse meeting, I blew in and took over.

Now, I sat on the step, rolling my uniform stockings. "Where were you yesterday, Leo?" Rickey asked, leaning over me.

"I went to the race track, Branch," I answered, without batting an eye.

If I had hit him with a club, I don't think he could have reacted worse. "Ju-das Priest!" he thundered.

He put both hands on his Homburg and yanked it down

over his ears, like a man going out in a blizzard. Without another word, he stomped out of the room. He couldn't bring
himself to talk to me again for three days.

As I look back on it, that was the closest I ever came to
being fired by Branch Rickey. He suspected where I had gone.
If I had told him anything but the truth, I think I would have
been bounced for sure.

I got out of that scrape alive. On the Western trip which
was coming up, we were very nearly killed—literally and
figuratively.

In Pittsburgh I ran into triple trouble. On September 6, Umpire Dunn kicked me out of the game, the Pirates beat us,
17–5, and the King's County Grand Jury held me for feloni-
ous assault in the Christian case. I was later acquitted, but for
the time things looked awfully bad.

They became worse. After our Pittsburgh and Cincinnati
stops, we dropped ten and one-half games behind. Gregg, trying for his sixteenth victory, lost six straight. Branca was wild,
and unlucky, too. In Cincinnati he pitched a dandy, fanning
ten men, but Olmo, failing to chase a foul fly, gave the Reds
two runs. They hung on then and beat us.

As we moved into St. Louis, the smarties were betting that
the Cardinals, only a game and a half back of the Cubs, would
again sneak in to snatch the pennant. A lot depended on these
three games.

They beat us in the first game. The second day it rained
and the third day it poured. Sam Breadon, however, wanted
to play those two games, at any cost. They were to cost him
plenty.

With the war emergency still crippling transportation, we
were anxious to have the games called off. We could get to
Chicago on the evening train and sleep in our hotel that night.
If we played the Cardinals in the rain and mud, we would get
away so late we would have to sit up all night riding to Chicago; no Pullmans were available.

There was another important angle. In addition to the regular game scheduled, we had an incomplete game to finish in Chicago the next afternoon. If Breadon called off our games with the Cards, we would have Gregg and Lombardi, our two best pitchers, ready to fire at the Cubs.

Breadon chose to make us stay and play that twi-night double-header in a cold drizzle. By making that decision he chose to face our two best pitchers—and also to send us in the next day against the league-leading Cubs tired out after an all-night sit-up ride.

We were mad as hornets when we took the field. I pointed out to the players that we had a chance to make St. Louis pay for mistreating us.

Lombardi pitched well, and Gregg shut the door in the Cardinals' faces. We beat them twice, and that certainly made a difference. For, although the Cardinals later caught up within one game of the Cubs they never did overhaul them. Those two defeats we administered were the margin.

The Cardinal players did not really want to play that rain-soaked double bill any more than we did. They figured they would have to sweep the two games to do themselves any good, and they didn't think they could make it, what with the rain, and our two best pitchers facing them, and a team as mad as we were. After the game, Red Barrett, whom we had belted out of the box, practically cried in our clubhouse. That night we broke the Cardinals. Before dawn, we were almost broken ourselves.

We were lucky to get a chair car to Chicago. It was nearly midnight when the train pulled out. Most of the boys passed up the chairs to stretch their weary bodies on the floor. All night we pitched and swayed in the darkened car; only a few hardy ones sat up and played gin rummy.

Dawn was just breaking. I was dozing in my chair.

Suddenly the whole train shook. It shuddered, hesitated as if it were going off the track, and rolled on, with a sickening, bumping glide. I jumped up. Everything was confusion. It made your heart jump and bounce inside you. The windows on both sides were solid walls of flame. You could hear the hissing and crackling of the fire and the night was as alive as Hell must be when they're stoking the furnace.

The boys who had been asleep in the aisles scrambled to their feet, and blindly started to stampede to the vestibule.

I had not been sleeping as soundly as the others; maybe that was why I reacted more quickly. "Stop! You're going the wrong way!" I shouted.

The rear of our car, which had the observation platform, was the safest way out.

We seemed to have run through the fire. At least the big, roaring flames were gone at our car. As the train came to a jolting stop, we tumbled to the ground. The car had nearly become a tomb for all of us. Every window was cracked or busted from the heat. As we flung ourselves into the air, the cloying, nauseating smell of burning flesh engulfed us.

You couldn't tell what was going on. The night was torn by the light of the fires, by frightened cries and heartbreaking moans. Half a mile behind us down the track was the burning town of Manhattan, Illinois. Ahead, on the front of the blackened locomotive in whose cab lay the charred body of the engineer, was the shell of a gasoline truck. That truck had started the whole tragedy. Like a dry cocoon the train had split it open at a grade crossing. The impact had caused thousands of gallons of high octane fuel, bursting into flame, to spray back over the speeding train. Had the train been derailed, we would all have been broiled. Fortunately, the wheels had rolled through the fire area, though the engineer was dead and no one was at the controls.

A pitifully weak voice reached us. "Help me, help me!"

On the off side of the train we found the fireman in the ditch where he had jumped. His clothes were singed. Big patches of his skin had blistered from the heat, torn, and shrunken away.

He sat there in the early-morning chill, a horrible wreck of a figure. "Doc" Wendler, our trainer, did what he could to ease his terrible pain. Even to have a finger laid on him was torture; he was just a mass of seared wounds. It was especially touching that the poor victim's only thought was for his pal, the dead engineer.

Wendler and Art Herring, the pitcher, finally helped him walk down the track to an ambulance. They would have carried him, but his back and sides were in unbelievable agony. I'll never forget the sight, for that man—George Ebert—walked back down the track to his death. His burns were too severe to allow him even a thin chance to live.

A few weeks later we had a letter from his widow. She thanked all the players for having made her husband as comfortable as possible in his dying moments. We wiped the tears from our eyes as we read it. Honestly, those lines will remain in my mind longer than anything else I've ever read.

Three men—the truckdriver died later—were killed in that wreck. By the time they got the crumpled locomotive off the track and pulled us in to Chicago we were almost dead ourselves.

The next day we played as badly as we had the night after our harrowing airplane adventure coming home from Cherry Point. Not counting the incomplete game, we lost three in Chicago. The Cubs, who had set a new National League record by sweeping eighteen double-headers that year, rolled ahead.

We finished third. Some of the baseball experts said it was my finest accomplishment, that to have driven this patched-up, mixed-up team, with its jumble of sagging veterans and too-eager kids, as high as we did, was a record by itself.

As I sum it up, Walker was the one who had the really surprising year. He won the run-driving leadership with 124, bringing in more than Camilli ever had, and coming close to the 130 record held by both Babe Herman (1930) and Jack

Fournier (1924). However, these men had all been recognized home-run hitters, and Dixie was not. But he was a tough man to fool when the ducks were on the pond, as the ballplayers say.

Galan had a good year, too. Clyde King, the kid collegian, had a remarkable relief record in the first half of the season, although he later lost his touch. The seven wins that Art Herring hung up after reporting in June were also important.

But, at least, the elevator was on the way up. During the banquet season, Eddie Dyer, the Cardinal manager, even named Brooklyn, rather than the champion Cubs, as "the team to beat in 1946."

After talking to me like an angry father, Rickey signed me again. He had not forgotten that Kingston episode. Still Branch, Junior, was right. Though I might have deserved it, his Dad could not bring himself to fire me.

So things looked bright for 1946. The most unusual prospect in the picture was Jackie Robinson.

Chapter 25

1946—YEAR OF PROMISE

ALWAYS SENSITIVE TO THE PULSE OF THE NATION IN SPORTS, Rickey had seen the "color line" begin to waver. Times were changing. A war had been fought to bring more, rather than less, freedom to the world. Sports call for sportsmanship, and a lot of folks who wouldn't have lifted a finger to change things were not too happy about "restrictions" against this group or that one. A player is as good as his performance, not as his religion, his color, or what he prefers for breakfast. Rickey wasn't planning a crusade. His interest was in keeping baseball the top American game. There was a situation here that lent itself to his purpose of building a better ball club. Maybe he *couldn't* help thinking in terms of fairness, but he did not start out with any grand notions of becoming a great emancipator.

"Leo," he said to me, "it is my great ambition to win a pennant for Brooklyn. I aim to use anybody who can help me do it, be he white, green, blue, or black. The Cardinals have several years' start on us in material and experience, so we must employ unusual methods to overtake them faster than we might ordinarily have to do."

"Unusual methods" is right. Rickey knew there was an untapped supply of talent in Negro baseball. For several years he had spent thousands of dollars scouting it in this country and outside. If he could find the man or men he needed, he would use him or them.

The job called for unusual scouting. Each player had to be looked over for muscular talents—running, hitting, and throwing. Moreover, he had to be scouted for his personal traits—

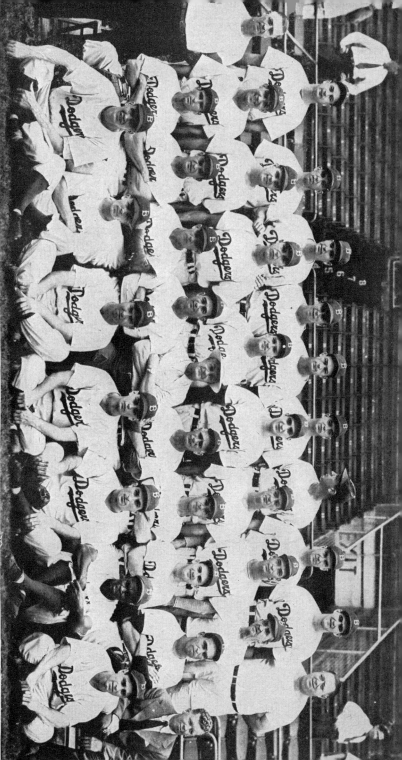

The 1947 pennant-winning Brooklyn Dodgers.

International News Photos

Incident of 1947 Series. Umpire Goetz (left) holds back Eddie Stanky as Edwards (10), Reese (1), and Suke-forth (15), argue with Umpire Rommel.

One of the great plays of baseball history. Al Gionfriddo nabs Joe DiMaggio's 415-foot drive in 1947 World Series Game.

strength of character and ability to withstand the bitter wave of prejudice which would seek to engulf him.

When Rickey was ready, he declared himself. Naturally he got the full weight of criticism. . . . Much of his mail, revolting in its contents, came unsigned.

Baseball men hammered at him openly and behind his back. Even within his family there was opposition when he announced that he would bring the first promising Negro to a place from which he could move into a major-league position.

Mrs. Rickey pleaded with him on another score. "Branch," she said, "you've fought and battled all your life. You're at the point now where you should be getting a little ease and comfort, instead of getting everybody mad at you again."

A man on the Montreal club asked Rickey, sincerely, "You don't really think Negroes are human like the rest of us, do you?" I think that guy has a few things to learn.

The complete story would take a book. There was the big-league magnate who pompously told his colleagues that by bringing in a Negro Rickey would jeopardize their investments. He prophesied that attendance would fall off, as white people would shun the parks. There were plenty of private sessions; naturally, for this was unprecedented. As time passed more and more came out. . . . All I want to do is to pause for a quick snicker at those false prophets and their muddied crystal balls.

Jackie Robinson's appearance helped to set attendance records at Montreal and at Brooklyn, and every club in the National League made money on him in 1947. If Robinson had flunked out, little more would have been said. But he proved to be a crackerjack player, and the fans like to see top performance, whether it's in baseball, track, or boxing.

All the comment was not bitter, of course. Several of the New York writers who had hit hardest at Rickey now lined up with him. In their February show the baseball writers kidded him good-naturedly about the Robinson experiment.

They had a "Glory, Glory, Massa Rickey" number, which ran:

> Mine eyes have seen the glory
> And the opportunity
> In the racial situation
> And the fact that men are free.
>
> It invited ostracism
> And severe impunity
> But Rickey marched right on.
>
> Glory, glory, Massa Rickey, Glory, glory, etc. . . .

Certain towns in Florida acted as though Robinson were a typhoid carrier instead of the fine athlete and gentleman that he is. Several times the Montreal club found the ball park padlocked and the games called off—without explanation. That is to the discredit of those towns. Nobody else.

Besides Robinson, Rickey had other problems. Jorge Pasquel, a Mexican with a bank roll big enough to choke a horse, began to make menacing gestures toward the structure of organized American baseball. He not only threatened to lure some of the stars south of the border, he actually got a few. One of the first to listen to his wiles was Olmo. Luis had seen too many beanballs in the National League, and besides he could talk Pasquel's language.

Branch figured that Luis would not leave before meeting some club official to talk it over. The Brooklyn club, having spent a large sum correcting an ailment which had troubled Olmo, had a sizable investment in the Puerto Rican at the end of the 1945 season. Furthermore, his running speed and power fitted in with Rickey's ideas for the rebuilding of the club.

Nevertheless, Olmo jumped in mid-February. He was reported to have made a deal for $40,000 for three years. We chalked that off as a loss; Olmo had hit .313, with ten home runs, the year before.

The next to go was Mickey Owen. He confessed that he

had not been tempted, but had opened negotiations with Pasquel himself. In the Tamale circuit in Mexico, however, Mickey
lost heart. He called Rickey, and was told to come back.

Branch, however, told Mickey and the newspapermen that
he would trade him, because he had "thrown over" his team.
"I'll give you the $20,000 you want," said Rickey, "but you'll
never play for me again."

Hearing this, Mickey plunged back into the Mexican loop
up to his neck. He was soon to be sorry.

Despite the Robinson and Mexican problems, Rickey
pushed ahead with his plans for restocking the Dodgers.
Reese and Reiser were back, and Lavagetto checked in. But
the real "finds" were among the hundreds—yes, hundreds—
of boys who had played in the minor leagues, in the Brooklyn
farm system, before the war. Some, like Henry Behrman, who
had never pitched higher than Class B before the war, had a
chance to play ball on Army teams all over the world. Little
known outside of Glendale, Long Island, where he had
pitched for the local Tigers, Behrman had come up fast. He
hurled thirty-six games for his regimental team in Germany.

Other boys never had a chance to swing a bat during the
tough war years. But they were bigger and stronger, and had
improved athletically, even though they had not played. Dick
Whitman, injured in the Ardennes offensive, was a case in
point. He made our ball club, although he hadn't been in the
game for four years.

Our problem was to appraise this new horde of boys, and
properly classify them. Obviously we couldn't look them all
over in the Dodgers' spring camp.

Rickey conceived the idea of a gigantic "clearinghouse"
training base in the celery belt of Florida, at Sanford. It
opened before the big club began to train. Many a long day
I spent there looking at kids I had never seen before.

Out of that welter of talent, which assembled in one big
rambling hotel as at a prep school, I got four boys who had

never played in the majors before. All four, Whitman and Furillo, outfielders; Behrman, pitcher; and Ferrell Anderson, a colossus-like catcher, made the Dodgers. They helped us stage one of the most spectacular finishes in National League history—that breathless finale that locked us for the first time in baseball history in a tie with the Cardinals.

Testing those youngsters was no small task. One long day I saw about eight ball games between picked teams. We were dog-tired. In the last game one team was getting its ears knocked off. A relief pitcher came in. Nobody paid much attention to him until he began to throw. Then everyone sat up: he was just so much faster than the rest who had pitched that you couldn't help noticing him. Behrman really had that extra something.

Furillo first attracted attention with his throwing arm. Today, I would say, it is probably the outstanding arm in baseball. His throws came in low, but with unusual accuracy and rifle-like speed.

I asked Rickey where he had got Furillo.

"We bought a franchise in Reading, Pennsylvania," chuckled Branch. "My son paid five or six thousand dollars for it and sometimes wondered if he had been stung. He got Furillo, two others who are now in our minor-league system, two sets of uniforms, and a bus. Also a tip on a ballplayer Reading had owned and released. We quickly got after him and signed him. His name is Hermanski."

All the good boys did not show up immediately in the brief month at Sanford. The "clearinghouse" was designed to let them play into better shape and to teach them the fine points, as well as to get them rated. Some had been through tougher hitches in the war than others. Furillo, for one, had been on practically every island in the Pacific.

One prospect who did not look too good at the time was a catcher named Bruce Edwards. He was sent to Montreal, which, in turn, farmed him out to Mobile. But how that boy was to rise and shine before 1946 was over!

Meanwhile, other events were shaping up. John L. Smith, with Walter O'Malley and Rickey, now owned 75 per cent of the club, their deal finally having gone through. Smith, the genius who pushed the development of penicillin, was the bank-roll man in the deal. He now undertook the improvement of Ebbets Field. Before the season opened, a total of $425,000 was to be spent for new seating arrangements, rest rooms, and general repairs.

As usual, with the Dodgers, there was plenty of excitement. Reiser held out. Then Branca held out, although in 1945 he had won only five games and lost six. Then the Pasquels sent an agent, one Señor Jaimes, right into our club's Daytona Beach lair to tempt more Dodgers.

Rickey caught this spy on the job, and there was a terrific clash. Babe Hamberger hovered in the background in case real trouble developed, but it takes two to make a rhubarb, and the Señor moved out of range as quickly as he could.

"I am an old man!" Rickey thundered. "But I'll take you outside this baseball park and—" Hamberger, talking about it later, said in awe, "I had often heard MacPhail talk like that. But I didn't dream Mr. Rickey knew all those cusswords."

The Mexicans were not through. They tempted Reiser later on, and also Stan Rojek. Then, with the make-up of our club worrying me, another thing happened— It seemed a very small incident, but how it snowballed!

We went to Miami to play an exhibition game. As far as our secretary, Harold Parrott, and I knew, everything was going smoothly. However, when the hotel bills came in later that month, an item alongside Billy Herman's name stopped us. It read: "Extras, $30.00."

Parrott asked Billy. Herman claimed he knew nothing

about it. So Parrott wrote the hotel, refusing to pay for that item.

The hotel addressed Rickey directly, and gave the details. They revealed that it had taken thirty dollars to "repair" the damages to the room occupied by William Herman and another player.

Rickey could not forgive that. If there is one thing he is strict about, it is that the ball club be well-mannered and keep training rules. For the moment he kept his peace: time, as always, was his ally.

All spring we used Jack Graham at first base. The big fellow, who had played in the Dodger farm system before the war, had tremendous power, but he did not hit frequently enough. In the field he had a good enough arm, and he could run fairly well. But he did not diagnose plays quickly, and his reflexes seemed to tag after him.

Branch looked at him longingly. He declared, "All the parts are there, Leo, just like for some powerful tractor. But what good are all the parts when you can't get them assembled?"

Graham never pulled himself together, and was marked to go. So was Goody Rosen. He had hit .325 for us the year before, but he wasn't getting any younger, nor any better. We were committed to the youth movement. At the eleventh hour, Dick Whitman and Carl Furillo were brought up to the parent club to join our other juvenile, Gene Hermanski.

Rickey convinced Horace Stoneham that Rosen and Graham were better than what the Giants had, so the men were invited to the Polo Grounds, instead of being allowed to slip to the minors.

Mike Sandlock had figured to do most of the catching. But in spring training Ferrell Anderson, a football tackle from Kansas, who was playing with the Montreal club, had hit a few balls over the wall. I liked Anderson's hustling. He had a defective eye and had to crook his neck at an odd angle in order to see straight. Still, Anderson did almost all of our catching in the early part of the season.

Rickey was pictured as the "Old Woman Who Lived in a Shoe," and as a cradle snatcher. His "Youth Movement"—it was mine, too—was the most discussed topic of the new season.

The first of the youngsters to bite the dust was Hermanski. Gene had trouble playing the sun-field in Boston. Then, in a game against the Giants at Ebbets Field, Dixie Walker pinch hit in the eighth, with New York in front by one run. The "Peepul's Cherce" hit the first ball into Bedford Avenue. We won the game, and Dixie had won the battle for right field again. He stayed there for the rest of the year.

In April, we won eight and lost three. So did the Cardinals, a sign of things to come. We were terrific at home, winning our first nine in Flatbush. But on the road we had trouble, and at the Polo Grounds the "Youth Movement" ran into its first squalls.

Goody Rosen had a big day when he met us, as traded players so often do. He got four singles and a home run! Meanwhile, Furillo got only two hits in sixteen trips. The experts began to holler that our kindergarten was flopping on the job.

Curt Davis was gone. But Ed Head's arm seemed to have come back. Ed flipped a no-hitter against the Braves at Ebbets Field and, the next time out, pitched a game that was every bit as good. The last one, at Wrigley Field in Chicago, we lost because, with two out in the last of the ninth, Furillo could not pick off a fly ball he should have put in his pocket. The wind whipped the flags in toward the diamond, and all afternoon I moved Furillo in. Now I failed to notice how far out he had drifted. He could not make the catch, and it cost us the game.

That encounter and the one Stanky and Walker handed

the Reds in August—when they collided under an easy fly ball with two out in the ninth—are the two mistakes that dragged us back into a tie for the pennant with the Cardinals.

Meanwhile, Jackie Robinson had begun his sensational year with the Montreal club. His fans cried that he ought to waltz right on to the Dodgers. Level-headed, Jackie had no such illusions. "If I can't make Montreal, I'll play wherever Mr. Rickey sends me," he told the writers.

He had an answer for everything—except for what had happened to Parrott the first time Harold went to fetch him from his Harlem hotel to come to Rickey's office.

"Mr. Robinson is in Room 204," the clerk at the hotel desk said. "House phone over here."

"He's expecting me," said Parrott, "I'll go right up."

"Sorry," said the Negro clerk, "no white people allowed above the lobby floor."

Somehow Dan Parker got hold of that item. Parrott had been barred, he joked, and now the discrimination was on the other foot!

But there was no joking about the way the California Comet broke into the International League, where he hit .350 and stole half a hundred bases. In his first game for Montreal, Robinson got four hits—one a homer—stole two bases, and cut such antics on third base that the opposing pitcher twice balked him home. As "Bojangles" Bill Robinson later remarked, the fans were seeing "Ty Cobb in technicolor."

Stanky was having another great year at second. He walked every other time up, and still made them mad. Stevens wasn't hitting often, but when he did the ball got lost, and he drove in more than twenty-five runs with his first twenty-five hits. He seemed to have the first-base job cinched. At short, Reese was getting into his stride. At third, Billy Herman was all right, because he did not have to move much.

I suspect that Branch had made up his mind early that Herman should leave us. Not only because Billy was heading for thirty-eight, but because he couldn't get about in the field. Billy had hit hard at the start, but he tapered off.

"Herman would have to hit .330 all year to have me keep him in the game," said Rickey. "Ball game after ball game is going past him at third. He is the typical anesthetic ballplayer. He grabbed the first ninety chances without an error. Why? Because they were hit right at him. He did not reach the balls he might have kicked."

That June he insisted on trading Herman, a trade that caused more discussion than any other baseball swap in a decade.

Miksis, the kid from Trenton, was returning from the war. We wondered about Cookie Lavagetto. Cookie was old and because of bone chips in his elbow couldn't throw very well.

Rickey called him in. "How about an arm operation?" he asked.

"I want to play now," said Cookie. "Let's wait until the end of the season."

"No," countered the boss. "Right now we can get by with what we have all right. But I think this team is going to get better. I think we'll be in a position to make a bid for the pennant in August. If you are in tiptop shape then, after your arm operation, it might make all the difference. You may win it for us."

When the Cubs came to Ebbets Field, Ed Stanky and Merullo, the Cub shortstop, got into a rhubarb. Peewee Reese tried to break up the fight and received plenty of abuse from Merullo.

The next day Peewee was getting ready for his batting practice swings when Merullo, wandering up near the cage—where he shouldn't have been—said something that revived the argument. Just then Dixie Walker, thinking Merullo was going to pop Peewee, beat him to the punch. In a few seconds the Cubs had ganged up on Dixie. Two Cubs punched him as he tried to get up from the dirt.

I had been in our clubhouse. By the time I got out to the battleground the cops had things pretty well under control. But Walker had lost a tooth, and his face was cut and bloody. Somehow Red Smith, the Cub coach, landed in bad with the gendarmes, and was about to be marched off to the station house when we squared matters.

Throughout the melee, Anderson, our big catcher, carried the Cub outfielder, Peanuts Lowery, around on his back, like a jockey. Peanuts beat on the young giant like on a bass drum, but Anderson ignored him and fought his way into the knot of struggling players, under which Dixie Walker lay.

As Anderson burrowed in, he came up beside Paul Erickson. The Cub pitcher was saying in a loud voice, "I'm going to take a poke at that Walker myself. I've always wanted to."

"I wouldn't, son!" boomed Anderson. "I've picked you for my own playmate!"

Erickson looked around. When he saw Anderson, topped by the flailing Lowery, heading for him, he suddenly lost his belligerent feelings.

Jim Gallagher, the Cub general manager, was indignant. Two of his men, Merullo and Smith, were fined $150 apiece, while Walker was the only Dodger to draw a penalty that large. Cavaretta and Reese were each fined a hundred dollars. Walker was suspended for five days, Merullo for eight.

"The Dodgers," said Gallagher bitterly, "are running this league!"

Walker soon got over his mauling. He hit in sixteen straight games, and brought his average up to .376. Stanky was working his way onto the bases, too. In one stretch he got on base in twenty-six straight games. At the end of May we were in first place with twenty-five won and twelve lost. We were two games ahead of the Cards.

There were danger signs. Head's arm went bad again. We warmed him up in Chicago to start a game, but when his shoulder tightened, Rex Barney had to rush in. Branca had a sore arm, and so did Gregg.

In Cincinnati, we had to start forty-year-old Art Herring; after five innings his arm tightened up, too. Herring had not allowed a hit in the five innings he worked, and the press box said I was daffy for lifting him when he had a chance to enter the Hall of Fame. But I wanted to take the game more than I wanted to win laurels for Herring. Besides, I wasn't going to wait until he got his brains knocked out. Perhaps it was the first time in baseball history that a no-hit pitcher was yanked.

But it worked. Casey came in, protected our lead, and we squeaked through to win a thriller. We beat the Reds twice that day, to jump three and a half games in front of the Cards. Incidentally, that was the first time in three years that we had won a series in Cincinnati. That I should have had to yank a no-hit pitcher to do it seemed quite in line with the zany Dodger tradition.

Now that we had started to play night ball, Anderson began to have his eye trouble. We lost a game in St. Louis when he had a man hung up between first and second, but never saw him out there on the limb. Sandlock could not do the job behind the plate, either. So we tried to make a trade.

The Cardinals had four catchers: Garagiola, Rice, Kluttz, and O'Dea. We made Sam Breadon a nice offer for either Rice or Kluttz. "I'll sell one," he said, "if it's all right with my manager."

I called Eddie Dyer. He declared, "Sure, Leo, we have to get rid of a catcher. I can't carry four. But I'm not going to help you. No, you can't have either Kluttz or Rice."

Well, it was nice to know they were scared of us, anyway.

In Chicago, we ran into more trouble. The radio announcers in the big village on Lake Michigan whipped the populace into a frenzy about Dixie Walker. He was alleged to have hit

Merullo and then to have tried to run away. They called it the "Battle of Brooklyn." Nice going.

Big banners denouncing "toothless" Walker were flaunted in the right-field bleachers at Wrigley Field. Dixie was showered with fruit and refuse. A set of false teeth was delivered special delivery to Charley Grimm, the Cub manager, with the request that they be delivered to Walker. Later on some misguided Cub fan who wanted to deride Dixie, shipped a set of crutches to Ebbets Field for him.

What hurt us more that day was the way Claude Passeau beat us. The game was still scoreless in the last of the ninth with two men out. The Cub pitcher himself was at bat. Two strikes were on him. He hit one into the left-field seats and beat Hatten. The next day the Cubs shut us out again.

In our very next series in St. Louis, Higbe fanned seven and had a two-hit shutout cooking in the seventh. But they made three in the last two frames to beat us. The next day after leading 3-0 Hatten was again knocked off. We had lost five straight now, and our lead was down to one game. After trailing 7-6 in the eighth, we rallied in the ninth inning of the final game against the Cards, and made four runs to win.

Still we looked wobbly. On the road we were around the .500 mark, and we couldn't win consistently. At home we had won fifteen out of twenty games.

The crowds were terrific. On this Western trip we drew 265,000 in thirteen games. In our twenty games at Ebbets Field we pulled 435,000. Generously, Rickey tore up the contracts of Gregg, Stanky, and Rojek, and gave them more cash. Rojek, like Reiser, had been offered $100,000 in Mex money to join Owen, but he had fought off the temptation. The Tamale circuit had tried to tempt Jackie Robinson, too, but he was making the most of his big chance in the International League, and he was happy.

Reiser, his injured collarbone getting better, was really galloping. He stole home seven times in nine tries, and in the press boxes around the league they were saying the greatest, most dramatic play in baseball was his steal of home.

Yet our team was not "set." I felt it in my bones and begged Rickey for a catcher. I looked for one in the major leagues. He knew where one he wanted was: down in Mobile. He had Scout Wid Matthews following Bruce Edwards. Wid wrote, "This boy will do the job for you right now in Brooklyn. He's ready!"

Rickey told Matthews to throw in a few more adjectives and send me a copy of the report.

When I read those glowing accounts of Edwards, who was hitting .338 and catching like a champion, I said, "Let's have him!"

"There's only one difficulty," warned Rickey. "I have to give Mobile a very tempting deal to get them to part with this youngster. He is their whole team."

He made the deal. But it did not come off quite the way he had planned it.

Chapter 26

ON THE SEESAW WITH THE CARDS

COMING HOME FROM THAT BAD WESTERN TRIP, EVERYONE HAD a feeling that there was a trade in the wind.

Saturday, June 15, was the trading dead line. As Augie Galan came into Ebbets Field that day, a fan barked, "I hear you're gonna be traded, Augie."

"Yeah," returned Galan, "an usher just told me all about it!"

Everybody right down to the batboy had a deal cooked up. But nobody guessed the right one. We made it with less than an hour to spare before the midnight dead line . . . Billy Herman was sent to the Boston Braves; we were to get Stu Hofferth, a thirty-one-year-old catcher who had once managed in the Brooklyn farm system.

Rickey had hoped to synchronize the deal. He wanted to bring Edwards up from Mobile and send Hofferth down there. But Hofferth set his heels and refused to go to the minors. He wasn't kidding either, and quit baseball to prove that he meant what he said.

Seven days passed before Edwards reached Brooklyn. The first time up, he made a lucky hit, but he caused no great stir. He took none of the heat off Rickey, and it was on, something torrid, because Branch had cut Herman and his big salary off the Dodger pay roll.

At third base it was to be a sad summer for us. I had thought young Miksis could do the job; but I was wrong. Rickey thought Lavagetto would be the man after the arm operation; but Cookie didn't hit, and we had to take him out. Bob Ramazzotti, a youngster who had played in the Dodgers' minors before the war, broke in at second when Slaughter busted Stanky up, and hit so well that we tried him at third.

When he faded, we tried Rojek. When the latter flopped, we got around to Galan, our wartime third baseman. We were so badly off we finally used Galan against both left- and right-handed pitching.

These failures made the writers and the fans continue to harp on the Herman deal. Billy had been hitting .296 when we sent him to Boston. I recall how angrily he ripped his stuff out of his Dodger locker and packed for his trip, that Sunday morning. Now in Boston he was hitting steadily. Every time we played the Braves, Billy murdered us. That didn't help matters any with the writers and the fans.

Our pitching had gone haywire. In fifty-four games, we could show only sixteen complete efforts; I had run in nine different relief men. The big laugh came when we beat the Cards two out of three, and in one game Casey went eight and two-thirds innings as a relief.

Higbe led a charmed life. He couldn't get anybody out, but Lady Luck handed him some soft touches. He would give up two runs, and we would make three to win for him. He pitched badly, yet his record was eight wins and no losses. When the tide turned, as usually happens, it swamped him. Higbe, as a relief pitcher, lost two games in three days.

My old pal, Joe Medwick, came to me for a job. I talked Rickey into signing him as a pinch hitter—on the theory that Babe Herman had helped us the same way the year before.

While we waited to clear a spot on the roster for Joe, Bill Boylan, the press-club bartender, pitched to Ducky every day. In that practice, Medwick whaled the ball to every corner of Ebbets Field. He looked great.

The first day Medwick was eligible—Reiser was out of action—I stuck Joe in left field. Rickey nearly died.

"What have I done?" moaned Branch. "This will set our youth movement back a whole year!"

I am glad Branch wasn't present the night in St. Louis when I got fed up with our first basemen a few weeks later and started Joe Medwick on first against the Cards. He played it on his hands and knees, as if begging for help.

But Joe did all right the first night; so did we. At the end of June we jumped way out in front, as the Cards hit a low spot. They lost five in a row and the lead we had held since May increased to seven and one-half games. A lot of people thought the race was over. We had been tied for the lead with the Cards on May 24, when they lost Lanier, Martin, and Klein to the Mexican League, and now we were seven and one-half in front.

The *Brooklyn Eagle* asked brazenly, "What ever became of the Cardinals?"

But we weren't out of the woods—or should I say bushes?— yet.

It took a little more than two weeks for the Cardinals to knock us out of the league lead. During that time, they ripped off thirteen victories in seventeen starts.

It was early for them to begin streaking, but what they did to us in St. Louis on that trip shouldn't happen to a sand-lot team. Even before we got that far, our luck turned bad.

Reese was the first to crack up. After taking enough X rays to start a heat wave, the doctors decided that a vertebra in his neck was chipped. Peewee had done it four years before, lifting his wife onto his shoulders. It had to show up now when we needed him.

Higbe, despite his strange winning record, was debunked in the All-Star game in which the National League was blanked, 12-0. "Ted Williams told me my knuckler was the best he ever saw," said the irrepressible Hig. He didn't add that Ted had belted the knuckler for one of the longest homers of the year.

On the way down from the All-Star game, Charley Dressen and I went to St. Paul to see if Walt Nothe, a big left-hander we had there, could help us. We wired our veteran coach,

John Corriden, to take charge of the club in the opener against the Cubs. We said we couldn't reach Chicago in time.

It was a gag, of course. We knew that Corriden didn't care for that kind of responsibility, and we wanted to kid him. That night he must have worked out one hundred different line-ups. He did not sleep a wink, figuring how he would run the team the next day.

Maybe he should have run it, at that. When I took charge, the Cubs beat Hatten again in the last of the ninth, 1-0. We couldn't seem to get Joe any runs against the Chicago club. We hadn't provided him with one in thirty-one innings!

But the pendulum swung for others, too. The Cards had dropped five in a row to the Giants in St. Louis. Now they whipped the New York club twice. We had only four and one-half games of our lead left as we marched into St. Louis for a vital four-game series.

Lombardi, probably our best pitcher at this time, opened that series. Vic was a classy little performer, but he wasn't aggressive enough to suit me. I was always begging him to brush those tough hitters back from the plate, to make them respect him, to keep them guessing, and to prevent them from getting set to slash at his fast ball.

As we went into the last of the eighth we had a one-run lead. Before Little Vic marched out to the mound I said, "Musial is up this inning. Brush him back from that plate!"

Vic got two strikes on the Cardinal slugger. I signaled for an inside pitch.

Instead, the ball went over the plate. Musial plastered it up against the fence, and sped into third. A moment later he scored, and the game was tied.

In the eleventh, I again pleaded with Lombardi to get tough with Stan Musial, to keep him from taking a toe-hold.

This time Musial hit a home run and school was out.

In the clubhouse afterwards I made a speech. "Lombardi," I said, "I'll never ask you to pitch tight to anybody again, because I can see you haven't the nerve to do it. You let them take the bread and butter right out of your mouth. Well, tomorrow I'll start somebody who will make them respect him!"

I did, too. I started Casey for the first time since 1942. He lasted a couple of innings.

When Joe Hatten pitched the final game of the series—we had lost three straight—I was a thousand miles away in a Harlem beanery, listening to Red Barber describe the play over the radio. I had been suspended for five days.

Shoving his head into the loud-speaker alongside me was Rickey. We were on our way up to a Boy Scout camp in the mountains, where Rickey was to address a few thousand youngsters. With this man you never know where you're likely to find yourself next.

I had been suspended because I rushed out and spun Umpire Al Barlick around after he gave a decision in short left field in St. Louis. Pete Reiser had made a sliding catch of a line drive. Barlick ruled that Pete had dropped or trapped the ball. That cost us an important run.

Reiser had really caught the ball. Irately, he charged at Barlick and grabbed him. As I rushed from the dugout, I had visions of Reiser getting a ten-day suspension, or maybe more. We couldn't afford to lose him; we were battling for that pennant. I thought to myself: I'll have to do something drastic!

When I got to the fracas, I seized Barlick. In fact, I pulled him away from the indignant Reiser, who was raving mad. I distracted the umpire. Barlick forgot about Pete, and concentrated on me, instead. He did such a good job that Ford Frick tossed me in the clink for five days. I didn't care; Reiser was still playing!

That was how I happened to be listening to the radio as Hatten rolled along in that fourth game. He was leading, 4-2, in the top of the ninth. It looked as though we'd get out of St. Louis alive after all!

First thing we knew, there were two men on and none out. Dusak was sent up to sacrifice. He fouled two off. The next one he hit deep into the seats in left center for a three-run homer and the ball game was theirs, 5-4.

Rickey and I left the restaurant numb. We drove fifty miles before either of us could say a word.

The club left St. Louis with a half-game lead. In the next two games they ran our losing streak to six straight in Cincinnati. On July 18, we were in second place for the first time since May 25. We had won only four of our last fifteen games.

We were glad to see Ebbets Field again. At home, we had won thirty out of thirty-nine. Now we got two big fat runs for Hatten against the Cubs who had been murdering him by 2-0 and 1-0. He made it by the skin of his teeth to win, 2-1. We were a half game in front again.

By the end of July, we had built our lead back to two and one-half games. Then the Cardinals came to town.

Instead of shooting an ace against Howie Pollet in the opener, I used Rube Melton.

"A sacrificial goat," Dick Young in the *News* called Melton.

Rube resented it so much that he pitched a classic to beat Pollet. Even with that advantage, we lost the series, two games to one.

It seemed that we just could not beat those Cardinals. In 1941, we had held them even in the season's series. Since then, they had beaten us thirty-three times at Ebbets Field and thirty-five times at St. Louis. We had won only sixteen games from them in each park.

Now our lead was down to a game and a half. We were sick at third base, where Miksis had got one hit in twenty-three tries.

But whenever we played the Phillies, we got well again. We had beaten them eighteen straight in Philadelphia. The

Giants, too, were our doormats. All Li'l Vic Lombardi had to do was lift his glove on the mound and the Giants rolled over dead. He had beaten them eight straight!

In Chicago, Gallagher was screaming. "The other clubs in the league faint when they see the Dodgers," he charged, in a newspaper interview. "Brooklyn is winning the pennant off the Phillies and the Giants."

"What difference does it make to you?" one nervy writer asked. "You're nine games behind, anyway!"

Then somebody was unkind enough to point out that the Cubs had won the 1945 pennant only because the Reds had played patsy twenty-one times in twenty-two games with the Chicago club.

Still, that did not stop Gallagher from hollering. Before the year was out, we were to hear loud noises from Bill McKechnie of the Reds and from Eddie Dyer of the Cards, too.

On August 8, we beat the Giants in a dandy. In the ninth, they needed a run to tie. They got men on first and second with one out. Rigney hit to Reese, who flipped to Stanky for another out. The 50,000 fans in the Polo Grounds craned their heads toward first to see if Stanky's throw would double Rigney to end the inning and the game. But Rigney beat the throw. What throw? Stanky had gunned the ball to Lavagetto on third, to cut down the Giant runner, who had carelessly turned third. Casey won the game, and, with Lombardi, reached the ten-win mark.

Incidentally, Casey was the only pitcher I would allow to use his own judgment. For the others, we called the pitches from the bench. I would tell Dressen, "curve," or "fast ball," and he would signal the pitcher. Edwards, in turn, would get the sign from the pitcher

But the Phils, whom we had beaten eighteen straight in their own park, turned on us twice on a Sunday. This was the historic occasion when Magerkurth kept his right hand out like a meat chopper, after calling strike three on Stanky, and refusing to let Eddie pass between himself and the catcher. Then he pushed Stanky.

I ran out and told him he couldn't shove my players around. First thing you know, he shoved me right out of the game.

The Cards beat the Reds twice as we were dropping two, and again our lead was down to half a game. This tight race was filling the parks. We came home and played an afternoon-night double bill, beating the Giants twice and drawing 58,691 fans into Ebbets Field in one day. We had drawn 832,-000 before the Fourth of July, and now, with 1,236,162, were past the 1941 record already.

For the entire season we drew 1,750,000 fans, which meant that Ebbets Field operated to 75 per cent capacity, every day of the season. Again I hit the jack pot because of my bonus contract. I earned close to $50,000.

On our last trip we took a game and a half lead west with us. Two days later our margin was gone. Vander Meer shut us out and the Cardinals won two.

There was some yelping in this encounter. Rube Melton brushed Grady Hatton, the kid third baseman, back from the plate and Bill McKechnie came out of the Reds' dugout hollering bloody murder. He waved his arms at Melton and shouted, "Moron!"

We gathered that Hatton didn't like to be pitched "tight." So we decided to give him the same treatment from then on.

There was a funny thing about all this yammering. We had had trouble with the St. Louis club; now McKechnie was hollering, and his coach, Jimmy Wilson, was telling writers that dusters were all right in daytime games, but should be barred at night.

Still, while everybody else was hollering, we were getting the works. Medwick had been beaned again, and was out for a couple of weeks.

We kept even with the Cards by beating the Reds in the final game of the series. This game at Cincinnati was close.

Joe Hatten pitched for us. In one episode Bert Haas was on second with the tying run when Grady Hatton came up.

Haas was stealing our signs from second base, so before each pitch I had to run out to the mound and tell Joe what to throw. Making sure that Grady Hatton would hear me, I said, "Just get the ball over to this guy. These .230 hitters can't hurt you."

I had no love for the boy anyway because he had admitted that he had turned down more money from Brooklyn and signed with Cincinnati for less—just because Jackie Robinson was in our organization.

Now Grady Hatton was so mad at me he could hardly see. Joe Hatten struck him out easily.

We moved into St. Louis, August 25, and split a double-header. For us, the game we won, by 3 to 2, was one of the big ones of the year, even though we used four pitchers.

In the sixth, with the score tied, Slaughter led off with a double against Lombardi. With none out, Whitey Kurowski, the next hitter, figured to sacrifice the runner to third. If Whitey bunted, I would leave Lombardi in; if he swung, I would bring in a right-handed pitcher.

Kurowski fouled off two attempted bunts. Knowing that Kurowski would swing now, I brought Harry Behrman in.

Whitey guessed on a curve, and Harry got that fast ball past him for strike three. Behrman got the next two hitters. After we scored, Gregg came on in the ninth to stop them cold.

In Sunday's second game, the Cards led 10-0, but as we began to tee off they, too, had to use four pitchers. When Umpire Babe Pinelli called the game in the eighth, I squawked.

"What are you griping about?" the Babe wanted to know. "You couldn't possibly win this one!"

"Maybe not," I said. "But Brecheen is pitching, and I want him tired out in case he tries to come back at us in the Tuesday game."

We got no breaks in the third game of the series. Melton started it, and gave up two runs in the first. Joe Hatten, who had shown nothing the day before to let the Cards get that 10-0 lead, now shut the door with three hits. We lost anyway, 2-1.

I rode Murry Dickson, the little Cardinal right-hander, hard in this game. I wanted very badly to win it.

Everybody in the National League had squawked at us this season. Now the first-base umpire, Lee Ballanfant, chipped in. "You're riding that kid too hard," he warned, "why not let up on him a little?"

"Listen," I said, "after the game tonight I'll buy Dickson a steak and beer. Right now, I want to beat him any way I can!"

In the fourth game of the series Higbe did beat them. It was only the third win for us in eleven games in St. Louis. Still it was a big one, for it got us out of St. Louis still tied for the lead.

In the St. Louis series, they had sent a big guy named Walter Sessi up to hit against us. He is the biggest fellow I have ever seen in a baseball suit.

When Sessi came to the plate, I hollered, "Hey, where is the wagon that goes with that horse?"

That probably got his nanny because he fanned twice in that series on six pitched balls, which may be a record.

As we went back to Chicago and into more trouble, the Giants came into St. Louis. With two out and one on in the last of the ninth, and the Giants ahead, 2-1, this same Sessi hit against them. I'd bet Giants Manager Mel Ott never hollered anything improper at Sessi; Mel is too nice a guy. But Sessi hit a homer to beat Voiselle and the Giants, 3-2. That hurt us at least as much as it did Ott.

I figured that it was working out as I had laid it out for Frank Graham one day at the Polo Grounds. I said that the

Giants were nice guys, but that was why they were last. I wanted the competitive boys playing for me—the boys who would sit up all night figuring how to beat the other team.

Now Ott and his boys were down around the cellar.

The Cards whacked the Giants three times, while we lost two to the Cubs—which made Gallagher very happy. But these losses pushed us two and a half games back of the Cards, the worst position we had been in. With only a month of the season left, and the Cards building up a head of steam, it looked like curtains.

We came East to play a series at the Polo Grounds, and ran into another rhubarb. Goody Rosen, trying to stretch a hit into a double, was shot down by Walker's arm. Angry at himself and the world in general, Goody kicked at Stanky as Eddie applied the ball. That was a mistake. Well, it was a pretty good fight while it lasted. But it only heightened the feelings of the Giants who would have sacrificed one hundred points off their percentage in the standings to knock us down in the race. We won the series.

We were mighty anxious to get home, where we had won forty-three and lost only fifteen. We were just a .500 ball club on the road. One of the big reasons we thought we'd win the flag was that we were scheduled to play only five more games away from Ebbets Field.

Right now, however, we faced a rugged series in Boston. For us it was tough to score up there. We won both games, 3 to 1 and 1 to 0, yet didn't gain an inch on the Cardinals.

Chapter 27

THE "ASSISTANT MANAGERS' ASSOCIATION"

DURING THIS EXCITING PENNANT RACE, WRITERS FROM NINE metropolitan papers traveled with us. They were chiefly younger men, like Herb Goren of the *Sun*, Bill Roeder of the *World-Telegram*, Arch Murray of the *Post*, Bob Cooke of the *Herald Tribune*, and Dick Young of the *News*. Perhaps that was what gave an "eager beaver" air to the press boxes wherever we went. For these industrious youngsters were always trying to "scoop" each other.

As a result, newspapermen figured in almost all of our big episodes. As younger men, the writers weren't as blasé as those who had been through dozens of pennant battles. When we lost they bled with us. They also second-guessed me both in the clubhouse and in their papers.

I contributed a lot to this situation. Unlike Joe McCarthy, who would say to an inquiring newspaperman, "Let me worry about that," I popped off on everything. I was always talking and it seemed there was always a writer around to hear what I had to say. If I had made no remark about certain guests Larry MacPhail had in his box in Havana in the spring of 1947—or if no young and eager writer had been on the job to take it down—a lot of baseball history might have taken a different course.

But this combination of zealous reporters and human-interest material monopolized the sports pages for us. We outdid any other two teams, I think, in lineage, "yardage," in the columns, year after year.

In MacPhail's day, largely because of his unpredictable moods and stormy ways, covering the Dodgers had been a twenty-four-hour proposition.

Eager writers helped along, of course. Some rival news-papermen still think that Eddie Zeltner of the *Mirror*, just to give himself a scoop, played a part in talking an indignant Van Mungo into jumping the Dodgers in Pittsburgh in 1939. At least, Zeltner lent a hand, and took the plane for New York with the befuddled pitcher.

Newspapermen were in deep in many of our big headaches. I'll never forget that it was Tim Cohane, who had poked his head into my dressing-room door and got the Newsom "spit-ter" story which led to the Vaughan "strike" the next day. If Cohane had given the game the routine treatment and re-mained in the press box to write his story, nothing unusual would have happened. But Cohane hustled, and things popped. I don't blame anybody. The newspaper game has its angles, the same as baseball does.

Like Cohane, who graduated to *Look* magazine, Young, Goren, Roeder, and Murray were all young writers with great ability and brilliant futures. I got a wallop out of the youthful Goren writing a column under the by-line of "The Old Scout" in the *Sun*. It reminds me of *PM*'s war expert, who wrote under the title of "The General"—until he was drafted into World War II as a private.

Most rabid of all the Dodger writers is Murray, known as "Tiger Arch" in the trade, because he is a Princeton man, from the soles of his feet to his crew haircut. Murray roots so hard and writes so hard that sometimes he becomes good copy himself to the other writers. In September, 1946, as we headed down to the wire in the thrilling race with the Cardinals, a Chicago writer wrote a whole column about Murray. He told how Arch would not change his clothes if the Dodgers were on a winning streak, how Parrott, the traveling secretary, made sure the hotels never put him in a room on a high floor when the team was going badly. And, of course, he made much of the fact that Arch wigwagged "signals" to me in the dugout from his press box perch, telling me who should relieve, and who should pinch hit.

Hatten was on the mound for the first game in Boston on September 4. He nearly caused a breach between the "Assistant Managers' Association" and me. In the ninth inning Murray almost blew his top because I did not yank the left-hander.

We had a 3-1 lead, but Hatten seemed tired—at least to Murray. The Braves had Masi on second, another runner on first, and none out. Johnny Hopp, one of the better hitters in the league, came to the plate.

With his first two pitches, Hatten was wild. Murray began to wigwag frantically from the press box, which is easily seen from the dugout in Boston.

I paid no attention. I had Casey warming up, but I knew that if I yanked the left-handed Hatten and came in with the right-handed Casey, the batter, Hopp, up there to sacrifice, would swing away. I knew, too, that three fine left-handed pinch hitters who had been kept on the Braves' bench— O'Dea, Rowell, and Padgett—would be ready to go to work if I brought Casey in.

So I stuck with Hatten.

Edwards tried to pick Masi off second, and threw wild into center field. Our hearts sank. Furillo charged the ball. He threw a line drive into third, and Masi became a dead pigeon. Hatten seemed to get a lift from that. He threw three straight strikes and fanned Hopp. He also fanned Connie Ryan to end the game.

I couldn't wait to meet Murray and the other "Assistant Managers" that night. I had had the last laugh.

Instead of blasting me, as they would have if Hatten had "blown" the game, the writers took apart Jim Gallagher, whose "collapsible" Cubs were playing dead for the Cardinals by scores of 10-1 and 8-1, while we had to battle the Braves so furiously.

The next day, Lombardi beat Sain, 1-0, on a wild pitch, and we came into Ebbets Field on September 7 for our final lunge at the pennant. We were still trailing the Cardinals by two and a half games.

Higbe, who had been sensational in his last five outs, now pulled a one-hitter out of his rubber arm, and fanned nine Giants to shut them out. It was a big win, for the Cardinals lost, and now we were only a game and a half back.

When Higbe had control, nobody could touch him. He was fast, he had a great knuckler, and his overhand curve was great against left-handed hitters. This day, oddly enough, every one of the nine Giants fanned were left-handed hitters. Normally one would expect them to do well against a right-handed pitcher.

Reiser had been in and out of the game with one ailment or another. But Furillo had been sensational as a fill-in against both types of pitching, right and left. In one double-header he had bagged six hits.

But Pistol Pete Reiser was still the big gun. Whenever he wasn't out of order, we had to get him into the line-up. Now he told me he was ready, and we turned him loose against the Giants. He stole three bases, including his seventh theft of home, and led the league with thirty-three sacks.

It was Eddie Stanky day. The feature was a pair of boxing gloves which good-natured Goody Rosen, Stanky's sparring partner of a few weeks before, presented at home plate with a nice little speech.

Although we won easily, as our boys pinwheeled around the bases on Schnozz Lombardi, and stole eight times, we had bad news that night. The Cardinals had won two, and led us by two full games.

On September 10, after both the Cards and the Dodgers had enjoyed a day off, the unpredictable Melton spun a three-hitter over the Reds. That allowed us to keep pace with the St. Louis club, which also won its game.

The next day Bill McKechnie shot Johnny Vander Meer, whom he had primed for this big battle, at us. We did not exactly murder Johnny. He held us scoreless for nineteen innings, to complete his string of twenty-six scoreless innings against Brooklyn. Meanwhile, in this dramatic battle, Gregg went ten innings, Casey five, Herring three, and Behrman one.

The Reds had two men thrown out at the plate, but they never did score. Both plays were sensational, Edwards making lightning-quick tags with those fast hands of his.

Eddie Lukon had rocketed a ball off the right-center wall. As the little outfielder spun around the sacks, the ball rolled all the way to left field. He passed third and headed for home. Reiser got the ball, lined up a perfect relay with Reese, and they nailed Lukon at the plate.

The Cardinals lost. Since we played a tie, we trailed again by a game and a half.

Now we had two worries. We had to get the Reds to come back to Brooklyn to replay the nineteen-inning tie, and we had to face the Cardinals.

Against the Cards, I opened with Higbe. His only defeat in his last six starts had been by 2-1, on a Chinese home run by Buddy Kerr, at the Polo Grounds.

But Higbe, our big hope, was out in the first inning, before the Cardinals were. He had two strikes on four straight Cardinal hitters, but they all reached base. At two strikes and no balls he gave Musial a fat pitch and Stan hit the fence. Then Slaughter hit Higbe, and Kurowski topped a ball past the mound. To that one Higbe tipped his hat, instead of fielding it. The pay-off was a home run by Joe Garagiola, who shouldn't have hit Higbe with a paddle. That five-run first inning sunk us two and a half games back of the Cards.

Afterward, Arch Murray asked Higbe, "Didn't you have your stuff, Hig?"

"Sure I did," said Kirby, "but I bounced it off their bats. That's all."

Chapter 28

THE DODGERS AND CARDS TIE

FRIDAY, SEPTEMBER 13, BEFORE THE SECOND GAME OF THE Cardinal series we had a big clubhouse meeting. When it was over, our bunch did not trot out on the field—they charged out and ripped into the Cards for a ferocious first inning.

In that clubhouse meeting I read a letter I had received from Whitlow Wyatt, who used to be our spearhead in these big "money" games.

"I see by the papers," Wyatt had said, "that they're complaining to Ford Frick because you're playing too 'rough.' Well, Skip, I'm sorry I am not there with you to hand it to them. But for my sake, give it to them a little harder, and make those crybabies moan."

I put it to our bunch this way: "It's your bread and butter that they're taking away from you!"

Right at the start we gave it to Eddie Dyer as he coached on first base. "Yes, Mr. Frick," we teased. "What did teacher's pet hear from the President's office today?"

We had a big first inning. Pete Reiser made one of the great plays of the year. Del Rice had the ball at the plate, but Pete came around behind him to score, touching the plate with his hand as he swept over it.

We got four runs, and kept up the riding. Our gab bothered Ken Burkhart, their relief pitcher, and he complained to the umpires. When he went in to talk to his catcher, Higbe cracked, "What an intelligent conversation that must be. When you two guys get your heads together, it reminds me of a rock garden!"

The Cardinals got three runs, and inch by inch crept up on

us. But we kept battling and talking, and they didn't know whether they were going or coming.

Musial was on third with none out. On a fly to Furillo, he broke for the plate. It was a bad play to make with none out, for by this time everybody in baseball knew what a gun Furillo had up his sleeve. Musial was out. That was a big run the Cards didn't get, for we won the game, 4-3.

Afterward, the Cardinals battled among themselves about that play. Musial claimed that Mike Gonzales, the veteran Cuban coach, had said "Go! Go! Go!" as the ball was hit in the air to Furillo. Gonzales insisted that he had cried "No! No! No!"

"Go" or "no," it pulled us back to within a game and a half. Still it was an expensive victory, because Reiser, skimming around third during the first-inning rally, stepped into a patch of soft turf and pulled a leg muscle. He got up from that great slide at the plate limping so badly he could hardly walk.

On Saturday came the big rubber game of the Cardinal series. In the dressing room before the game I told two of the "Assistant Managers"—Arch Murray was one of them—my secret plans.

I figured to start Ralph Branca, and to get all of Eddie Dyer's left-handed hitters into the starting line-up. After Branca had pitched to the first hitter, my plan was to have Ralph "hurt" his arm, so that Lombardi could rush in as a "relief." With his left-handers in the line-up, Dyer would be handcuffed. He couldn't very well take them all out, because if I relieved later with Casey or with some other right-hander, he would be stuck with his right-handed hitters.

I pledged Murray to secrecy.

Ralph Branca warmed up well. He was relaxed, because he knew he was only a decoy. There wasn't a thought in his mind about going any further than the first batter, because he had warmed up for ten straight innings during the nineteen-inning game against the Reds on Wednesday, and this was Saturday. He hadn't started a game in a month, and he hadn't pitched more than seven innings all season!

As the game got under way, big Ralph was "loose." The ball was going into Edwards' mitt with an audible "whump!" I called Dressen over. "Is that ball really jumping, Charley," I asked. "Or am I seeing things?"

Dressen saw it too. And now Edwards turned to us and indicated that Branca had terrific stuff.

Ralph got Schoendienst out and then, according to plan, began to hold his shoulder, and grimace in "pain." Lombardi who had begun to warm up in the bull pen as soon as the game started, was ready. The fans looked down toward him, expecting the little left-hander to come into the game any minute.

But I told Lombardi to sit down, and motioned to Branca to go right ahead. I wanted him to keep pouring that fast ball and that big overhand curve of his in there. This was a new turn, and I wanted to make the most of it.

The park was full. Suddenly the fans were amazed to see Big Ralph, who a moment before obviously had been in pain, drop his grimaces and go ahead with the game.

Meanwhile we got five runs off Harry Brecheen. The "Cat" got peeved because Dressen, coaching at third, "called" his pitches, and tipped off our hitters. Ford Frick, who had become so indignant about "dusters," watched as Brecheen threw a ball right behind Bruce Edwards. But Branca was superb. He fanned ten and shut them out with three hits!

So now we were within reach of the Cards at last, only half a game back.

But only for a day. The Cards beat the Giants twice on Sunday, September 15. We had a hectic time with the Cubs and by splitting a double-header, dropped back a game and a half again.

Brooklyn Dodgers fan Albert L. Esposito snapped this view of the stands during the fifth game of the 1947 World Series.

Dodgers Band prepares an enthusiastic reception for the 1947 pennant-winning Dodgers team at the Grand Central Terminal.

A tremendous crowd gathered around Borough Hall in Brooklyn to pay homage to the 1947 pennant-winning Dodgers team.

After the Dodgers won the fourth game of the 1947 World Series, Manager Burt Shotten joyfully hugged Lavagetto, hero of the game

That Sunday is worth remembering. Joe Tepsic had been a Penn State football and baseball star. A lot of clubs had been after him. Rickey went high—to $16,000—to sign him, when he put on a one-man exhibition at Ebbets Field around mid-season, after a game with the Phillies. The boss watched him throw like Furillo and run like Reiser. When Tepsic hit several balls, thrown by bartender Bill Boylan, into the upper deck in left field, Branch signed him.

There was only one catch in this deal. Tepsic was an incredible character, who believed he was good enough to star in the major leagues right away. He would not sign a Dodger contract unless Rickey promised him that he could stay with the team for the full 1946 season, at least.

He was an astonishing athlete, with amazing confidence in himself. He reminded me of some of those great "I am" characters that Ring Lardner used to write about.

I saw the boy's natural ability as soon as he joined us. But I was taken aback to hear him say, "There isn't an outfielder on this club I can't outplay, Mr. Durocher."

"What about Pete Reiser?" I asked.

"Him, too!" said the amazing Mr. Tepsic.

He bet on himself in races against some of our fastest men —and won. He bet he could hit balls farther than they could —and won. But those things were done in practice, when it didn't mean anything. In the games, the pitchers threw him curves. He looked like a man rocking a rowboat. He just did not know what a curve was. I could not use him much, except where it meant nothing.

But now we had reached the final few weeks of the season. A pinch hit here or there might win the flag for us. However, with Tepsic, our roster was full, and we could not bring up the man we wanted: Tom Tatum, an experienced outfielder on the Montreal club.

The players, especially Dixie Walker, talked to Tepsic. They told him honestly that he needed more preparation in the minor leagues. They practically begged him. Wouldn't he please consent to go down now so we could get the pinch hitter we needed?

"Listen," returned the still-amazing Mr. Tepsic, "I am no infielder. But I can play third base better an' hit better than the guys you got tryin' to play the bag now!"

That meant Lavagetto, Miksis, Rojek, and Galan. Mr. Tepsic lost friends fast—but very fast!

When the boys divided their share of the World Series money, they wanted to leave Tepsic out entirely; and no wonder. But at my insistence, they included him. They gave him one-eighth of a share. They gave more to Jean Pierre Roy, who had jumped to the Mexican League!

So Tepsic, ignored by the rest of the club, stayed on. In this double-header with the Cubs we really got into the spot where we needed a pinch hitter. We had the score tied in the last of the ninth, three on, one out. Even a fly ball would rack that game up. But Medwick was sick that day, and not in uniform. Instead of Tatum, I had to gamble on Ferrell Anderson, who had almost as much trouble with a curve ball, after the pitchers got to his weakness, as Tepsic did.

Andy would come back to the bench after looking bad on a curve, and say, "Skip, they don't throw me the straight one any more." That's what he called the fast ball—the "straight one."

Now, Johnny Schmitz fanned Anderson with a curve, and we never got the run in. Instead of winning the game in nine innings, we lost it in ten.

In the second game that day we had a 2-0 lead in the bottom of the fifth inning. But Higbe was shaky. We had been catching all their line drives and only a double play had saved Kirby in the bottom of the fourth. I did not think we could play another inning and get by with Higbe, and yet I had nobody for relief that I could depend on. It was already late, and the shadows were lengthening. If we could waste a little time during our turn at bat in the fifth, I thought, perhaps they'd call the game.

"Come on!" I said to the gang. "Get on these Cubs, all of you. A good rhubarb is all that can save us."

They got our first two hitters, and I realized that I'd have to do something quickly. So I offered, "I'll show you guys how to raise a rhubarb."

Mickey Livingston, the Cub catcher, was near by, nice and handy, so I started on him.

"You can tell the Cubs are out of the pennant race," I trumpeted. "Livingston is catching today."

Mickey turned my way. Inside his mask I could see his features twist into an insult.

"Pressure's off," I needled, "so Grimm can afford to use you!"

Immediately, Livingston whipped off his mask and let me have a good blast. Some of the things he said would have made me pretty mad ordinarily, but now they were music to my ears.

Beans Reardon, the umpire, hopped on Livingston. "Get in there and catch!" screamed Beans. "Time's getting short."

Livingston and Reardon now tangled. I could see Mickey waving in the direction of our dugout.

Manager Charley Grimm was blowing his top. I heard him bellow, "Why don't you get after Durocher? He's the one who started this whole thing!"

"I'm running this game," quavered Reardon in his girlish voice, "and I don't need you to help me, Grimm. Now get out of here!"

But Grimm wouldn't leave. Pretty soon they were at it hot and heavy. Meanwhile, Livingston was still fuming and glaring, letting off occasional explosions at me like a pinwheel that was burning itself out.

About this time a tremendous swarm of gnats, which had been feeding on the fans near the visitors' bull pen in left field, advanced to do battle with Reardon and Livingston, and with Stanky, who was our hitter. Nature was going to be on our side this time.

By the time Beans had things straightened away and the Cubs got Stanky out, it was too dark to continue, and we all went home. The rhubarb had insured our victory—although the papers the next morning said it was the first time a game had been called on account of gnats.

With an even two weeks to go, we were a game and a half out. We couldn't afford to make mistakes. But in Monday's game with the Cubs, we made several. They belted everyone I put in to pitch. I was so mad I was sick.

Big Bill Nicholson, the powerful Cub outfielder, came up with three men on. He pulled a ball down the first-base line that was so hot it would have torn Stevens apart if he had reached it. I always hate to see Nick come up there in a jam, because he is such a power hitter. His attitude, too, scares you. If you say hello to him, he just grunts. He lets you know that he didn't come to the park to act social. He came there to pound that baseball over the fence and to beat your brains out, if possible.

Now when Nick pulled a shot down the line, I watched Umpire Reardon for his decision. Beans flipped his lapels and watched Walker run the ball down. Meanwhile, three runs pattered over the plate and Nick pulled up at third. We were trailing 5-0.

I went out to challenge Reardon.

"Well," I asked, "what was it? Fair or foul?"

"What are you doing out here?" snapped Beans, quite surprised.

"What did you call it?" I barked.

"What difference does it make?" shrilled Reardon. "You're so far behind—"

" 'What difference?' " I repeated. "Call it! Was it fair or foul?"

"I guess—" Beans started to answer.

"YOU GUESS!" I exploded. I drowned out his protests, kicked a little dirt on him, and began to work my way to the dugout. But as I was about to duck out of sight I let him have some choice expressions he hadn't heard before, a few which I had picked up around Fourth and Atlantic, in Brooklyn.

"Wait a minute," said Beans, running up to get within my range. "Did you say I was a—"

"What!" I boomed, "can't you hear, either?"

"If you said what I think you said," Reardon went on, his face getting redder and redder, "you're out of here!"

"You really want to know, Beansy?" I smiled.

"Yes, I do!" he snapped.

"Well," I said, "you've been guessing all afternoon, so guess what I said!"

That little speech cost me a hundred dollars. But the game was much more expensive. We pulled up to tie it at 5-all, but then, with the bases full, Nick hit one out of the park off Paul Minner, a kid left-hander. That was all, brother.

That night things looked pretty black because we were now two games back.

We won Tuesday; so did the Cardinals. Time was running out. I hammered at the boys that we couldn't afford to make even one more mistake. Still, we made it in the first game of a double-header against the Pirates on Wednesday.

It was Ostermueller who came back to beat us by one run, 3-2. Edwards had led off one of the late innings with a triple. But we couldn't bring him home. Again it was the lack of a pinch hitter that made the difference.

Branca won the second game that day, and we got a real break when the Cards lost. So we were a game and a half behind.

On Thursday, September 19, Gregg shut out the Pirates

with three hits, and Stanky passed the 130 mark in walks. The Cardinals made news by asking the Braves to move their night game in Boston up to the afternoon, so they would be able to leave for home sooner. That request gave everybody a laugh. The St. Louis club, which liked to play everything under the lights, now wanted to call off a night game!

The Cards won it and held their game and a half margin.

On September 20, Rube Melton warmed up to start against the Reds in the replay of that nineteen-inning tie. I didn't think Rube had enough stuff and switched to Herring, who hadn't started a game since the five-inning no-hitter he had pitched in Cincinnati in June.

McKechnie had saved Vander Meer for us again. I began to wonder if we were ever going to score on the Jersey left-hander; he had a string of twenty-six scoreless innings against us. Now he ran it to twenty-nine before he finally gave up one run.

In the same inning, Dixie Walker came up with two men on. "I'm going to guess, Skip," he whispered to me. "I'll either hit one out of here or get hit on the head!"

Walker guessed for Vandy's curve, and stepped in to get around on it. A fast ball would have caught him all tangled up, and might have skulled him.

But Dixie guessed right, and his eighth homer of the year looked pretty as it went over the wall into Bedford Avenue.

Casey had to enter the game for some fancy relieving. He got Lonny Frey with the bases full and, later, fanned Mueller with the tying runs on second and third. We won it 5-3, and were only a game behind.

At Boston, in the first half of a Sunday double bill, we pulled a play that really had them talking. I called for Hatten to squeeze a run home with two strikes on him. We had done it before, with Stanky the bunter, to beat the Giants. We were trying everything we knew to win the flag: gambling, scrambling, praying, jockeying.

We had Sain in the coffin, ready to nail the lid down, but nobody had the hammer. There were three men on, none out, and Lavagetto, Galan, and Walker coming up. We didn't get a run in, and Sain escaped to pitch the rest of the way and win the game. We won the second. When the Cardinals lost, our split pulled us to within one-half game of the top.

What a wearing struggle it was! We had won eighteen of our last twenty-four games, and yet had gained only two games on the Redbirds, as we plunged into the final week of the season.

On Monday we won, and so did the Cards.

At this point help came from an unexpected quarter. The Reverend Benney Benson, pastor of the Greenpoint Reformed Church, turned up on the steps of Borough Hall and prayed that we overhaul the Cardinals. "I have three million people with me, O Lord!" he intoned. "Give to the Dodgers an even break!"

I felt like telling the Reverend that an even break **was no** good. We had to win them all to get the pennant.

On Tuesday we were idle again. The Cards won theirs in ten innings. Now they led by a full game. The strain was terrific. My stomach felt as though Steve Owen's football Giants were scrimmaging inside it.

On Wednesday I thought we had lost once and for all. Going into the ninth we led the forlorn Phillies 9 to 6. But they put up a battle, and I had to yank Higbe and relieve with Lombardi because two left-handed hitters, Wyrostek and Northey, were coming up. Lombardi walked one, and bounced a base hit off the bat of the other. We blew that game, 11-9, in an incredible series of mistakes, and we were really sunk in gloom. Perhaps the Reverend Benson's prayer helped, for the Cardinals also lost, so we did not fall back any farther. We still trailed by one full game.

That night I could not sleep. I kept trying to see where I

had made a mistake. The fact of the matter was that Branca, Gregg, Behrman, Higbe, Lombardi, and Herring had all failed in that weird game with the Phillies. Had any one of them pitched well, we could have won.

Thursday was another black day; Reiser broke his leg. He slid back to first base, trying to favor the muscle he'd pulled in the game against the Cardinals, and he snapped the bone. That youngster had been through everything. He had suffered a shoulder separation, a cracked skull, a burned hand, a sore back, and a pulled muscle in his leg. The broken leg was the cruel climax. It had been a bad year for him all around, for while he had stolen thirty-four bases, he had hit only .283 in 121 games.

We lost Reiser, but we won the game, and Higbe bagged himself his seventeenth win. Frank McCormick, the Phils' first baseman, and Ben Chapman, their manager, did not think we had really won the game. They insisted that Reiser had been tagged out as he broke his leg. Umpire Al Barlick maintained that Reiser had returned safely and that time had been called before Pete rolled off the bag in pain. It just went to prove how the Phillies, going nowhere except down, fought to knock us off! Chapman and McCormick were still kicking up a storm after the game, when Reiser was already in the Caledonian Hospital.

On Friday we beat the Braves. The Cubs shut out the Cardinals. Result: Brooklyn and St. Louis were tied at ninety-five victories and fifty-seven defeats each.

The fans went crazy. Photographers and newspapermen haunted Ebbets Field, and followed the players home at night to get feature stories and human-interest yarns. "Dem Bums" were headlined on front pages everywhere.

A young couple, just married in their native Chicago, came to Brooklyn and spent their honeymoon waiting with thousands of others on the bleacher line outside Ebbets Field.

The Reverend Benson chartered a plane and prayed for a Dodger victory as the ship cruised over Ebbets Field.

On the Saturday before the final game of the season, Joe Hatten outpitched Johnny Sain again. The Cards won theirs, too.

We did not win another game that year.

Chapter 29

WHAT ARE "DODGERS"?

ON SUNDAY, THE BOSTON MANAGER, BILLY SOUTHWORTH, shot a red-hot Mort Cooper at us. He had shut out the Giants on Thursday, and was coming back with only two days of rest.

We never did get a run off Mort. It might have turned out differently if Eddie Stanky had not swung at a ball over his head with the count three and two in the first inning. It's hard to find fault with a player who has walked 140 times, but the fact is that Eddie should have got on. I had planned to sacrifice with Lavagetto: Galan actually did single.

If we had got that run, I believe they never would have beaten Lombardi. They had earned only one run off him; the others in that 4-0 defeat came after I had taken Vic out.

That potential run was moved to third by a double which Billy Herman hit off a high outside curve ball. So Herman still pestered us, providing the newspapermen with plenty of ammunition to shoot at Rickey for having made that deal which sent him to Boston. The final score was brought in by Mort Cooper himself on a fly.

Having lost that game, everything seemed over for us. All the Cardinals had to do to win the flag was to beat the Cubs. But as we sat around our clubhouse, it began to be apparent that the Cards might not take it. They lost; we felt pretty good as we took the train for a Tuesday play-off game in St. Louis!

The army of newspapermen traveling with us asked me for an interview. I told them that what impressed me most was the way Grimm and the Cubs, hating us though they did, had hustled to beat the Cardinals two out of three in that final series; and the way Mort Cooper, who was bitter toward Breadon and the Card management, still beat us, though it saved the Redbirds' chance at the flag.

The Cardinals were not too chipper themselves. They had planned a big victory celebration in St. Louis with Roy Stockton, a local newspaperman, as master of ceremonies. But, as Herb Goren remarked, they forgot to bring the victory along.

Now they had to fight us before they could bring home the bacon, and St. Louis was bitter. Stockton's paper ran a box saying that Rickey had broken a rule by giving the Dodger players automobiles as presents. One of our own writers retorted that if the Cardinals gave their men less rules and more automobiles they might be happier.

The first play-off game in October was a miserable exhibition. When Lavagetto crossed in front of Reese on an easy chance, we gave them a run. Two more came in on a Garagiola fly that Furillo had time to autograph as well as catch; he did neither. Then Branca, who hadn't pitched badly, got tangled up in the box and a ground ball went through him for another run. We lost 4-2.

We came back to Brooklyn on Thursday, October 3. We had won fifty-six games and lost twenty-two at Ebbets Field. What did they do to us? They beat our brains out. Six pitchers couldn't stop the Cards, though we provided a typical Dodger finish. We had three runs in, one out, three men on, with Eddie Stanky and home-run hitter Schultz coming up. But Stanky and Schultz both struck out, and we lost, 8-4.

We trudged back into the clubhouse to find Branch Rickey waiting. He did not talk to the players often, but did he rib us because the Cardinals had taken the pennant! This time he really gave us an earful.

"Don't think about this defeat," he advised. "Forget it right now. Don't get the idea you are losers, because you are going to win next year, and after that."

Then he came to something that really choked him up. He said that a columnist had written something that had hurt him more deeply than anything else that had happened to him in his long lifetime of baseball. We thought he was referring to Jimmy Powers, who considered any day lost on which he did not take a poke at Rickey.

However, Branch was not thinking of Powers. He declared that Powers' jibes were nothing alongside of the paragraph that Joe Williams had written for the *World-Telegram*.

Williams had reached the conclusion that Rickey had traded Herman because he did not want to win the pennant, and desired only to come close. Why? It was better business at the gate that way, said Williams.

Now Rickey, speaking softly, but with deadly meaning, went on, "That was a lie! I want none of you young men to leave here and go home with the idea that I don't want to win *every day*, every year. Because I do, with all my heart!"

He was talking to a team of men, young and old, to which he was closer perhaps than any he had put together in the past. And he was crying openly and unashamedly.

Then he confessed something he had never admitted to the critical press. "I say to you that the Herman deal may have been a mistake," he admitted. "I don't think it was, but I may be wrong. If it was a mistake, it was an honest one. I thought we would be stronger without him."

What happened after that, during the fall and winter, seems like a dream now.

In December I called Rickey. "Something is happening to me, Branch."

"I know, Leo, you're in love again," he sighed.

"I am," I said, "with a person so lovely that I have no right to know her, much less think of marrying her."

The first time Laraine Day and I were in the same room

together was at the Cub Room in the Stork Club. Her escort pointed me out to her. "Leo Durocher!" he whispered.

"Who's he?" asked Laraine.

"The manager of the Brooklyn Dodgers, of course," he said.

"And what are they?" asked the girl who was later to become the manager's manager.

It was a hectic winter. Larry MacPhail offered me the job as manager of the Yankees. I told him it was my hope that I'd spend the rest of my career in Brooklyn.

In Columbus, Ohio, I told Rickey how I felt about managing his club, in 1947 and forever, if he would have me. That evening, to escape the swarms of newspapermen, we went to his real home, the Ohio country around Duck Run, and Hog Wallow, at Lucasville. We wound up at a square dance. Dressed as I was, I felt as much out of place among those earnest country farmers as Spike Jones would at the Metropolitan Opera.

Rickey was the center of attraction. He introduced me to one leading citizen in the community who declared bluntly that he had never heard of me, and what branch of the Rickey family was I from, ennyhow?

My refusal of his Yankee offer embittered Larry MacPhail, and he began to attack Laraine and me. That led to a series of events which culminated in the hearings at St. Petersburg and Sarasota before Commissioner Chandler.

Then the big blow fell— I was suspended for a whole year. All that remained for me to do was to go into the clubhouse, wish the boys good luck, and tell them good-by. It was my team; Rickey had built it for me, sure, but I had suffered with it through the diaper stage. I had thrilled to see it grow and improve, and now that it was striding about on its own legs, I had to leave it.

It was the toughest thing I have ever had to do, and I almost broke down. But through my tears I asked them to have faith in Rickey. He had always kept his word to me, and to every other ballplayer I knew. "If you have troubles, go to him," I urged. "You'll find him a lot different from the prejudiced pictures you see of him in some sports columns. Place your faith in him."

The good-bys were tough all around. The Dodger Knothole Club Dinner, annually a welcome-home affair for our team, with thousands of fans in attendance, turned into a farewell for me. Rickey missed it because of illness. But Walter O'Malley, one of the club's directors, speaking for Branch, declared warmly, "Leo, we aren't saying 'good-by' to you and Laraine. We say, 'We'll be seeing you soon!' "

I had an hour's talk with Barney Shotton, the smart old friend Rickey had brought in to pinch hit for me as manager. I told him he'd have to spot Lombardi against the left-handed hitting clubs, and that Furillo could not hit a sidearmer with a paddle. In that short time I added dozens of other hints which I had picked up in my years of managing the boys. I felt very much like a mother must feel when she abandons her infant on a doorstep, as I left my Dodgers with Barney. How very, very wrong I was—he won the pennant with them, didn't he?

Chapter 30

THE MEMORABLE YEAR '47

I went home with Laraine to our house in Santa Monica, California. I began to transplant flowers and to landscape the grounds. But my heart wasn't in the work. I just couldn't get Brooklyn out of mind. I kept a radio near by, tuned in always for the play-by-play rebroadcast of the Dodgers' games. Did I say *a* radio? I broke more than one before I learned to take things calmly when Peewee Reese took a called third strike through the middle with two out and everybody running.

The club won eight of its first ten games, and the Cardinals lost eight of their first ten. So we were on top, and our old rivals were at the other end of the league. Then things began to happen, and before I knew it we had dropped to fifth place, only one game over .500 with a 14-13 record. And all I could do was dig the ground or chew my nails.

That first Western trip nearly ruined us, as we lost two straight to the Reds and three out of four to the Pirates. Then we—how else can I put it except "we"?—went into St. Louis and Enos Slaughter broke Stanky up in a play at second base, just as he'd done a year before. Miksis took Ed's place.

We went East to the Polo Grounds. When Stanky got in a rhubarb with Umpire Beans Reardon, Miksis had to go in again. About that time I would have given my right arm for a few words with Reardon. Three thousand miles away it sounded to me as though Beans were taking advantage of my boys.

In that game with the Giants we kicked one, and Harry Taylor, the good-looking kid with the sharp curve ball, blew up, or seemed to. He walked two more to fill the bases with one out, and up came Mize. The score was tied at 1-all.

"Where's Casey?" I kept repeating to myself, tearing my hair.

I'm glad nobody except Laraine saw me during those days. I nearly went daffy with my ear in the radio loud-speaker. In thirty-one games only six pitchers had gone all the way for Barney. Now another needed quick relief. Surely Barney wouldn't let the kid stay in there and pitch to Mize?

When Mize hit that ball I felt the tremor all the way out on the coast. It was a screaming line drive. But Miksis took it, and turned it into a double play, to save Handsome Harry that inning. Taylor had no more trouble and won the game from the Giants 14-2!

Then Hatten pitched a complete game. And Branca made it three in a row.

Maybe, I thought, Shotton's patience with Taylor had had a settling influence on the whole staff.

Shotton also went a lot farther with some of the others than I might have. He left skinny Johnny Jorgensen, whom I had asked for from the Montreal club just before I left, in at third base against both right- and left-handed pitching. Then it developed that, although he was a left-handed hitter, the kid also hit southpaws very well.

After that life-saving double play, Taylor went right on. In three starts he gave only twelve hits and three runs. I danced on the lawn in Santa Monica. Shotton had certainly found himself a pitcher.

We traded Kirby Higbe, one of the standby Dodger pitchers, to Pittsburgh, and my heart sank. But then the boys, coming up against him, beat Higbe once, and beat him again! One of the writers said Kirby turned out to be a better pitcher for Brooklyn in a Pirate suit than he ever had been in

Dodger colors. That wasn't quite right, but it meant that the club had not made a mistake in the trade.

It was an amazing deal: Higbe, Hank Behrman, Gene Mauch, Cal McLish and Dixie Howell, for $325,000 and a half-pint outfielder named Al Gionfriddo. . . . But the Pirates had a "look" agreement on Behrman, and could get a refund on him if they decided to send him back. I thought the Behrman I remembered from the year before might turn into the most important man in the lot.

Then we beat Behrman and Higbe in a double-header, and people began to wonder if Rickey was psychic. For he had been trading away only the lemons.

One of the gang wrote me that, one day, as Higbe was getting ready to pitch against Brooklyn, Casey had entered the Pirate dressing room.

"What you fussin' so about gettin' dressed for, Hig?" said Casey to his old roomie. "You'll be undressin' again in 'bout half an hour."

"Not me, Fat Stuff!" retorted Higbe. "I'm shuttin' you guys out today. An' maybe with no hits, too."

"Your Pittsburgh owners ain't so smart," needled Casey with a grin. "How could they ever make half a deal like they made when they got you?"

"Whaddya mean, 'half a deal?'" Kirby grumbled suspiciously.

"Why," laughed Casey, "they forgot to get me. What good is Higbe without Casey to mop up for him?"

There was a lot of kidding about Gionfriddo, a little Italian who ran in the real Rickey tradition. "Rickey got Gionfriddo just to carry over the $325,000," said Arch Murray. "Al can run fast and get to Brooklyn with it quicker!"

At the moment Gionfriddo was a laugh. But he was to make two of the most dramatic plays in the World Series that fall—a vital steal of second and a miracle catch on DiMaggio.

Still, in June and July, it hardly seemed that the Dodgers

could make the World Series—without buying themselves tickets. Reiser ran into a wall again and cracked up his head. Rain piled up the double-headers. In the first two months, the club had eight postponements. The loss by rain was over $150,000. The club lost a Saturday and Sunday game with the Cubs at Ebbets Field, and the glooms predicted that that would kill Brooklyn's chance to draw 1,700,000 again. We drew better than 1,800,000 anyway.

The "difference" at the gate and on the scoreboard, too, was Jackie Robinson. He was having a rough time, no question about it. From the opposing dugout, most everybody gave it to him. But he was driving the catchers and the outfielders crazy, stealing and taking those extra bases. His lightning moves had them hurrying their throws and making mistakes.

By July 4, Jackie was hitting .317. He had stolen thirteen bases and was in an eighteen-game hitting streak.

In the Polo Grounds, as 53,000 fans roared, Jackie got five straight hits, and blew a game wide open with his daring on the bases.

When they "rode" him, Jackie bit his lip. Yet, when the newspapermen interviewed him, he always said the sporting thing.

"I notice you sit alone in the Brooklyn dugout," commented Bill Roeder of the *World-Telegram.* "Do the other Dodgers shun you?"

"That's my fault, not theirs," replied Jack. "I am a loner. I never palled around even with Negro boys. Everybody has been nice to me up here, even fellows on opposing teams, like Hank Greenberg, and Joe Medwick, too."

Still the tirade of abuse poured out at him.

"Let them keep it up," said Rickey to me over the phone. "If the other clubs ride Robinson, it will make a fighting unit of our club quicker than anything else possibly could. It will be the making of our team."

It worked that way, too. When Enos Slaughter spiked Robinson's outstretched foot in a play at first base that wasn't even close, Hugh Casey, who lives in Georgia, charged at the Cardinal outfielder.

"I saw a Georgia Cracker defend a Negro boy!" marvelled one writer. "It can be said that Robinson 'made' the team today!"

Branca pitched his thirteenth victory. This one was a one-hitter over the Cards. St. Louis had quit the cellar, and had begun to make threatening gestures. In the rubber game of that series, one victory having gone to each club, I thought I'd go crazy. As Shotton juggled hitters in a welter of strategy to win the game, we made three in the last of the ninth. Miksis drove in the winning run with a pinch-hit single.

But Ford Frick took that victory away because an umpire talked too much. Beans Reardon, who is always talking, had told Cardinal outfielder Ron Northey to slow up as he rounded third in the top of the ninth in that game. Because, said Beans, the ball which Northey had hit off Casey was in the bleachers for a home run.

How much Northey slowed up nobody could really tell: he runs like my Aunt Kate. But Reardon was wrong. The ball had not hit in the bleachers. Umpire Goetz, who had run out to center field to cover the play, said the ball was in play. When the relay came home, Northey, who had speeded up again, was out a mile.

That night I remembered the other talkative umpire—remember the one whose job I'd saved when he spoke out of turn?—and I wondered how Ford Frick could possibly take this victory away from Brooklyn. The Cardinals never did get three Dodgers out in the bottom of the ninth, and if we had played it out, we might have rung up a dozen runs. Yet, Reardon was the one I wondered about most. I wrote him a hot telegram—and tore it up.

At the end of July we went into St. Louis and beat the Cards three straight. Taylor, the pitcher Burt Shotton had developed by being patient, shut them out in the first game and, with a bunt and a triple, drove in four runs. We blew a 10-0 lead with Branca. Casey was knocked out in relief, and finally with the score 10-10, King got the Cards out just when their winning run was on third in the last of the ninth. That nightmare we won 11-10, on a hit by Peewee Reese.

Peewee won the third game for Lombardi with a hit-and-run double to right, beating Pollet. How I loved that kid! So, we led both the Cards and Giants by ten games. Everybody said it would be a waltz from there in. The Pirates had got a refund on Behrman, and Hank, a flop with them, was back with us and pitching well.

But in building our lead to ten games, we had been on a thirteen-game winning streak. Now, with that over, the reaction set in. On August 18, when the Cards came into Brooklyn, we were only four and a half in front. We had a four-game series to play, including the game which Frick had ordered replayed because of the Reardon-Northey incident.

On that big Monday we beat the Cards twice. Little Lombardi, with his wife in the hospital because of an emergency appendectomy, stopped them cold in the afternoon. That night Taylor hurt his arm, and spunky Lom went right back in, relieved him, and held the lead.

Again I thought it was all over, but two days later I wasn't so sure.

The next day Hatten had his ears beaten back. In the final game Branca had a one-hitter and a two-run lead in the top of the ninth. He became wild, and so into the pitcher's box came Casey. With two out, Casey got Kurowski to hit a one-hopper to Jorgensen. But the kid took a look at it, backed up instead of coming in, and "blew." That inning, the Cards got two runs to tie. In the twelfth Kurowski, who had reached base eleven straight times in the series and had hit two homers, hit another, and we blew the game. That afternoon even the beautiful Santa Monica countryside looked like the Sahara to me.

All year, Brooklyn had been a running team. Robinson and—when he was in shape—Pete Reiser, had spun around those sacks like madmen. Even Dixie Walker had turned into a base-stealer as he pinwheeled around the bases on the heels of Jackie and Pete.

Everybody had something to say about the Negro boy. Wherever the club went, they talked about him.

In Chicago, with the game a scoreless tie in the top of the ninth, he drew four balls and sprinted, not walked, to first base. He made the turn, and was on second before the Cub catcher could pull himself together. That piece of daring tore the game wide open, and we got four runs that inning.

In Pittsburgh, with the score tied at 2-all late in the game, Jackie stole home on Ostermueller. Later, on an infield out, he sped in from second.

Time and again he raced from first to third on a sacrifice bunt. In Brooklyn, facing Johnny Sain, who was always tough, he bunted, went to second when Sain threw badly, and instead of stopping there, sailed right into third. Sain blew up, and was out of the game in the first inning. Brooklyn went on to win.

Everybody watched Jackie Robinson. He was on base when Dixie Walker hit a big homer in the Polo Grounds. It's customary to wait at the plate to shake the hand of the homer hitter. But Jackie did not shake hands. He walked to the bench.

"Robinson snubbed Walker," buzzed the gossips. "They still don't get along."

But Dixie could have told the story. Robinson knew that pictures of Walker shaking hands with a Negro boy—however much Dixie might have wanted to, privately—would hurt Walker's hardware business in Alabama. He knew the cameras were focused on the plate, and that those pictures would go all over the country. Always thoughtful, Robinson ducked out of the picture.

Yes, the Dodgers had been a running club all year long. Now Shotton gathered them for the final dash for the pennant.

Chapter 31

THAT MAN'S BACK AGAIN!

EWELL BLACKWELL, THE BUGGY-WHIP RIGHT-HANDER, CAME in with the Reds right after the Cards had walloped Brooklyn in those last two games. That made it tough, because the team was "low" after Jorgensen had been benched for kicking the game away. . . . And Blackwell was extra tough, the best in the league.

Now Blackwell went to work on us. Reiser was on third. The Reds' subcatcher, Hugh Poland, let the ball get away. Reiser began to come in. Blackwell took a high throw, covering the plate. His arms were stretched upward to full length when Reiser hit him, and he folded up like an accordion.

The Reds screamed bloody murder. Blackwell, limping, had to be taken out of the game. Brooklyn got four runs on three stolen bases: a passed ball, a balk, and an error.

After the game, Blackwell shouted at the Dodger players that he would "get even."

"Shucks," said Reiser after the game, "I saved that kid. I could have come in spikes high, and put him out for the year. But I turned them aside, and took him out with my knees. That's baseball. What's he crying about?"

But the Dodgers were crying before long as the Reds did even the score. Bert Haas stepped on Peewee Reese, and severed one of Peewee's arteries. Our kid shortstop was on crutches when our boys needed him most.

Subbing for Reese, Stan Rojek came in to give an imitation of Honus Wagner. Earlier, Miksis, filling in for Stanky, had hit three home runs in three days. That great reserve strength that Shotton had in his club made the difference.

Sitting at my radio I couldn't help but wonder if this last

Western trip would be a nightmarish repetition of 1941 and 1942. For we headed into the badlands with only a five and one-half game lead.

In Chicago, we had a ball game won with Vic Lombardi, who was going along smoothly. But we got into a jam with three on, one out.

Lombardi fanned McCullough. Two were out, the bases were full. All Lom had to do was get rid of Aberson, a muscle-bound football player from the Western Association.

But Aberson hit one high and far into the seats, for four runs and the ball game. How it reminded me of the double-header we had lost at the start of the last 1941 Western trip!

In the second game at Chicago, we beat the Cubs and took our four-and-one-half-game lead into St. Louis. This three-game series was "for the money," and everyone knew it.

Branca won the opener, 4-3. The Cards made a pincushion out of Robinson. When Garagiola spiked him, Jackie quickly let him know that he understood what it was all about.

We lost the second game 8-7, after Casey walked three men in a row. But we held on and won the third, also 8-7, although the Cards rallied for five runs in the last two innings, with the help of a dazzling sun that blinded Reiser, Walker, and Stanky and made them drop fly balls. Perhaps, working an afternoon game rather than the usual arc-lights battle in St. Louis was too much.

Anyway, that was the works. We finally won the pennant by five games, with ninety-four victories and sixty defeats. Here I cannot emphasize too strongly that it was a great feat for Manager Shotton. He took a team he knew nothing about and triumphed over such hard luck as Taylor's sore arm— Harry had not pitched during the last month and a half—and Reiser's injury. Still Barney could not have won the flag without Robinson. Jackie's twenty-eight stolen bases represented more than the total thefted by the entire Yankee team we were to face in the World Series.

For drama, it was a great series. But it was not good base-ball. As I watched them, the Yankees were ripe to be knocked off. Our side played even worse.

In the first game, the Yanks got Branca after he had pitched four perfect innings. He went wild, and "blew," with 70,000 people yelling—something that might happen to any boy of twenty-one.

With good outfielding Lombardi might have won the second, but Reiser had a bad day.

In the third game Hatten staggered and Casey relieved him to win.

In the fourth game, Taylor started. But with the bases full in the first inning, Coach Clyde Sukeforth rushed out to yank him.

"But I've been saving my arm," protested Harry, "I haven't started to throw hard yet, Sukey."

"When were you going to start?" barked the other, staring at the loaded bases. "There isn't any more room to put anybody!"

Gregg, a flop all year, came in to pitch a great relief game. But the Yankees' Bevens was better, and with two out in the ninth and Gionfriddo on first base, he had a no-hitter. Gionfriddo stole second, Bevens walked Reiser intentionally. Then Lavagetto made baseball history with a game-wrecking pinch double off the right-field wall.

Shotton was at the bottom of the pitching barrel. He had to start Rex Barney in the fifth game—which we lost—and Gregg again in the seventh. Those two hurlers hadn't won ten games between them all season. But by the seventh game, our big winners—Branca, Hatten, Lombardi, Taylor—were out of it.

No one could have come closer to winning a pennant, and then fail, than we did in 1946, when I was manager and we tied the Cardinals. And nobody could have come closer to winning the world championship, without actually doing it, than Shotton did in 1947. I could hardly say which failure made me feel worse

In the clubhouse later, I felt the same as Rickey did. Branch shouted, "I hope we meet these Yankees in 1948. You boys made me proud in this series. But when you're a year older, you won't have to take second honors. Don't worry about this defeat. Go home and think about next year's victory!"

Now I practiced what I had preached. I put my faith in Branch. Everyone assured me that, this time, I was out in the cold for good. I would never get my job back. In the face of pressure that would have made it much easier for him, had he made a change, Rickey quietly gave me the manager's reins again. But I could have told you that Branch was never one to trade his ideals for a plush ride through life. At sixty-five he was so full of fight that the idea of an easier way out never entered his head.

In December, Bob Hope had introduced me to his pals as "Burt Shotton's winter replacement." Now I became lovable Barney's summer replacement, too.

That's all of it, I guess.

Maybe I haven't put in all you'd like to know about the spring of 1947, and the rhubarb that led to the abrupt subtraction of a year from my baseball career. Yet, for the first time in my life, I really have nothing to say. But not by choice.

For the last line in the Commissioner's ruling, which Rickey had summarized so dramatically that April morning in his office, took care of that.

It said briefly.

"All parties to this controversy are silenced from the time this order is issued"!

That's all, brother!

LEO ERNEST DUROCHER (Lippy)

(Hung on him by Yankee teammates during first training trip because of his freshness and continual popping off.)

BROOKLYN DODGERS

Height, 5:09. Weight, 175. Blue eyes and brown hair. Throws and bats right-handed. Nationality—French. Born, July 27, 1906, at West Springfield, Mass.

Married Laraine Day   Hobby—Golf.

Outstanding performance—Equaled major league record of two two-base hits in one inning, first game, August 25, 1936. Led league in runs and total bases, 1942.

Year	Club	League	Pos.	G.	AB.	R.	H.	2B.	3B.	HR.	RBI.	B.A.	PO.	A.	E.	F.A.
1925	Hartford	East.	SS	151	536	60	118	13	4	1	....	.220	317	502	59	.933
1925	New York	Amer.	PH	2	1					0	0	.000			0	.000
1926	Atlanta	South.	SS	130	408	62	97	9	5	0	33	.238	245	393	43	.937
1927	St. Paul	A.A.	SS	171	594	60	150	27	10	2	78	.253	420	559	56	.946
1928	New York*	Amer.	2B-SS	102	296	46	80	8	6	0	31	.270	158	274	25	.945
1929	New York*	Amer.	SS	106	341	53	84	4	5	0	32	.246	197	299	22	.958
1930	Cincinnati	Nat.	SS	119	354	31	86	15	5	3	32	.243	212	380	24	.963
1931	Cincinnati	Nat.	SS	121	361	26	82	11	5	3	29	.227	240	344	24	.963
1932	Cincinnati	Nat.	SS	143	457	43	99	22	5	1	33	.217	283	429	30	.960
1933	Cinf.-St. Louis†	Nat.	SS	139	446	51	113	19	4	1	44	.253	275	422	29	.960
1934	St. Louis	Nat.	SS	146	500	62	130	26	5	3	70	.260	320	407	33	.957
1935	St. Louis	Nat.	SS	143	513	57	136	23	5	8	78	.265	313	420	28	.963
1936	St. Louis	Nat.	SS	136	510	46	146	22	3	1	58	.286	300	392	21	.971
1937	St. Louis‡	Nat.	SS	135	477	41	97	11	3	1	47	.203	279	381	28	.959
1938	Brooklyn	Nat.	SS	141	479	42	105	18	5	1	56	.219	287	399	24	.966
1939	Brooklyn	Nat.	SS	116	390	42	108	21	6	1	34	.277	228	322	25	.957
1940	Brooklyn	Nat.	SS	62	160	10	37	9	1	1	14	.231	102	131	9	.959
1941	Brooklyn	Nat.	SS-2B	18	42	2	12	1	0	0	6	.286	17	28	4	.918
1942	Brooklyn	Nat.								(Did not play)						
1943	Brooklyn	Nat.	SS	6	18	1	4	0	0	0	1	.222	23	11	0	1.000
1944	Brooklyn	Nat.								(Did not play)						
1945	Brooklyn	Nat.	2B	2	5	1	1	0	0	0	0	.200	3	4	0	1.000
1946-47	—Did not play.															
	Major League Totals			1637	5350	575	1320	210	56	24	567	.247	3237	4643	323	.961

*Claimed for waiver price by Cincinnati, February, 1930.

†Traded with Pitchers John M. Ogden and Frank J. Henry to St. Louis Cardinals for Pitchers Paul Derringer and Allyn Stout and Infielder Earl J. Adams, May 7, 1933.

‡Traded to Brooklyn for Infielders James Bucher and Joseph V. Stripp, Outfielder John W. Cooney and Pitcher Roy Henshaw, October, 4, 1937.

WORLD'S SERIES RECORD

Year	Club	League	Pos.	G.	AB.	R.	H.	2B.	3B.	HR.	RBI.	B.A.	PO.	A.	E.	F.A.
1928	New York	Amer.	2B	4	2	0	0	0	0	0	0	.000	1	17	0	1.000
1934	St. Louis	Nat.	SS	7	27	4	7	1	1	0	0	.259	13	18	0	1.000
	World's Series Totals			11	29	4	7	1	1	0	0	.241	14	35	0	1.000

ALL-STAR GAME RECORD

Year	League	Pos.	G.	AB.	R.	H.	2B.	3B.	HR.	RBI.	B.A.	PO.	A.	E.	F.A.
1936	National	SS	1	3	0	1	0	0	0	0	.333	4	0	0	1.000
1938	National	SS	1	3	1	1	0	0	0	0	.333	0	3	0	1.000
	All-Star Game Totals		2	6	1	2	0	0	0	0	.333	4	3	0	1.000

LIFETIME RECORD OF BROOKLYN
IN THE NATIONAL LEAGUE

Year	Finished	Won	Lost	Pct.	Year	Finished	Won	Lost	Pct.
1890	First	86	43	.667	1919	Fifth	69	71	.493
1891	Sixth	61	76	.445	1920	First	93	61	.604
1892	Third	95	59	.617	1921	Fifth	77	75	.507
1893	Sixth *	65	63	.508	1922	Sixth	76	78	.494
1894	Fifth	70	61	.534	1923	Sixth	76	78	.494
1895	Fifth *	71	60	.542	1924	Second	92	62	.597
1896	Ninth *	58	73	.443	1925	Sixth *	68	85	.444
1897	Sixth *	61	71	.462	1926	Sixth	71	82	.464
1898	Tenth	54	91	.372	1927	Sixth	65	88	.425
1899	First	88	42	.677	1928	Sixth	77	76	.503
1900	First	82	54	.603	1929	Sixth	70	83	.458
1901	Third	79	57	.581	1930	Fourth	86	68	.558
1902	Second	75	63	.543	1931	Fourth	79	73	.520
1903	Fifth	70	66	.515	1932	Third	81	73	.526
1904	Sixth	56	97	.366	1933	Sixth	65	88	.425
1905	Eighth	48	104	.316	1934	Sixth	71	81	.467
1906	Fifth	66	86	.434	1935	Fifth	70	83	.458
1907	Fifth	65	83	.439	1936	Seventh	67	87	.435
1908	Seventh	53	101	.344	1937	Sixth	62	91	.405
1909	Sixth	55	98	.359	1938	Seventh	69	80	.463
1910	Sixth	64	90	.416	1939	Third	84	69	.549
1911	Seventh	64	86	.427	1940	Second	88	65	.575
1912	Seventh	58	95	.379	1941	First	100	54	.649
1913	Sixth	65	84	.436	1942	Second	104	50	.675
1914	Fifth	75	79	.487	1943	Third	81	72	.529
1915	Third	80	72	.526	1944	Seventh	63	91	.409
1916	First	94	60	.610	1945	Third	87	67	.565
1917	Seventh	70	81	.464	1946	Second	96	60	.615
1918	Fifth	57	69	.452	1947	First	94	60	.610

TOTALS: Games won, 4266.   Games lost, 4315.   Percentage, .497.

* Tie.

MANAGERS OF THE BROOKLYN DODGERS

1890	WILLIAM McGUNNIGLE
1891—1892	JOHN MONTGOMERY WARD
1893—1896	DAVE FOUTZ
1897	WILLIAM BARNIE
1898	WILLIAM BARNIE, MIKE GRIFFIN, and C. H. EBBETS
1899—1905	NED HANLON
1906—1908	PATSY DONOVAN
1909	HARRY LUMLEY
1910—1913	BILL DAHLEN
1914—1931	WILBERT ROBINSON
1932—1933	MAX CAREY
1934—1936	CASEY STENGEL
1937—1938	BURLEIGH GRIMES
1939—1946	LEO DUROCHER
1947	BURT SHOTTON
1948	LEO DUROCHER